WORLD WAR I AND ITS CONSEQUENCES

A note for the general reader

War, Peace and Social Change: Europe 1900–1955 is the latest honours-level history course to be produced by the Open University. War and Society has always been a subject of special interest and expertise in the Open University's History Department. The appeal for the general reader is that the five books in the series, taken together or singly, consist of authoritative, up-to-date discussions of the various aspects of war and society in the twentieth century.

The books provide insights into the modes of teaching and communication, including the use of audio-visual material, which have been pioneered at the Open University. Readers will find that they are encouraged to participate in a series of 'tutorials in print', an effective way to achieve a complete command of the material. As in any serious study of a historical topic, there are many suggestions for further reading, including references to a Course Reader, set book and to two collections of primary documents which accompany the series. It is possible to grasp the basic outlines of the topics discussed without turning to these books, but obviously serious students will wish to follow up what is, in effect, a very carefully designed course of guided reading, and discussion and analysis of that reading. The first unit in Book I sets out the aims and scope of the course.

Open University students are provided with supplementary material, including a *Course Guide* which gives information on student assignments, summer school, the use of video-cassettes, and so on.

A318 War, Peace and Social Change: Europe 1900–1955

Book I   Europe on the Eve of War 1900–1914

Book II   World War I and Its Consequences

Book III   Between Two Wars

Book IV   World War II and Its Consequences

Book V   War and Change in Twentieth-Century Europe

Prepared by the course team and published by the Open University Press, 1990

Other material associated with the course

Documents 1: 1900–1929, eds Arthur Marwick and Wendy Simpson, Open University Press, 1990

Documents 2: 1925–1959, eds Arthur Marwick and Wendy Simpson, Open University Press, 1990

War, Peace and Social Change in Twentieth-Century Europe, eds Clive Emsley, Arthur Marwick and Wendy Simpson, Open University Press, 1990 (Course Reader)

Europe 1880–1945, J. M. Roberts, Longman, 1989 (second edition) (set book)

If you are interested in studying the course, contact the Student Enquiries Office, The Open University, PO Box 71, Walton Hall, Milton Keynes MK7 6AG.

Cover illustration: 'Subscribe to the Sixth War Loan' (Trustees of the Imperial War Museum)

WAR, PEACE AND SOCIAL CHANGE: EUROPE 1900–1955

BOOK II

WORLD WAR I AND ITS CONSEQUENCES

*Henry Cowper, Clive Emsley, Arthur Marwick,
Bill Purdue and David Englander*

**OPEN
UNIVERSITY
PRESS**

Open University Press
in association with
The Open University

**The Open
University**

A318 Course team

Tony Aldgate   *Author*
Kate Clements   *Editor*
Charles Cooper   *BBC Producer*
Henry Cowper   *Author*
Ian Donnachie   *Author*
Nigel Draper   *Editor*
Clive Emsley   *Author*
David Englander   *Author*
John Golby   *Author*
John Greenwood   *Liaison Librarian*

Tony Lentin   *Author*
Arthur Marwick   *Author and Course Team Chair*
Ray Munns   *Cartographer*
Bill Purdue   *Author*
Wendy Simpson   *Course Manager*
Tag Taylor   *Designer*
Bernard Waites   *Author*
Geoffrey Warner   *Author*

Open University Press
Celtic Court
Buckingham
MK18 1XT
England

and
1900 Frost Road, Suite 101
Bristol, PA 19007, USA

First published in 1990

British Library Cataloguing in Publication Data

War, peace and social change: Europe 1900–1955. – (A318)
  Book II, World War I and its consequences.
  1. Europe, history
  I. Cowper, Henry   II. Open University, *A318 War, Peace and Social Change course team*   III. Open University
  940

  ISBN 0 335 09307 8 (hbk)   ISBN 0 335 09306 X (pbk)

Library of Congress Cataloguing in Publication Data

World War I and its consequences / Henry Cowper . . . [et al.].
    p.   cm. – (War, peace, and social change; bk. 2)
    Material for an honours-level history course produced by Open University.
    ISBN 0-335-09307-8. – ISBN 0-335-09306-X (pbk.)
    I. World War, 1914–1918 – Influence.   2. World War, 1914–1918.
  3. Revolutions–Europe–History–20th century.   I. Cowper, Henry.
  II. Open University.   III. Title: World War I and its consequences.
  IV. Title: World War One and its consequences.   V. Series.
  D523.W74   1989
  940.3′1–dc20   89-23167 CIP

Designed by the Graphic Design Group of the Open University

This book is set in 10/12pt Palatino by Rowland Phototypesetting Ltd Bury St Edmunds, Suffolk

Printed and bound in Great Britain by Redwood Press Ltd, Trowbridge, Wiltshire

1.1

CONTENTS

Acknowledgements

Grateful acknowledgement is made to the following sources for permission to reproduce material in this book:

Text

R. F. Leslie (ed.) *The History of Poland since 1863*, Cambridge University Press, 1980; J. F. McMillan, *Housewife or Harlot: The Place of Women in French Society 1870–1940*, Harvester Press, copyright © J. F. McMillan, 1981; M. Travers, *German Novels on the First World War and Their Ideological Implications, 1918–1933*, H. D. Heinz, 1982; P. Fussell, *The Great War and Modern Memory*, Oxford University Press, 1975.

Tables

Table 7.1: D. Winter, *Death's Men: Soldiers of the Great War*, Allen Lane, 1979; *Tables 7.3 and 7.4*: P. Kennedy, *The Rise and Fall of the Great Powers*, Unwin Hyman, 1988; *Table 8–10.1*: B. R. Mitchell, *European Historical Statistics 1750–1970*, Macmillan, London and Basingstoke, 1981; *Table 8–10.4*: A. Marwick, *Women at War 1914–1918*, Macmillan, London and Basingstoke, 1977; *Table 11–13.1*: G. Vernadsky *et al.* (eds) *A Source Book for Russian History from Early Times to 1917*, Yale University Press, 1972; *Table 11–13.3*: D. Koenker, 'Moscow workers in 1917', unpublished PhD thesis, University of Michigan, 1976; *Tables 11–13.5, 11–13.6 and 11–13.7*: M. Ferro, *The Russian Revolution of February 1917*, Routledge and Kegan Paul, 1972; *Tables 11–13.10 and 11–13.12*: G. Hardach, *The First World War 1914–1918*, Penguin, 1977; *Table 11–13.11*: E. H. Tobin, 'War and the working class: the case of Düsseldorf 1914–18', *Central European History*, vol. XVIII, American Historical Association, Emory University, 1985; *Table 11–13.13*: R. Wall and J. M. Winter, (eds) *The Upheaval of War*, Cambridge University Press, 1988; *Table 11–13.14*: J. R. Wegs, *Austrian Economic Mobilization During World War I, with Particular Emphasis on Heavy Industry*, unpublished PhD thesis, University of Illinois, 1970; *Table 11–13.15*: J. R. Wegs, 'The marshalling of copper: an index of Austro-Hungarian economic mobilization during World War I', *Austrian History Yearbook*, vol. XII–XIII, Rice University, Texas, 1976/7; *Table 11–13.16*: R. B. Spence, *Yugoslavia, the Austro-Hungarian Army and the First World War*, unpublished PhD thesis, University of California, 1981; *Table 11–13.17*: R. Pearson, *National Minorities in Eastern Europe 1848–1945*, Macmillan, London and Basingstoke, 1983; *Table 11–13.18*: A. C. Janos, *The Politics of Backwardness in Hungary 1825–1945*, Princeton University Press, 1982.

Figures

Figure 8–10.1: A. Marwick, *Women at War 1914–1918*, Macmillan, London and Basingstoke, 1977.

UNIT 7   THE NATURE OF THE WAR

(Sections 1–4 by Henry Cowper; sections 5 and 6 by Clive Emsley)

Open University students will need to refer to:

Set book: J. M. Roberts, *Europe 1880–1945*, Longman, 1989
Video-cassette 1

INTRODUCTION

Until the outbreak of war in 1914 the term 'the Great War' had been used to refer to the twenty-two year struggle between Britain and France during the Revolutionary and Napoleonic period. Before the end of hostilities in 1918, however, the term was being applied to World War I. The global scale of the conflict was also immediately apparent. The fact that three of the principal combatants – France, Germany, and Great Britain – had overseas colonies, often in close proximity, ensured that the war would spread outside Europe, especially given the squabbles that had developed in Africa and elsewhere in the decades before 1914. The term 'World War' was also applied to the conflict early on; for example, the twelfth edition of the *Encyclopaedia Britannica*, published in 1922, was a facsimile of the 1911 edition with three additional volumes devoted largely to the 'World War'. However, when Colonel Repington, the war correspondent of *The Times*, published his book *The First World War* in 1920, there was shock and concern, since the title implied that another war on a similar scale could follow.

This unit is concerned with the nature and conduct of World War I. Its aims are to give you some knowledge of

1   the military events of the war;

2   how the war was fought in different theatres;

3   the extent to which the war differed from its predecessors.

The preparation of this unit was very much a joint effort, but Henry Cowper was primarily responsible for the first four sections and Clive Emsley for sections 5 and 6.

Before continuing with this unit it will be useful for you to get an overall grasp of the events of the war. Chapter 9, pp.278–318, of the set book (J. M. Roberts, *Europe 1880–1945*) will give you this and introduce you to some of the issues which we will explore in more detail here. Read those pages now.

The war, as we have already stressed, was global. In East Africa the German General Paul von Lettow-Vorbeck conducted a brilliant campaign throughout the war, inflicting three times as many casualties on British Imperial forces as they had suffered in the Boer War; in the Pacific, German colonies rapidly fell to the Japanese and British Imperial forces – in August 1914, for example, Australian troops captured German New Guinea in one week. Essentially, however, these campaigns were side-shows. The following chronology concentrates on the principal theatres of the war in Europe and its periphery. You will probably find it useful to refer back to as you work your way through this unit and the remainder of the book. Study it now, together with Map 3 in the *Maps Booklet*.

The Theatres of World War I

The western front

1914

3 August: Germany launches invasion of Belgium and France. French attacks in Alsace and Lorraine beaten back.

6 September: German troops about 50 miles from Paris. French mount counter-offensive; the battle of the Marne (6–9 September) forces German retreat.

October–November: 'The race to the sea' as British and French armies attempt to turn the German flank. At the end of this period the line of trenches stretches from the Channel to the Swiss border.

By the end of 1914 there was stalemate on the western front. The Germans occupied the entire length of their side. From the Swiss frontier northwards through the Vosges and the Meuse and up to Armentières the French held the line for the Entente powers. The Somme to Bethune and Flanders was held by the British, and the Belgians held the tiny area around La Panne, the only part of their homeland not occupied by the Germans. One tenth of France , including many of its coalfields, remained in German hands until the end of the war. Key dates in the conflict during this period are:

1915
April–May: Battle of Ypres and first major attack involving the use of poison gas.

1916
February–November: Battle of Verdun launched by German General von Falken-hayn in an attempt to 'bleed France white'.

July–November: In an attempt to relieve the pressure of Verdun the British Army launches the battle of the Somme; first use of tanks in battle (September).

1917
February–March: Germans withdraw in part of northern sector of the front, between Arras and Soissons, to the heavily fortified 'Siegfried Line'.

April: Abortive French offensive of General Nivelle leads to a series of mutinies in 68 out of the 112 divisions in the French army (involving 30,000 to 40,000 men); the mutinies reach their peak in June and July.

June: General Pershing (US Army) lands in France with his staff; American troops begin to be committed piecemeal to assist the British and French armies.

July–November: British offensive at Passchendaele.

1918
March–July: German 'Ludendorff Offensive', countered by

August–November: Succession of Allied offensives, including, in September, the first solely American operation at St. Mihiel.

3–4 October: German government offers armistice to US President Wilson. Allied response calls for an end to unrestricted submarine warfare, withdrawal from occupied territory, and authorized negotiators to discuss terms.

29 October: Mutiny in German fleet at Kiel.

7 November: Revolution in Bavaria.

9 November: Revolution in Berlin; announcement of Kaiser's abdication; procla-mation of a republic.

11 November: Armistice.

The eastern front

1914
August–September: German army scores massive victories over Russians at Tannenberg (26–30 August) and the Masurian Lakes (6–15 September).

August–September: Austro-Hungarian advance checked by Russians at Lemberg.

The front in the east remained far more fluid than in the west, with considerable areas of territory changing hands as a result of offensives and counter-offensives. It is also worth remarking that, until the end of 1916, far more German soldiers were killed on the eastern than on the western front.

1915

September: Tzar Nicholas II takes over supreme command of the Russian army.

1916

June–August: Beginning of the Brusilov offensive, initially successful for the Russians, but resulting in very high casualties.

1917

March: Rioting in Petrograd leads to revolution in Russia with Provisional Government (12 March) and abdication of Tsar (15 March).

July: New Russian offensive fails.

November: Bolshevik coup in Petrograd.

17 December: Armistice between Russia and central powers.

1918

3 March: Treaty of Brest-Litovsk.

The Balkan front

1914

12 August: Austria-Hungary invades Serbia, but by the end of September the fighting has reached stalemate and trench warfare has begun.

1915

October: Bulgaria enters war on the side of the central powers. British and French troops land at Salonika in Greece to help Serbians.

October–November: Pressed by Austro-Hungarian, German and Bulgarian armies, the Serbian army, with a large number of civilian refugees, retreats into Albania.

1916

January: Albania declares war on Austria-Hungary and is promptly defeated. The Serbian Army is evacuated from Albania to Corfu, where it is re-equipped by the French and then sent to Salonika.

August: Romania declares war on the central powers, but is rapidly defeated by Austro-Hungarian, Bulgarian and German armies. Most of Romania is then occupied, except for a strip in the north where the Romanians are supported by Russian troops.

1917

June: Greece declares war on the central powers.

1918

July: French and Italians begin an offensive in Albania.

September: Offensive by British, French and Greek forces in Salonika routs Bulgarian army.

30 September: Bulgaria agrees to armistice.

October–November: Allies reconquer Serbia.

29 October: Yugoslav peoples declared to be separated from the Austro-Hungarian Empire.

1 November: Formation of an independent Hungarian government.

3 November: Armistice between Austria and the Allies.

The Italian front

1915

23 May: Italy declares war on Austria-Hungary. The frontier between Austria-Hungary and Italy stretched along the Alps and only near the River Isonzo was the ground flat enough to launch major attacks. Between May 1915 and October 1917 eleven fierce battles were fought along the length of the Isonzo.

1917

24 October: Austro-Hungarians launch attack at Caporetto, routing the Italian army. British and French troops are rushed in to stem the Austro-Hungarian advance.

1918

June: Austro-Hungarians reach limit of their drive into Italy.

October: Italian and Allied troops finally regain the line of the Isonzo.

The Turkish fronts

1914

November: Turkey enters the war.

1915

December to January: Disastrous Turkish advance against Russia in the Caucasus.

February: British and Turkish troops clash over Suez Canal. British Imperial forces advance up the River Tigris in Mesopotamia.

23 April: British Imperial and French forces land at Gallipoli, fail to advance beyond the bridgehead, and trench warfare commences.

November–December: British advance in Mesopotamia is checked and Turks besiege a British Imperial army at Kut-al-Amara.

1916

8 January: Allied troops finally withdraw from Gallipoli.

29 April: British forces surrender at Kut.

6 June: Beginning of the Arab Revolt against Turkish rule in the Hejaz (Arabia).

August: British offensive from Egypt begins driving Turks northwards into Palestine.

1917

February: British recapture Kut and push on to capture Baghdad.

December: British capture Jerusalem.

1918

April: Turks take advantage of Russian defeat to move back into the Caucasus, but continue to be pressed by British Imperial forces pushing through Mesopotamia and Palestine, as well as by the Arab revolt.

September–October: Damascus and Beirut captured by Allies.

30 October: Turkish armistice with the Allies.

The war at sea

1914

4 August: British ships begin patrols in the North Sea and English Channel to prevent the passage of shipping to the central powers. Joint British-French patrols are established for the same purpose in the Mediterranean. In November the British declare the North Sea a war zone.

November: German naval victory at Coronel (off Chile).

December: British naval victory off the Falkland Islands.

1915

February: Germany declares the waters round the British Isles a war zone and begins submarine attacks without prior warning on shipping in these waters.

7 May: The passenger liner *Lusitania* is attacked by a U-boat and sunk. Of the 2,000 passengers aboard 1,198 died, including 291 women and 94 children. 128 of the dead were US citizens.

18 September: Following American protests Germany agrees to restrict submarine warfare, but in

1916

March: Germany actually intensifies the U-boat war.

20 April: USA threatens to break off diplomatic relations with Germany.

24 April: U-boats instructed not to sink vessels without warning.

31 May–1 June: The Battle of Jutland. The major fleet action of the war which ends in a draw, but the German High Seas Fleet withdraws to harbour, never to take to sea again during the war.

1917

1 February: Germany resumes unrestricted submarine warfare.

3 February: USA breaks off diplomatic relations with Germany.

6 April: USA declares war.

April onwards: a convoy system is developed for merchant shipping which helps beat the U-boat blockade; the successful Allied blockade of the central powers remains in force until 1919.

Exercise The war began in the Balkans, but can you detect anything from the above chronology and from your reading of Roberts which suggests that the war fought in this area was different from that fought on the western front in particular? ∎

Specimen answer The fighting in the Balkans was not as continuous as that on the western front; Bulgaria did not join the war until 1915, Romania not until 1916, and Greece not until 1917. States were decisively defeated, and were often defeated rapidly: Serbia was destroyed in the winter of 1915–16; Romania was almost entirely overrun in a matter of months. □

Discussion The events of the war (perhaps 'wars' would be more apt) in the Balkans will be discussed in more detail in Units 11–13, but for the moment it is important that you recognize the difference between the war here and that on the western front. Human losses in the Balkans were enormous; economies were devastated by invasion and plunder, as well as by the needs of war; states were destroyed by their enemies, and new ones were created by victors.

1 THE CONDUCT OF THE WAR ON LAND

In Book I, Unit 2 it was pointed out that none of the wars fought in Europe since the 1850s had lasted for more than ten months. The last big war between two major European powers had been the Franco-Prussian War of 1870; in that war casualties were heavy, but the fighting was over in nine months. The British, French and Italians had fought colonial wars; the British had drawn some sharp lessons from their experiences in the Boer War; and Russia had suffered a humiliating defeat at the hands of the Japanese. Austria-Hungary had not been involved in war since it became a dual monarchy in 1867. As a consequence the battle experience of most troops in 1914 was non-existent. When war did break out it was predicted with some confidence, and with much apparent justification, that it would be 'over by Christmas'. The 'short war illusion' was widespread in military and naval circles as well as among politicians and the public. But this does not mean that the military did not expect heavy casualties; it was the duration that was unexpected.

Exercise There is, I think, one abiding image of the conduct and environment of World War I. Write a few brief notes describing

1   your own abiding image of the conduct and environment of the war; and,

2   anything in the preceding chronology which makes you feel that you must qualify that image. ∎

Specimen answer 1   You might disagree, but I think the abiding image of World War I is of a conflict fought in muddy trenches.

2   Some kind of trench warfare featured in most of the theatres of war between 1914 and 1918, but the chronology does note that the war on the eastern front was often fluid with large tracts of land changing hands, while the war in Mesopotamia and Palestine was not characterized by the stalemate of the fronts in France. □

Discussion The experience of trench warfare varied on the different fronts partly for climatic reasons, but also because the combatant armies appear to have approached the construction of their trench systems in different ways. Drawing on a range of examples, Paul Fussell suggests that

> There were 'national styles' in trenches as in other things. The French trenches were nasty, cynical, efficient, and temporary. Kipling remembered the smell of delicious cooking emanating from some in Alsace. The English were amateur, vague, *ad hoc*, and temporary. The Germans were efficient, clean, pedantic, and permanent. Their occupants proposed to stay where they were. (Paul Fussell, *The Great War and Modern Memory*, 1975, p.45)

The trench system on the western front ran for a length of some 400 miles from the Belgian coast to Switzerland. It began as a series of primitive shelters, but in spite of the 'national styles' these soon became much more sophisticated, with deep dug-outs capable of resisting heavy artillery. Each army constructed its trench system in three lines – 'front', 'support' and 'reserve' – linked by communications

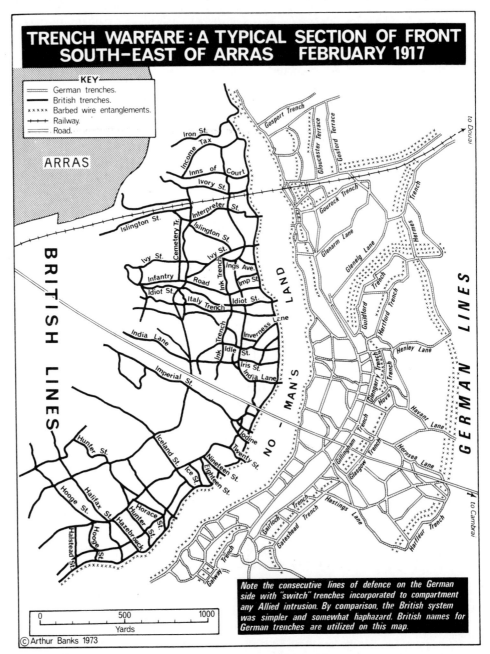

TRENCH WARFARE: A TYPICAL SECTION OF FRONT SOUTH-EAST OF ARRAS   FEBRUARY 1917

KEY
- ═══ German trenches.
- ─── British trenches.
- ××××× Barbed wire entanglements.
- ┼┼┼┼ Railway.
- ═══ Road.

Note the consecutive lines of defence on the German side with "switch" trenches incorporated to compartment any Allied intrusion. By comparison, the British system was simpler and somewhat haphazard. British names for German trenches are utilized on this map.

© Arthur Banks 1973

Source: Arthur Banks, *A Military Atlas of the First World War*, Heinemann Educational Books, 1975.

trenches. Troops did not spend their entire service in the trenches. For example, a British infantry battalion (between 900 and 1,000 men) would be at the front for up to six months, but would spend only periods of up to ten days actually confronting enemy positions in the front-line trenches. One officer gave a detailed breakdown of his service in 1916 which seems fairly typical. He was under fire for a total of 101 days, though he was only in the front line proper for 65 days; he spent another 120 days in reserve and 73 in rest. The remaining ten weeks were made up of ten days in hospital, 17 on leave, 23 travelling, and 21 on courses.

Conditions in the trenches were generally foul, especially when it rained; the combination of these conditions with lice, vermin and a poor diet led to a large number of troops going sick. The list of British admissions to hospital on the western front in 1917, given below in Table 7.1, only takes account of the most severe cases, since the army was hard on 'malingerers' and, as you will notice, it does not include battle casualties.

Table 7.1   *British admissions to hospital, 1917*

Anthrax	8
Dysentery	6,025
Enteric	1,275
Frostbite	21,487
Meningitis	162
Nephritis	15,214
Pneumonia	2,157
Tuberculosis	1,660
VD	48,508

Source: Denis Winter, *Death's Men: Soldiers of the Great War*, 1979, p. 99.

It is, of course, most unlikely that the cases of VD were contracted in the trenches, though many of them were probably contracted in France.

While we can recognize trench warfare as the central image of World War I, we have to try to understand why, given that the generals, politicians and general publics of the states of Europe were expecting a short war, and a war of movement, the conflict in the west especially became a stalemate. The efficient German general staff were contemplating knocking France out of the war in a matter of weeks with the Schlieffen Plan. What went wrong?

Alfred von Schlieffen became Chief of the German General Staff in 1891. As alliances between the European powers developed and solidified, Schlieffen was faced with the problem of how to fight a war on two fronts, against Russia in the east and France in the west. His solution was to strike a lightning blow at France, encircling its armies in a great arc through Belgium and swinging south towards Paris, before the Russians had time to mobilize their enormous manpower. Only about 10 per cent of the German Army was to be deployed against the Russians; the attack through Belgium was designed to give the Germans a seven to one ratio over the French. Schlieffen retired in 1905, and his successor, Moltke, modified the plan for two reasons: first he believed that a French attack into Alsace-Lorraine had to be taken seriously and met with a stronger force than Schlieffen had planned; second, he thought it important to strengthen the number of troops in the east, given Russian military improvements. As a result of the modifications the German sweep through Belgium and into France in August 1914 saw the Germans with a superiority of only three to one; nevertheless the four German armies deployed for this manoeuvre amounted to about one million men.

Exercise   There is debate about exactly why the Schlieffen Plan failed in 1914, but, bearing in mind that the bulk of the German army was infantry, can you think of any problems that would affect a fast attacking arc swinging through Belgium and down towards Paris? ■

Specimen answer   I think there are four major problems. First, you might have identified the exhaustion of the troops, especially those on the extreme right flank of the German advance who were expected both to march and fight and to keep up with those closer to the centre of the arc who had less distance to cover. Second, there was the problem of keeping the men supplied, especially those who had the longest route to cover. Third, there was the deadliness and efficiency of new weaponry, such as the machine gun, which the attackers had to face. Finally, even though the German General Staff was the best in Europe, the control of one million men engaged in the same enterprise was bound to be fraught with difficulty. □

Discussion   I shall look in more detail at the new weaponry and the question of supply shortly, but in case you had difficulty with the above question I can indicate some of the problems by describing what actually happened. On the extreme right of the Schlieffen arc was the German First Army commanded by General von Kluck. The plan required this army to cover some 300 miles in three weeks, which meant marching about fifteen miles a day as well as fighting. The field kitchens could not keep up with the march; one regiment had no bread for four days. Radio was still in its infancy – there were only two transmitters with Kluck's army and only one receiver at headquarters, the codes took a long time to decipher, and the French had quickly become adept at jamming transmissions. Furthermore, motorcycle dispatch riders tended to get lost on roads crammed with troops, artillery and supplies. The consequences of all this were that Kluck's army lost contact with German headquarters; it advanced too far, became separated from Bülow's Second Army to its left, and was itself enveloped by the French.

Technological innovations in the second half of the nineteenth century had revolutionized man's ability to fight wars. The basic infantry weapon in 1914 was a breech-loading rifle. The effectiveness of these weapons had been amply demonstrated by the French Chassepot rifle during the Franco-Prussian war. The different general staffs in Europe were all aware of the new firepower; the directorate of military training in the British Army, for example, forecast 65 to 75 per cent casualties in the army if it was engaged in a war lasting a year – but of course, no war was expected to last that length of time. It was the effectiveness of the new firepower which encouraged the generals to explore flanking attacks. The problem which rapidly developed on the western front was that there were no flanks that could be turned by an infantry attack. The situation was rather different in the east, where the front was twice as long and where men were much thinner on the ground; flanking attacks were possible here, though were not always attempted.

If the general staffs of 1914 appreciated the effectiveness of the rifle, they were not yet sure of the machine gun. Should it be used primarily for offence, to cover a final assault, or for defence? Furthermore, the more machine guns, the fewer men who could be deployed in a final assault with fixed bayonets; and machine guns were new, not always reliable or robust, and they used enormous amounts of ammunition. Most of the machine guns used during the war had a rate of fire of between 500 and 600 rounds per minute – thirty times the rate of the best infantry rifle. Artillery had also been considerably developed during the second half of the nineteenth century, but in the expectation of mobile warfare, most armies were principally equipped with light, quick-firing field guns. However, these guns fired on a low trajectory, and were of little value when it came to destroying trenches and dug-outs. The war consequently witnessed the development of heavy artillery designed to drop large, high-explosive shells into trench systems or to explode shrapnel over a trench. In 1914 the French army had only 300 heavy guns; by 1918 this number had risen to 7,000, of which 400 were mounted on railway carriages. The scale of the bombardments prior to infantry assaults became phenomenal. Before the British attack at Passchendaele in 1917, 320 train-loads of shells were brought up for the artillery; there was one gun for every six yards of front, and some four million shells were fired.

Exercise Can you think of any difficulties which the demands of machine guns and artillery might create both for armies and national economies? ∎

Specimen answer In the first place the different national economies would have to be structured to provide for the demands of the new weaponry. Secondly, the armies would have to ensure that the ammunition got to the front when and where it was needed. □

Discussion Supply was one of the major problems of World War I. No one had contemplated the amount of ammunition that would be required, and the munitions industries of pre-war Europe were simply not prepared to produce on the necessary scale. When the British government established its Ministry of Munitions in June 1915 the production of high-explosive shells was 92 per cent in arrears. In the pre-war arms race it seems that, on average, 4 per cent of national income was devoted to armaments; to meet the needs of actual war this was increased to 25 or 33 per cent. It was this need which compelled governments to take command of industry and to enter into alliances with business and labour, thereby creating what some historians, notably Gerald Feldman (with reference to Germany), Keith Middlemas (with reference to Britain) and Charles Maier (with reference to France, Germany and Italy) have referred to as a new kind of corporate state. (This issue will be explored in detail in subsequent units.)

Producing the weaponry and equipment was only half of the problem, though. The equipment still had to reach the men who needed it. Railways were important, but they could not run right up to the artillery, still less up to the trenches. The armies of 1914 relied mainly on horse-drawn vehicles to supply troops on the move and then to pull supplies up to the front. But the problem with horses was forage: a horse consumed ten times as much in weight each day as a man, and armies were using one horse for every three men. Kluck's army required two million pounds of fodder a day; this, in turn, created massive logistical problems for the military planners. Motorized vehicles began increasingly to take on supply tasks. In 1916 Verdun was supplied by motor transport; some 300 trucks a day travelled on a minor road south of the town to Bar-le-Duc. The route came to be known as the *Voie Sacrée*, the Sacred Road, and took on the character of a national myth. But motorized transport had its own problems of supply: it needed fuel, oil, spare parts and skilled mechanics.

Two new forms of weaponry were introduced on the western front: gas and tanks. The suggestion that chlorine gas should be used against the enemy was raised both at the time of the Crimean and the American Civil War. The French were the first to use toxic weapons during World War I, firing tear-gas grenades from rifles in August 1914. On 27 October 1914 the Germans bombarded the British at Neuve Chapelle with shrapnel shells containing chemical irritants. However, it was another six months before the first major gas attack of the war took place. On 22 April 1915 the Germans discharged chlorine gas from cylinders which the wind carried over French and Canadian trenches at Ypres. The attack came as a total surprise to the Allies, who were totally unprepared and unprotected. Choking chlorine gas causes intense irritation of the lungs and can result in death when inhaled even over a short period. The attack caused 15,000 casualties, of which 5,000 were fatal, and it created a four-mile gap in the line. The German press was to boast of this 'triumph of chemistry', although the success came as something of a surprise to the Germans too. They had decided to use the gas because of a munitions shortage and because of the general ineffectiveness of artillery against earth fortifications like trenches and dug-outs; they did not expect, and were therefore not prepared, for a strategic breakthrough. Within a few days Allied troops were equipped with a crude form of respirator which could cope with gas discharges. Both the French and the British were quick to retaliate; indeed, the Germans were more vulnerable to gas attacks than the Allies since the prevailing winds over north-west Europe blow from the west or south-west, but the wind was an unreliable ally and could drop, or even blow gas back over the attackers.

New forms of gas were introduced as the war progressed: phosgene at the end of 1915, and mustard gas in July 1917. The latter soon became the most widely used gas weapon, since it is virtually colourless and odourless and it evaporates slowly; it causes vomiting and burning. New means of delivering gas were also developed; by 1917 gas shells were fired by the artillery and were used as much to neutralize enemy artillery behind the trenches as to assist infantry attacks. At the same time new respirators were developed, and troops were drilled in how to respond to gas attacks. After 1916, when figures were kept for British gas victims, only 3 per cent of them were listed as having died. In all, however, there were around 800,000 casualties caused by gas and chemical warfare on the battle fronts between 1914 and 1918.

Tanks were first employed in significant numbers at the Somme in September 1916, but they were thrown forward in unco-ordinated fashion. They were used sporadically until Cambrai in November 1917 when, without the usual preliminary bombardment, an attack was launched by the British with 378 tanks. These early machines were unwieldy, and the attack was to some extent ill-conceived, since there were no infantry reserves to exploit any breakthrough; as German reinforcements arrived, the attack petered out. However, the tanks did prove effective: at the end of the engagement 10,000 Germans had been taken prisoner and 200 guns had been captured. Cambrai was regarded as a great victory, and in London bells were rung for the first and only time during the war. Tanks quickly caught the imagination of the public after Cambrai; one contemporary poster issued in Britain and aimed at war savings proclaimed:

> The tank is a travelling fortress
> That clears the way for our soldiers
> It cuts through the wire under fire
> It saves lives
> It is our war discovery
> It is a matter of pride to help to build tanks.

Yet some of the military hierarchy remained sceptical, regarding tanks very much with Kitchener's jaundiced eye as 'pretty mechanical toys'. The French were quick to develop their own tanks, but these, like the early British tanks, were often very slow; the heavy Schneider and St. Chamond machines were also poor at crossing trenches. The first French attempt to use tanks on a large scale was in the Nivelle offensive of April 1917, when German heavy machine guns knocked out 60 out of 132. The Schneider also proved to be a death trap for its crew if it caught fire. Ludendorff regarded tanks in much the same way as Kitchener had done, but after Cambrai the Germans speeded up their production, though their only operational model, the A7V, was not ready for action until March 1918. The Americans were keen on tanks and used the French Renault and British Mark V for their own forces, but the first American tanks did not arrive in France until November 1918. Neither Russia nor Italy, with its well-developed motor industry, ever managed to put tanks into production.

2 *THE WAR AT SEA*

Britain entered the war with the essential strategy that had served it well for centuries – a strong navy and continental allies. As the war continued, the size of Britain's armies and the extent of its involvement in the fighting on mainland Europe was to surpass the peak of its previous military endeavour during the Napoleonic Wars, yet supremacy at sea remained all-important. The challenge to British supremacy represented by the German High Seas Fleet, developed from the 1890s, had been an important factor in drawing Britain into the Entente with France and Russia. Once war had begun, the containment of German sea power in port was as effective as its destruction on the high seas, for the vital aim was the exercise of maritime supremacy. Liddell Hart has argued that upon British sea supremacy 'was based the whole war effort of Britain and her allies, because upon it depended the very existence of Britain' (*A History of the World War*, p.360).

Although the ships and their armaments were very different, the essence of naval strategy – to keep enemy fleets in port, to keep the sea lanes open, to blockade the hostile powers and to provide against invasion – was not very different from that of the French revolutionary and Napoleonic period, while the textbook tactics for battle had changed surprisingly little. Just as the fleets at Trafalgar had sailed past each other thundering their broadsides into each other, so, at longer range, had the Russian and Japanese fleets at Tsushima in 1905. As the most recent major naval battle, Tsushima was held to have underlined the centrality of the battleship to naval warfare. After the development of the Dreadnought class, the profile of a battle fleet was an elaborate chessboard arrangement, with heavily armed and armoured battleships ringed by protective destroyers, preceded by battle cruisers with their own attendant destroyers, while lightly armoured fast cruisers acted as the scouts of the fleet.

That there were so few major clashes between the British and German fleets during the war is largely explained by the British success in keeping the High Seas Fleet in port for so much of the time and the caution of British admirals. In late July 1914 the British Grand Fleet was at sea as part of a mobilization exercise. On 28 July it was ordered by Churchill, the First Lord of the Admiralty, to its war stations; from that moment its main role was to remain intact, and the destruction of the enemy fleet was secondary to this. David Howarth has described its main function as being 'the same as Cornwallis's in 1804, the dull and inglorious chore of simply existing in order to keep the enemy fleet in port'.

A great naval engagement was expected, however. Admiral Fisher, who had done so much to prepare the fleet for war and who was recalled by Churchill to be First Sea Lord in 1914, had prophesied that a major engagement would take place in September, and the British public, weaned on the idea of Britannia ruling the waves, expected victory. A clash between cruisers in the Heligoland Bight in

August 1914 was hailed in Britain as a victory; the defeat of a squadron off Coronel in November was a shock, but soon redeemed by the destruction of the offending Germans off the Falkland Islands; in January 1915 cruisers clashed again at the Dogger Bank, and again the Royal Navy could claim victory. These early battles undermined the morale of the German High Seas Fleet and discredited it in the eyes of the public; but the battles also revealed glaring faults on the British side in warship construction, in organization and in leadership, much of which was ignored and proved to be costly when the major fleet action of the war was fought at Jutland in 1916.

Exercise Can you think of any geographical advantages which the fleets of the Entente powers enjoyed over those of the central powers, especially in European waters? ■

Specimen answer and discussion Most of the coastline of Western Europe could be covered by the fleets of the Entente powers. If the High Seas Fleet had wanted to break out into the Atlantic, it would have been forced to go round the north of Scotland, or through the English Channel. Similarly, the much weaker Austro-Hungarian navy had only a narrow channel of access to the Mediterranean. An additional point which you may not have considered is that warships require refuelling. If the German or Austro-Hungarian fleets had succeeded in breaking out, they would have been at a disadvantage compared with the British and French, whose imperial possessions gave them many more coaling stations around the globe; for the central powers a return to base would have required the fleets' having to run the same gauntlet as when they broke out. The British Grand Fleet was able to maintain a successful if loose blockade of the High Seas Fleet for most of the war; neither side was prepared to offer battle unless it considered itself to have the advantage, and this led to a stand-off which largely favoured the British. The Battle of Jutland confirmed this pattern. □

Another sphere in which British naval power could have been effectively brought to bear on the enemy was the eastern Mediterranean. Turkey entered the war in October 1914 after being progressively nudged towards entry by the German government, whose battleship *Goeben* and cruiser *Breslaw* had been allowed to enter the Dardanelles Straits after being pursued by the British fleet in the Mediterranean. An immediate attack by the Royal Navy on the Dardanelles, whose defences were obsolete and incomplete, would have stood a good chance of success, but the opportunity was missed. The naval attack on the Dardanelles that did eventually take place began with a bombardment of the outer ports in February and culminated in an attempt to force the Straits on 18 March by British and French minesweepers and battleships. Due to a failure to sweep all the mines, three Allied battleships were sunk and three more badly damaged, and the operation was called off. The Dardanelles, it was now decided, were to be subjected to a land attack. Some have seen the attempt to force the Straits by a battle fleet as an improper and inappropriate use of naval power, and yet the operation may well have been close to success. Liddell Hart suggests that a widely held opinion among Turkish and German officers was that a renewed attack could not have been long opposed. The loss of men – sixty-four – was small in comparison to the numbers that would be lost in the Gallipoli land attack, while the sunk battleships were old and obsolete. A renewed naval attack on 19 March might have succeeded and opened up Constantinople to the guns of the Allied fleets.

As with the war on land, it was in the western sector that the decisive battle was fought. Jutland was where Jellicoe and the Grand Fleet could have lost the war and where matters between the Royal Navy and the German High Seas Fleet were put most dramatically to the test. At the end of May 1916 Admiral Scheer led the High Seas Fleet out of port. Over two days (31 May/1 June) it fought the Grand Fleet, inflicting the heavier losses (as Table 7.2 shows). But at the end of the battle, Scheer went back to port and the Royal Navy resumed its blockade; furthermore the German Fleet remained in port until the end of the war. Scheer's reluctance to move out of port after 1916 was partly prompted by the removal of his submarines. Scheer relied on these for spotting the superior enemy fleet and for crippling it; indeed, fear of German U-boats meant that the Grand Fleet became increasingly reluctant to move without a large destroyer escort. In August 1916 Scheer's submarines were directed to leave the High Seas Fleet and to join the blockade of British commerce in a campaign which almost brought Britain to its knees.

Table 7.2   *Battle losses at Jutland*

	British	German
Battle cruisers	3	1
Armoured cruisers	3	—
Old battleships	—	1
Light cruisers	—	4
Destroyers	8	5
Ships' tonnage	112,000	61,000
Men killed	6,000	2,500

In the final analysis battleships and Grand Fleets were good for sinking other battleships, and they were sometimes used for coastal bombardment. Battleships required destroyer escorts to act as a screen and protection, which left the merchant navy with insufficient destroyer protection. At the height of the German submarine onslaught on British merchant shipping in the spring of 1917, the idea of convoys with destroyer escorts was suggested, but Jellicoe opposed it: merchant ships could not keep station, and in any case the navy did not have enough destroyers to protect them. Lloyd George, on advice from a junior naval officer, overruled his First Sea Lord. Convoys worked: whereas in April 1917 one ship out of four leaving British ports never returned, less than 1 per cent of convoyed ships were lost from all causes. Nevertheless, over 500 British merchant ships were lost between May and December 1917. The entry of the United States into the war (itself partly a result of the U-boat attacks on neutral shipping) certainly helped Britain's position. British shipyards could not produce the number of destroyers which the Admiralty demanded for the protection of surface ships, but United States shipyards, with the enormous economic potential of that country behind them, could and did.

While U-boats attempted to blockade Britain, the Entente mounted a counter blockade of Germany and Austria-Hungary. The Entente's blockade brought a confrontation between Britain and Sweden in 1916, with Britain having to tread carefully since it needed Swedish iron ore and pit props. The Dutch, too, resented the restrictions which the British in particular sought to impose upon them. However, the Entente's blockade was more successful than that of the U-boats, and it grew steadily tighter as the war progressed, increasingly depriving the central powers of food supplies and raw materials from neutral Europe, the Far East, Africa and America. The Allied blockade was already beginning to bite in Vienna before the end of 1914. The impact was a little slower in Germany, but became particularly serious in 1917 and 1918. Pre-war Germany imported 20 per cent of the total calorie intake of its people, and by 1917 the Professor of Political Science at Giessen University, Goetz Briefs, was convinced that 'the German household' was living on the poverty line. While demographic trends are notoriously difficult to estimate, there were approximately 300,000 deaths among German civilians aged between 15 and 59 during the war years that would otherwise not have occurred; 'excess' deaths among the young and the old would probably have been proportionately even greater. Of course, the blockade was not directly responsible for all of these deaths or the general debility of the German people, but it made a significant contribution.

3 THE WAR IN THE AIR

The first aeroplane to be used for aerial warfare was deployed by the Italians against the Turks in Libya in 1911. At the same time the French and the German armies were experimenting with aircraft, while Britain's Royal Flying Corps was formed in 1912 with less than a dozen pilots. In 1914 the belligerent nations possessed between them rather less than 2,000 planes; in spite of the experiments, quite what the effect of aerial war would be remained a mystery. Sir John French felt it necessary to warn members of the British Expeditionary Force that, 'should it appear inevitable that an aeroplane flying low must strike any individuals they should lie down in order to avoid being struck by the propeller'.

The role of military aviation at the outset of the war was perceived essentially as one of reconnaissance, but reconnaissance aircraft soon found themselves attacked by enemy fighters and needed fighter cover of their own. By the middle of the war fighter planes were being sent up specifically to win superiority in the air so that reconnaissance, artillery spotting from the air, and bombing raids could be carried out.

During World War I bombing raids were primarily conducted against military targets. Early in 1916 the Italians began launching long-distance bombing raids over the Adriatic against Austro-Hungarian towns and military bases. The first of these raids involved Caprioni bombers flying alone; later they were escorted by fighters. The Germans bombarded military targets from the air in 1914 using their fleet of eleven rigid airships. London was attacked twelve times by the Zeppelins between May 1915 and October 1917, and there were raids over other parts of Britain – in April 1916, for instance, a Zeppelin raid on Edinburgh and Leith resulted in the deaths of eight people, including three children. Over 800 civilians were killed and 1,500 injured by aerial bombardment in London between 1914 and 1918. The worst raids came in late September 1917 when Gotha and Riesen aircraft were used. People took shelter in the Underground and, to reduce panic, the government persuaded newspaper editors to cease publication of pictures showing bomb damage. British raids on Germany were never on the same scale, although a raid on Karlsruhe as early as June 1916 left 26 women and 124 children casualties.

Bombs were not the only thing that could be dropped from the air. In the early afternoon of 30 August 1914 a German aircraft dropped four small bombs and a bag on Paris between the Gare du Nord and the Gare de l'Est; the bag contained a number of copies of a leaflet warning Parisians that the German army was at their gates and urging them to surrender. Although the Germans were first off the mark in this new style of propaganda, the British and French became better organized, dropping leaflets advising German soldiers that they would be well cared for as prisoners and, on the French part, small books and newspapers designed to undermine German morale. Italian aircraft dropped leaflets and proclamations in the language of, and to, the subject peoples of the Austro-Hungarian Empire, urging them to break from Habsburg rule. The Germans dropped a few leaflets on Russian troops and the Russians responded in kind, but overall it was on the static western front where this new kind of propaganda was most employed.

Aerial warfare must be kept in perspective, however. During the war airpower made great steps forward: aircraft and their armaments (notably the synchronized system enabling a machine-gun to fire through a propeller) were significantly improved, and the numbers of men in the different air forces were increased. But airpower played a minor role, and was generally employed in support of traditional military tactics on the ground or at sea. There were 'dog fights', anti-aircraft guns were quickly developed and deployed, and the loss of life was high: perhaps 50,000 airmen were killed during the conflict. Even at the end of the war concepts such as the aircraft carrier and strategic bombing were still only in embryo, but they were to be developed both theoretically and in practice during the inter-war years.

4 PERCEPTIONS OF THE WAR

The Battle of the Somme was the biggest battle on the western front before 1918. Preparations for it were massive. On 24 June 1916 a seven-day artillery barrage commenced during which 1,500,000 shells were fired on German fortifications. But this massive bombardment, which could be heard in England, failed to destroy the German dug-outs, which were deep and well fortified. It also failed to destroy the miles of barbed wire stretched in front of the German trenches. At 7.30 a.m. on 1 July, the British Third and Fourth Armies, and the French Sixth Army went 'over the top' from their trenches and advanced into 'no man's land'. To their surprise the German resistance was fierce, and the advancing waves of troops were mown down by machine-gun fire. On this first day of the battle 20,000 British troops were killed, amounting to 60 per cent of the officers and 40 per cent of the other ranks committed to the action.

Just over seven weeks after the first infantry waves went in, the film *The Battle of the Somme* opened at thirty-four London cinemas on 21 August; a week later it appeared in major provincial cities, and it was shown extensively throughout Britain and the Allied countries. The camera had been used to record wars before. Still photographs were taken of the Crimean and the American Civil War. Some moving film was shot during the Boer War, the Russo-Japanese, and the Balkan Wars; during World War I filming took place on a much wider scale, but the technical and practical limitations of heavy, hand-cranked cameras still restricted what could be filmed. *The Battle of the Somme* was the work of two British cameramen, Geoffrey Malins and J. B. McDowell, who joined sections of the British Fourth Army on 28 June 1916 specifically to film the new offensive.

On the morning of 1 July Malins filmed the explosion of a giant British mine under a German strongpoint; he then followed men of the 1st Lancashire Fusiliers up the approach trenches to their attack positions. As the men went over the top they were mown down and Malins was unable to follow without being killed himself. He therefore rejoined McDowell at the Minden Post dressing station. Here they filmed the wounded of both sides. Later in the day, or perhaps the following day, they filmed German prisoners and captured German trenches. Finally they filmed the troops who had initiated the attack on 1 July coming out of the line to rest.

Exercise Turn now to video-cassette 1 and watch item 5, the extract from *The Battle of the Somme*. As you watch the extracts, note down anything which you feel the film tells you about the conduct of the war and of the Somme battle in particular. ∎

Specimen answer and discussion This was not meant to be a trick exercise, but I feel that the extracts tell you little about the battle itself. There is no pattern, the events are rather bewildering and there is no guide to what is happening; many of the soldiers from both sides look bewildered, too, which is hardly surprising considering what they had to go through. For the reasons noted above there could be no scenes of actual combat, though of course you do get an idea of what men looked like who had just emerged from combat. □

We do not know what the first audiences made of the film, although it is clear that many were shocked to see men fall dead as they went over the top. Sequences from the film have been used again and again to show 'images' of what war was like on the western front. S. D. Badsey, who has made a detailed study of the film, comments:

> What the camera showed, both to the British public for the first time and to historians ever since, was a war in which men suffered but achieved nothing. Soldiers were pictured marching, often in high spirits to the front line trenches. There, as the moment of attack came, they waited faces strained with tension. They then vanished out of the camera's sight until it found them again collapsing with pain at a dressing station or fatigue at a rest camp. The bewilderment felt by the common soldier in a major battle, stemming largely from his inability to see its overall shape, was certainly not exclusive to the First World War, and even less so to film as a means of recording war, but in this particular case, the novelty increasing the impact, the technical limitations of the film record reinforced the shapelessness of war, and the helplessness of individuals in war, far beyond the point of objectivity. (S. D. Badsey, 'The Battle of the Somme', *Historical Journal of Film, Radio and Television*, 1983, pp.105–6)

Film is, of course, only one of the media which helped to construct both contemporary and historical perceptions of the war. There was a vast amount of literature published in all countries during the war; one bibliographical study of English poetry of the war, dealing only with printed books and ignoring the thousands of poems which appeared in newspapers, shows that some 2,225 people published verse on the theme of war, and over 500 of these were women. Some of the more important novels to emerge from the war will be discussed in

Units 8–10, but here I just want you to consider briefly the value of literary works for historians, and to put their images alongside some more 'popular' culture. Creative writers of the war period tended to come from the upper or middle classes; those who wrote directly about the rigours of battle were invariably junior officers. How typical was their reaction to events? Does a poem about poison gas describe it any more accurately than a newspaper report or a letter from a private soldier?

Exercise   The following is a family letter in my possession. Read it now and then answer the following questions. What picture does Lance Corporal Fraser give of battle? How does this picture compare with the more graphic descriptions usually found in poems or novels? ∎

> 8131
> L/C W. Fraser
> C Company
> 9 Platoon
> 2nd A & SH
>
> 29/4/17
>
> Dear Mrs McGuinness, I was looking for your brother but could not find him hence my writing to you regarding Jim. Your husband is amassing what had happened to him, I do not know he may only be slightly wounded which I hope and trust is the case. We had made an attack and Jim with a few more were sent up to support another company, when the enemy made a counter attack it was here that I saw him last. I had asked for a magazine for the gun and it was him that supplied me with some. We were being pushed back a little hence the reason for my losing sight of him, but I pray God nothing serious has happened to your husband, and my best pal.
> I remain
>
> Yours in anticipation
>
> William Fraser

Specimen answer and discussion   What strikes me about the letter is how matter-of-fact it all is; asking for a magazine for a gun seems like asking for a pen or a tool at work (and in a sense perhaps it was). There is no mention of the squalor of the trenches, nor the savagery and brutality of battle. No doubt Lance Corporal Fraser did not want to upset Mrs McGuinness, but remember also that the letter was not meant for publication; it was written by a simple man, and was therefore not 'tainted' with artistic description and convention. (As a matter of interest Mrs McGuinness's brother was killed later in 1917; her husband was made a prisoner of war, but survived to die in 1957.) Of course, it is never advisable to generalize from one source, but the letters and diaries of ordinary soldiers are being analysed increasingly by historians, and they are tending to show that many of the traditional ideas about the combatants of World War I are erroneous. David Englander's study of the correspondence of French soldiers, for example, concludes:

> Peace at any price . . . was not desired. . . . The war was accepted passively as a defensive necessity without any ideological commitment beyond the removal of the enemy from French soil. While the *poilu* [the

French soldier] came to accept that the German soldier experienced comparable suffering, there was never any doubt that he was the author of his own misfortune. A fierce and undying hatred of the enemy remained a pronounced feature of correspondence from the front. (David Englander, 'The French Soldier, 1914–18', *French History*, 1987, p. 64)

At the same time French attitudes to their allies were coloured by a narrow calculation of advantage: 'Until 1916 the British were thought to have been indolent and not really serious about the war or willing only to fight to the last Frenchman' (Englander, p.66). The British soldiers' attitude to the French appears to have been similar, as were German attitudes to the Austro-Hungarians, and so on across the battlefronts.

In spite of the horrors and carnage of trench warfare, men came to terms with it. This is reflected in a British publication which came straight from the trenches. The *Wipers Times* (British soldiers never quite mastered the pronunciation of Ypres) was first published in February 1916 and appeared under various titles at fairly regular intervals until December 1918. Except for the very last issue it was never printed out of the front line, and at one time the printing press was within 700 yards of enemy positions. While it was produced and largely written by junior officers, other ranks contributed, and the paper was widely read by front-line troops. It also stands in sharp contrast to the war poetry and those memoirs written several years later. The illustration overleaf is a page from the *Wipers Times* which is clearly based on the traditional music hall advertisement.

The English writer Robert Graves estimated that a subaltern's life expectancy at the front was about two weeks. Officers faced greater risks than their men: about 20 per cent of those who served at the front were killed, compared to about 12 per cent for other ranks. Many soldiers experienced a bond of shared experience with their junior officers, and this comes over in the pages of the *Wipers Times*. Writing in 1973, the author Henry Williamson, who had fought at Ypres, commented:

> more than fifty years later, I can feel myself to be surrounded by the spirit of the Western Front in the pages of the *Wipers Times* . . . for every item is gentle in attitude to what was hellish – and this attitude, its virtue, was extended to the enemy. It is a charity which links those who have passed through the estranging remoteness of battle. (Henry Williamson, foreword to *The Wipers Times*, facsimile edition, 1973, p.ix)

The perception of World War I is generally one of unrelieved horror, of carnage and devastation on a massive scale. The perception is undoubtedly correct; but it must be remembered that when the front-line soldiers resumed their civilian lives after the war, for some of them at least, their home surroundings seemed drab. At regimental reunions, and in organizations like the British Legion, the *mouvement combattant* and the *Stahlhelm*, many came together, forgetting the horrors and remembering the comradeship. In some instances these groups acquired sinister political attitudes and attributes; but if sections of the *Stahlhelm* fed into the Nazi Party, the *mouvement combattant* was profoundly loyal to the French Republic, while the British Legion fostered an apolitical image and kept 'remembrance' alive.

Note that sections 5 and 6 are written by Clive Emsley.

THE NEUVE EGLISE HIPPODROME

GRAND NEW REVIEW, ENTITLED:

"SHELL IN"

POSITIVELY THE GREATEST SPECTACULAR PERFORMANCE EVER STAGED.

BRINGING BEFORE THE PUBLIC AT ONE AND THE SAME TIME THE FOLLOWING HIGHLY-PAID STARS:

THE CRUMPS.
LITTLE PIP-SQUEAK
DUDDY WHIZZ-BANG.
HURLA SHELLOG, etc., etc.

THRILLING OPENING CHORUS ARRANGED BY LEWIS VICKERS.

Exciting! Hair-raising!! Awe-inspiring!!!

SEE WHAT THE PAPERS SAY.   BOOK EARLY.   PRICES DOUBLE THIS WEEK.

TO HARASSED SUBALTERNS.

—o—o—o—o—

IS YOUR LIFE MISERABLE? ARE YOU UNHAPPY?

DO YOU HATE YOUR COMPANY COMMANDER?

—o—o—o—o—

YES! THEN BUY HIM ONE OF

OUR NEW PATENT TIP DUCK BOARDS

YOU GET HIM ON THE END—THE DUCK BOARD DOES THE REST

—o—o—o—o—

Made in three sizes, and every time a "Blighty."

—o—o—o—o—

" If once he steps on to the end,
'Twill take a month his face to mend "

—o—o—o—o—

WRITE AT ONCE & ENSURE HAPPINESS

THE NOVELTY SYNDICATE, R.E. HOUSE   Tel.: " DUMP '

A page from The Wipers Times, *vol. 1, no. 2, 1 May 1916 (reproduced from the facsimile edition, London, Peter Davies, 1973)*

5 *DIPLOMACY AND THE WAR*

Exercise Deadlock was achieved on the western front before the end of 1914, and although there was movement in the east, there was no sign of a decisive breakthrough. Why, given this situation, do you suppose that the belligerents did not seek a negotiated peace? ■

Specimen answer The explanation seems to be that both sides still thought that they could win. □

Discussion It was in the early months of the war that the German government began to develop a series of war aims, though Chancellor Bethmann Hollweg tried hard to prevent an early debate on these; in both the east and the west these war aims involved annexation and the domination of some smaller states. Such a realignment of frontiers, the German government and military believed, was necessary for the security and development of the Empire. While the Entente powers were much slower in devising war aims, opposition to German annexations always figured in their thinking, and negotiations on these German terms were unthinkable even before they published their war aims (which in the British case was not until early 1918). Furthermore, as the war dragged on, and as the human and economic costs mounted, governments appear increasingly to have felt that they needed some tangible and obvious results to convince their people that the sacrifices had been worth it; the defeat of the enemy was the best prize to present in these circumstances.

Exercise You are probably familiar with the phrase 'war is the continuation of diplomacy by other means'. But did diplomacy stop because war had started? From your reading of Roberts's Chapter 9, note down where, and over what issues, diplomacy continued; and I don't want you to think purely in terms of 'peace' diplomacy and negotiations. (You will probably find it helpful to refresh your memory by looking again at Roberts, pp.291–4, 299–302, and 310–14.) ■

Specimen answer and discussion Roberts shows diplomatic negotiations being conducted in four principal areas between 1914 and 1918.

1   The various belligerents negotiated with other powers to persuade them to join the war on their side. The most obvious example here is the attempt to bring Italy into the war; the Entente succeeded, essentially by promising the Italians other people's territory. Rather similar discussions were conducted with some of the different nationalities of Central and Eastern Europe. In particular Roberts notes the German negotiations for an independent Russian Poland. This kind of discussion naturally concerned the rulers of the multi-racial Austro-Hungarian Empire. An element which you may not have noted was the diplomatic significance of the idea of national determination in President Woodrow Wilson's 'Fourteen Points'; but in the last year of the war in particular the Allied governments of Britain, France and the United States were negotiating with Czechoslovak, Polish and Yugoslav leaders, and Czech, Polish and Yugoslav military units were fighting on different fronts – the two former in France and Italy (with the Czech Legion also creating problems for the Bolsheviks), and the latter in the Balkans.

2   Combatant allies had to negotiate with each other over war aims and war policy. The example of Germany and Austria-Hungary agreeing to an indepen-

dent Russian Poland obviously required discussion, especially given the concerns of Vienna. The Entente powers wanted the defeat of the central powers, but they did not have identical views about the best outcome of the war. While some attitudes and concerns would not have been voiced in diplomatic discussions, these nevertheless shaped the thinking of those involved. The French, for example, wanted the return of Alsace-Lorraine and a Germany sufficiently weakened that it would be incapable of invading French territory again. The British were not as committed to the return of Alsace-Lorraine; in the early stages of the conflict at least, they also felt that a strong Germany could have a role to play in restraining Russia, especially if Russia emerged from the war considerably strengthened. At the outset the British were also far less keen than the Russians about involving Turkey in the war, since trouble in the Middle East could spread into parts of the British Empire. The Russians were even more sensitive about their Polish territories; the issue could not be raised in official diplomatic correspondence between Russia and its Entente allies, and this limited the extent to which the Entente sought to subvert the Poles in Austria-Hungary. The situation changed with the Russian Revolution. In varying degrees the revolutionaries of the provisional government and the first soviets all recognized Polish claims to some sort of independence, and as a consequence the 700,000 Poles in the Russian army became the nucleus of a Polish army on Polish territory. These troops, together with the embryonic state administration which developed alongside them, and those Polish units and vocal diplomatic representatives in the West, provided the Entente with a potential new ally against the central powers.

3   The belligerent powers still had to negotiate with neutrals, particularly when their blockading policies caused offence or, worse still, the deaths of neutral citizens. Roberts concentrates on the impact of the blockade on the United States while it remained neutral, and on the diplomatic friction which developed between the Americans and the belligerents. But there were other neutrals, notably the Netherlands and Sweden, who were much closer to the actual fighting and who were drawn into difficult diplomatic negotiations because of their trade with Germany and the attempts of the Entente powers to limit or, better still, to end it. Both Sweden and the Netherlands, an imperial power in its own right with rich colonies in the East Indies and a large merchant marine, naturally objected to anyone telling them with whom they should trade. They also objected to having their ships stopped or delayed and their letters and cables censored. Geographically the Swedes were in the stronger position; they were further from the fighting and the might of the Royal Navy, and they could, if they wished, impede goods *en route* from Britain and France to Russia. Whatever their attitudes to the rights and wrongs of the war, the neutrals had to continue trading to keep their own economies alive. It was not simply a question of profiting from the war needs of the belligerents, since the war had dislocated the international economy and the neutrals suffered from both wartime inflation and war-induced shortages. The Netherlands also had to cope with 150,000 refugees and invalided soldiers. The American entry into the war worsened the situation of the neutrals in that it lost them their strongest champion and exerted greater pressure on them to co-operate with the Entente; yet negotiating this co-operation required deft diplomatic skills from both sides.

4   There were also attempts to bring a negotiated peace, sometimes by belligerents (notably the abortive discussions between Britain, France and Austria-Hungary in 1917–18), sometimes by neutral leaders (notably President Wilson),

and sometimes by outsiders such as the neutral socialists, who organized the conferences at Lugano in 1914 and Zimmerwald in 1915, and Pope Benedict XV, who issued his call for peace in August 1917.

The idea of a negotiated peace gained popularity in 1917 for a variety of reasons. First, among the combatant population there was an increasing degree of war-weariness and dissatisfaction with the war and the resulting privations. In Russia these problems led to revolution at the beginning of the year; in France the agony of Verdun and the disastrous Nivelle offensive led to army mutinies; in Italy economic privation provoked strikes and bread riots. Parts of Austria-Hungary, particularly the German lands, were suffering near-famine conditions. Britain and Germany were holding their respective alliances together, but they too were experiencing serious shortages and industrial disorders in 1917. In addition to the internal problems of the belligerents, certain political events seemed, in the eyes of some individuals and groups, to offer new hopes of peace. An initial effect of the Russian Revolution was to liberalize Russian war aims: the governments which replaced the Tzar were prepared to carry on the war against Germany, but declared that there would be no annexations or indemnities on Russia's part. President Wilson had sought to negotiate peace as a neutral on the lines of liberal nationalism and self-determination for peoples, and general democratic ideals. American entry into the war seemed to offer the chance of some negotiation, though Wilson's response to the Pope's peace proposal in August 1917 disappointed any such hopes. The Pope had suggested a return to the *status quo ante bellum*, with the Germans withdrawing from occupied Belgium and France and the Entente restoring captured German colonies. Wilson, however, assuming the leadership of the Allied cause, declared that there could be no peace with the present rulers of Germany, since their word could not be taken as a guarantee of anything.

Inspired by the Russian Revolution, socialists in Britain and Germany began making calls for a negotiated peace without annexation or indemnities. In July 1917 socialist deputies and the Catholic Centre Party came together in the *Reichstag* to pass a resolution for 'a peace of understanding'. Richard von Kuhlmann, the German Foreign Minister, subsequently elaborated a plan for a separate peace with Britain, but this foundered on the twin rocks of British suspicion and the hostility of the German military and those who were determined to annex territory. In Britain, the war cabinet faced the problem of one of its members participating in the arrangements for a meeting of socialists in Stockholm which appeared likely to make a call for peace through negotiation. Arthur Henderson, the Secretary of the Labour Party, had been brought into the war cabinet in December 1916 to give the labour movement some representation at government level; his involvement with the Stockholm meeting led to a confrontation with Lloyd George. Henderson resigned from the cabinet but, freed from collective responsibility, he began publicly to voice his feelings about the war and to win the Labour Party to them; this put additional pressure on Lloyd George to make a public declaration of British war aims.

Austria-Hungary conducted secret negotiations with Britain and France on and off throughout 1917. The leaders of the Dual Monarchy were worried by their internal economic situation, and they feared that defeat would mean the break-up of the empire. In March the new Emperor, Charles, began negotiations with the French through his brother-in-law, Prince Sixtus of Bourbon-Palma. The negotiations failed for a variety of reasons, some of which reflect the point made earlier about the differences that existed between allies as well as enemies. In particular, while the Emperor was inclined towards making a separate peace without Germany, his foreign minister, Count Czernin, was not; Charles was not a strong enough personality to act on his own over this. Moreover, Charles was reluctant to make peace if it meant yielding territory to Italy. The French were concerned that if Italy won concessions in a peace with Austria, then Italy might pull out of the war against Germany. Both the British and the French were not particularly anxious to conclude a separate peace with Austria-Hungary if it did not help achieve their other war aims, and if it encouraged calls for a general negotiated settlement among their populations. In August there were new talks with Czernin's blessing; on this occasion there was talk of increasing the Habsburg Empire at German expense, but again Charles was reluctant to cede land to Italy, and there were fears that the Entente powers really only wanted to upset the Austro-German alliance and were intending to reveal the negotiations to the Germans. Again in December there were secret negotiations in Switzerland between General Jan Smuts, the South African statesman who was also a member of the British war cabinet, and Count Albert von Mensdorff, a former Austrian ambassador to London; again the discussions foundered, with the Entente seeking to detach the Dual Monarchy from the alliance with Germany, and the Dual Monarchy seeking a more general peace.

The Bolshevik coup in Russia and the German negotiations to conclude the war in the east, which resulted in the treaty of Brest-Litovsk, put a different complexion on both military and diplomatic affairs. The central powers could now withdraw combat troops from the east, and economic arrangements, particularly with the Ukraine, looked like easing the effect of the Allied blockade. In addition, the Entente powers feared that Bolshevik propaganda, condemning the war as the work of capitalist imperialism, might strike a chord among their own populations, and worse still among their troops. At the end of January 1918, for example, the permanent under-secretary at the British Ministry of Labour reported:

> A good deal of treason is being talked, and the idea of 'peace by negotiation' is making headway, induced largely by the mental apathy resulting from war-weariness. Some of the leaders are talking very high and appear prepared to go to extreme lengths, and in the general atmosphere of sentimentality and unreason which is prevalent at the moment, the Russian Revolution has awakened much wider echoes than would have been the case at a time when men's minds were not unbalanced by the strain of the prolonged war conditions, and were more capable of seeing the facts in their true light. It would be rash to venture any prophecy as to what will happen. The Government has to a large extent lost its authority in the eyes of the workers, and there is a general impression that it is bound to obey their demands. (Quoted in Christopher Andrew, *Secret Service: The Making of the British Intelligence Community*, 1985, pp. 327–8)

Such fears were not matched by action on the part of the workers. Indeed, in Britain the news of Brest-Litovsk and the Ludendorff Offensive undermined opponents and critics of the war. However, these fears did contribute to the diplomatic moves of the Entente powers at the beginning of 1918. Lloyd George made a declaration of Britain's war aims on 5 January, outlining Britain's hopes for a peace based on moral principles and a new order focused on a League of Nations which would find an alternative for settling international disputes in place of war. Significantly this declaration was made not to parliament, but to the Trades Union Congress, and it was, at least in part, designed to draw the sting of opponents of the war and those demanding negotiations. Three days later Woodrow Wilson announced his celebrated 'Fourteen Points'. These were in keeping with the stand that Wilson had taken throughout the war, but they were also aimed at rousing the internal opposition to the governments of Germany and Austria-Hungary.

Diplomacy therefore continued during the war, sometimes partly for internal consumption, sometimes partly as a weapon of war; but it was not to decide the outcome.

6 BALANCE SHEET

Exercise Roberts, pp. 289–90 gives a rough outline of the comparative strengths of the belligerents in 1914. Compare these with Tables 7.3 and 7.4 below, which are from Paul Kennedy's *The Rise and Fall of the Great Powers*. What particularly strikes you about Kennedy's comparison in contrast to that of Roberts? ■

Table 7.3   *Industrial/technological comparisons of the 1914 alliances*

	Germany/ Austria-Hungary	France/ Russia	+	Britain
Percentages of world manufacturing production (1913)	19.2	14.3	+	13.6 = 27.9
Energy consumption (1913) million metric tons of coal equivalent	236.4	116.8	+	195.0 =311.8
Steel production (1913) in million tons	20.2	9.4	+	7.7 = 17.1
Total industrial potential (UK in 1900 = 100)	178.4	133.9	+	127.2 =261.1

Source: Paul Kennedy, *The Rise and Fall of the Great Powers*, 1988, p.333.

Table 7.4   *Industrial/technological comparisons with the United States but without Russia*

	UK/US/France	Germany/ Austria-Hungary
Percentages of world manufacturing production (1913)	51.7	19.2
Energy consumption (1913), million metric tons of coal equivalent	798.8	236.4
Steel production (1913) in million tons	44.1	20.2
Total industrial potential (UK in 1900 = 100)	472.6	178.4

Source: Kennedy, *The Rise and Fall of the Great Powers*, p.350.

Specimen answer   Kennedy's tables amplify Roberts's brief comments about the economic development and potential of the combatants. Table 7.4 demonstrates the enormous
economic power which the United States brought to the war against Germany;
this more than compensated for the loss of Russia. □

Discussion   Roberts emphasizes that his figures for troops and population have to be
qualified, particularly with respect to the Russian army, which was poorly served
logistically and felt that it had to keep large numbers of men in Siberia in case of
hostile moves by the Japanese. In the same way the industrial/technological
comparisons need qualification, since the potential of each alliance could not
always be met.

Russia again provides a vivid example. During the war the Russian economy
grew at a very fast rate, but the growth was uneven. Moreover, while overall
agricultural and industrial output increased – and the rise in arms production was
phenomenal – this was not matched by improvements in either the transport
system or the administrative bureaucracy. Uneven growth, poor transport and
poor organization led to massive bottlenecks: imports from the Allies were left
piled on docks, while weapons, ammunition and forage accumulated far from
where they were often desperately needed. The French industrial/technical
potential was adversely affected for other reasons. The German invasion of 1914
swiftly occupied that area of northern France containing 64 per cent of French pig
iron capacity, 24 per cent of steel and 40 per cent of coal capacity; this area
remained under occupation until 1918. To compensate, the French had to embark
on a massive relocation of industry in the south and west; Paris too was
transformed from a city of specialized crafts into a centre of mass-production
industries. A transformation on this scale required direction by the state. It also
required massive aid from Britain and then from the United States in the form of
financial loans, coal, coke, pig iron, steel and machine tools; the raw materials and
production equipment were carried, in large measure, by the British merchant
marine.

While the French lost industrial resources as a result of the German invasion,
the Germans, of course, gained. Occupied territories were plundered for the
German war machine. The successful invasion of Romania in 1916, for example,
provided Germany with significant oil and wheat fields to exploit; and workers
from the occupied lands could be drafted into German factories, something which
happened most notably in Belgium. An additional element working in the favour
of Germany and its allies was their internal lines of communication. Transferring
men and *matériel* from the eastern front to the western front, or to the Balkans or to
Italy, was much simpler for the central powers than for the Entente.

The above paragraphs give some idea of the relative economic advantages and
disadvantages of the great powers that went to war in 1914. Increasingly the
governments of the combatant powers felt the need to control and direct their
economies to ensure, and to hasten, victory. As Ian Beckett points out in the
Reader article which you read in conjunction with Book I, Unit 1, this has been a
central feature of twentieth-century total war. In World War I, governments took
control of railways and mines, set up agencies for arbitration at the workplace,
and regulated the recruitment and placement of workers. Of course, such control
and direction did not always guarantee efficiency. We have already noted the
Russians' inability to transport equipment to where it was needed. The French
government may be said to have presided over the successful relocation of
industry, but they also had to import foodstuffs into a country which, before 1914,

had generally produced an agricultural surplus. The reason was that the French government injured their agriculture by requisitioning too many men and horses from the land for military needs, and by investing too much in military equipment to the detriment of farm machinery and fertilizers. The other powers of continental Europe made similar miscalculations over agricultural needs, thus contributing to food shortages and the resulting unrest and disorders. But governments also recognized the need to enlist the assistance of the experts and of the interest groups working in their economies; this led to businessmen and industrialists, and also the leaders of organized labour, being consulted and drawn into government deliberations, though whether this amounted to state corporations is a debate which must be left to later units.

Much of the wartime government control was ephemeral, though it left a legacy in many of the states where it was most rapidly dismantled. In France, for example, the expansion of the economic power of the state encouraged the trades unions and the Socialist Party to develop a plan for the remodelling of the post-war economy that involved state management, long-term planning, and a mixture of nationalized industries and state monopolies. In Britain the experience of state management of the economy brought about an increase in trades union support for the nationalization of key industries, in particular coal and the railways; it also appeared to validate the socialist claim that private enterprise was not the only viable means of organizing the economy.

No balance sheet of World War I would be complete without drawing attention to the massive casualties caused by the conflict. Table 7.5 overleaf gives one estimate of the war casualties; these figures cannot be considered as definitive, but there is a substantial measure of agreement among the various authorities. The numbers are enormous by any standards, but they need also to be thought about in relative terms. Of the principal belligerents, for example, France mobilized 168 men out of every 1,000 inhabitants and lost 34; Germany mobilized 154 and lost 30; Britain mobilized 125 and lost 16. But given the demographic differences between the powers, these losses had different results. In the decade before 1914 the French and German birthrates were, respectively, 20.2 and 31.6 per thousand; during the period 1916–20 these rates fell to 13.9 and 17.9 – a smaller percentage fall for France, but starting from a lower base and with a smaller population, the French population declined even further in relation to that of Germany.

The statistics in Table 7.5 relate only to military casualties; civilians were also killed and injured during the war. The sinking of the *Lusitania* and the aerial bombing of towns and cities was noted above; civilian losses were also caused by naval bombardment – German warships bombarded the east coast of Britain a dozen times between December 1914 and June 1917 – by artillery fire, and also by the actions of troops on the ground. About 5,000 Belgian civilians were killed during the German invasion of 1914. Some of these were accidental battle casualties, others were shot in reprisal for snipers firing on German troops. The German soldiers, inexperienced in war, had been told stories of atrocities by French *francs-tireurs* (partisans) during the Franco-Prussian War. They appear to have expected civilian partisans to attack them in both Belgium and France, and consequently attacks by snipers – very often the work of Belgian soldiers – met a swift and brutal response. Hausen's Third Army shot 612 civilians at Dinant and, following an attack on Kluck's rearguard, Louvain was sacked and its medieval library destroyed. Such actions were embroidered by the British and French press

Table 7.5   *Military casualties in World War I*

	Total mobilized forces	Killed and died[1]	Wound casualties	Prisoners and missing	Total casualties	Total casualties in per cent of total mobilized
Allies						
Russia	12,000,000	1,700,000	4,950,000	2,500,000	9,150,000	76.3
France[2]	8,410,000	1,357,800	4,266,000	537,000	6,160,800	73.3
Brit. Emp.[2]	8,904,467	908,371	2,090,212	191,652	3,190,235	35.8
Italy	5,615,000	650,000	947,000	600,000	2,197,000	39.1
USA[3]	4,355,000	126,000[4]	234,300[4]	4,500	350,300	8.0
Japan	800,000	300	907	3	1,210	.2
Romania	750,000	335,706	120,000	80,000	535,706	71.4
Serbia	707,343	45,000	133,148	152,958	331,106	46.8
Belgium	267,000	13,716	44,686	34,659	93,061	34.9
Greece	230,000	5,000	21,000	1,000	27,000	11.7
Portugal	100,000	7,222	13,751	12,318	33,291	33.3
Montenegro	50,000	3,000	10,000	7,000	20,000	40.0
Total	42,188,810	5,152,115	12,831,004	4,121,090	22,089,709[5]	52.3
Central powers						
Germany	11,000,000	1,773,700	4,216,058	1,152,800	7,142,558	64.9
Austro-Hungary	7,800,000	1,200,000	3,620,000	2,200,000	7,020,000	90.0
Turkey	2,850,000	325,000	400,000	250,000	975,000	34.2
Bulgaria	1,200,000	87,500	152,390	27,029	266,919	22.2
Total	22,850,000	3,386,200	8,388,448	3,629,829	15,404,477	67.4
Grand total	65,038,810	8,538,315	21,219,452	7,750,919	37,494,186[5]	57.6

Notes
[1] Includes deaths from all causes.
[2] Official figures.
[3] Includes marines serving with the Army.
[4] Includes 'died of wounds' (14,500).
[5] See note 4.

Source: *Encyclopaedia Britannica*; figures are estimates of United States War Department.

into atrocity stories; particular favourites were the reports of 'Germhuns' hacking the hands off children and the breasts off women. The popular press had long recognized the value of sex and violence in selling newspapers to the newly literate public; these could now be enlisted to unite the public against the monstrous enemy. But it was not just the popular press which carried these stories. In December 1914 the British government appointed a committee under Lord Bryce to investigate German atrocities. The committee's report was published a few days after the sinking of the *Lusitania*; it contained graphic eyewitness accounts of German brutality inflicted on the civilians of 'gallant little Belgium'. None of the depositions allegedly made to the committee have ever subsequently been found. Both the Entente and the central powers continued to accuse each other of atrocities against civilians, as well as wounded and captured military personnel. The illustration opposite gives a good example of propaganda against the bestial hun. But the real atrocities in World War I were to be found not on the western or the eastern fronts, but in the Balkans and Turkish zones, where the war fed upon generations of ethnic hostilities intertwined with religious conflict.

The most appalling episode began in 1915, when the Turkish government instigated a policy against the Christian Armenians which was tantamount to genocide.

'Red Cross or Iron Cross?' (The Trustees of the Imperial War Museum, London)

Exercise   Look again at Table 7.5, and think back to the chronology included at the beginning of this unit. Is there anything that strikes you about the losses sustained by the Balkan countries? ■

Specimen answer   The Balkan countries did not fight continually throughout the four years of World War I; nevertheless their losses, particularly those of Romania and Serbia, were enormous. □

Discussion   From our traditional viewpoint in Britain, the First World War is generally perceived in the image of the trench fighting on the western front. But the war started in the Balkans, and it was in the Balkans and in Eastern and Central Europe that the upheaval and dislocation was probably the greatest. No one knows how many tens of thousands of Serbians – men, women and children – died on the great mountain retreat of December 1915; most died of exposure in the bitter weather, but typhus and the Arnauten tribesmen of Montenegro, seeking revenge for Serbian violence in the Balkan Wars of 1912–13, also claimed their victims. Romanian losses were so high partly because, like Serbia, they were heavily outnumbered by Austrians, Bulgarians and Germans, but also because their army was abysmally led and poorly equipped. At the crucial battle of Red Tower Pass in September 1916, for example, the Romanian army was pounded by 54 artillery batteries and could reply with only 18. Romania also relied on Russia for supplies, which put it at the mercies of the shambolic Russian transport system.

Lastly, of course, it was in Eastern and Central Europe that the war was to have its most dramatic political impact. The Tzar, the Kaiser and the Emperor of Austria-Hungary all abdicated, and their empires were torn by revolutionary violence. Further to the east, on Europe's periphery, the Ottoman Empire also fell victim to the war. All of these empires had weaknesses in 1914, and may have succumbed to internal disorder sooner or later. Nevertheless, it was World War I which provided the occasion of their collapse.

REFERENCES

Andrew, C. (1985) *Secret Service: The Making of the British Intelligence Community*, London, Heinemann.

Badsey, S. D. (1983) 'The Battle of the Somme', *Historical Journal of Film, Radio and Television*, vol. 3, no. 2.

Englander, D. (1987) 'The French Soldier 1914–18', *French History*, vol. 1, no. 1.

Fussell, P. (1975) *The Great War and Modern Memory*, London, Oxford University Press.

Hart, L. (1930) *A History of the World War*, London, Cassell.

Howarth, D. (1974) *Sovereignty of the Seas*, London, Collins.

Kennedy, P. (1988) *The Rise and Fall of the Great Powers*, London, Unwin Hyman.

Williamson, H. (1973) 'Foreword', in *The Wipers Times*, facsimile edn, London, Peter Davies.

Winter, D. (1979) *Death's Men: Soldiers of the Great War*, London, Allen Lane.

UNITS 8–10 THE DEBATE OVER THE IMPACT AND CONSEQUENCES OF WORLD WAR I

(Introduction and sections 2.5–2.10 by Arthur Marwick; sections 1 and 2.1–2.4 by Bill Purdue)

Open University students will need to refer to:

Set book: J. M. Roberts, *Europe 1880–1945*, Longman, 1989

Course Reader: *War, Peace and Social Change in Twentieth-Century Europe*, eds Clive Emsley, Arthur Marwick and Wendy Simpson, Open University Press, 1990

Documents 1: 1900–1929, eds Arthur Marwick and Wendy Simpson, Open University Press, 1990

Offprints Booklet

Maps Booklet

Video-cassette 1

Audio-cassette 1

INTRODUCTION

From what you have learned about the nature of World War I from Unit 7 you will appreciate why those who lived through the war felt, as far as can be established from such sources as we have, that it had had a profound impact on their lives. Many of those who left diaries, autobiographies or collections of letters (a very tiny minority, of course) stated clearly that they felt their world had been changed by the war. Historians, subsequently, have not always been so certain. In fact, it would probably be true to say that the main fashion in writing about war in the last ten years or so has been to argue that neither World War I nor World War II had any significant or long-lasting effects in the realms of social change. We saw in Book I, Unit 5 that changes were already taking place in most European countries before the war. Recent writers have tended to stress long-term structural and ideological trends, seeing the war as of little real significance compared with them, but rather as, perhaps, a temporary distortion, or even an interruption to long-term change. A substantial proportion of recent writers have strong socialist or feminist sympathies and have argued (perfectly correctly) that the war certainly did not usher in an era either of socialism or of complete equality between the sexes. They have pointed to the deprivation, misery and horrific slaughter involved in the war and have suggested that these are more compatible with regression than with change, certainly with change in any desirable direction. Some have stressed – and this is a particularly important point – that even if there were changes during the upheavals of war, what one must look at is societies as they settled down in the post-war years to see whether these changes really did last. It has also been pointed out that governments at the time, for propaganda reasons, greatly exaggerated the changes that were taking place and *would* take place once victory was won. Ordinary people, it has been argued, too readily fell victim to the idea that because the war was so horrific it must result in change.

For a long time it has been held that simple *post hoc ergo propter hoc* arguments simply will not do – that is to say, arguments that because something happened after something else it must have been caused by that something else – in this instance, post-war changes. Thus those who wish to argue that the war did bring social changes have not only to list social changes during, at the end of, or after the war, but have to show how they are related to the actual war experience.

To some extent the debate is over what one counts as change and whether one feels it more important to pin down the broader forces which would have brought certain changes anyway, or to pin down why certain precise developments took place *when* and *in the way* they did. Perhaps it is not necessary to become embroiled in a debate at all. Probably the task really is to establish the balance between the effects of the longer-term forces we have studied in Book I, and the particular circumstances of war in bringing about certain clearly identifiable changes.

There can be little doubt that both ordinary people and writers who perhaps ought to have known better, have created rather simplistic accounts of the war's effects. It is rather unsatisfactory to speak of the war doing this and the war doing that, as if the war was some kind of consciously motivated invasion from an alien planet, or a natural disaster like an earthquake (though some historians, including myself, would say that *in certain aspects* there are similarities between the effects of war and those of natural disaster). But the point to be stressed is that war is not something discrete and separate from society: we don't have society in one position, and war as a separate entity acting upon society. Societies are themselves involved in war; without societies there would be no war. If there is change, even temporary, that change comes not from war acting upon society, but from society's being involved in war, experiencing war. One suggestion that has been made is that the important distinction is between 'society not at war' and 'society at war', and that in trying to establish what changes, if any, can be attributed to the experience of war, one should try to isolate what happens in 'society at war' that does not happen in 'society not at war'. A concept much used in the debate over the consequences of war is that of *participation* (sometimes expressed, in the original formulation of the sociologist Stanislav Andreski, as *military participation ratio*). The basic idea of this is that in 'society at war' those whose participation in the war effort is vital (for example, certain skilled workers, or women replacing men in certain jobs) will tend to make gains in wages, social benefits, etc., other things being equal – which, of course, they are not, the very destructiveness of war always being a countervalent negative force.

However, as we have seen in Book I, the societies of 'Europe not at war' were by no means all identical to each other.

Exercise   What broad lines of distinction can be drawn between the different European societies as they were on the eve of World War I? ■

Specimen answer and discussion   1   We have the broad distinction made by Roberts (set book) between constitutional states and autocratic states.

2   We have the differences between 'developed', industrial states, and 'underdeveloped', predominantly agricultural states.

3   There is the distinction between nationally homogeneous states (like Britain and France), and multinational ones like Austria-Hungary and Turkey. □

Exercise   Why might these differences affect the possible consequences of involvement in war? ■

Specimen answer and discussion   Agricultural, underdeveloped countries might find it more difficult to support the enormous costs of total war, and might therefore suffer much greater negative effects and perhaps nothing in the way of desirable social change. Autocratic countries might be able to control the repercussions of war more effectively than constitutional countries. Multinational states might be more prone to falling apart under the pressure of war than nationally homogeneous ones. □

Exercise   Two other broad lines of distinction might be made with regard to establishing the effects of war on particular countries, the first to do with the society's attitudes towards involvement in the war, and the second to do with its actual experience of the war. What are these? ■

Specimen answer and discussion   Some societies, e.g. Britain, France and Germany, entered wholeheartedly and unitedly into the war, some much less so, particularly Italy, and probably Russia. With regard to experience of the war it might seem likely that in assessing the consequences of the war there would be a difference between whether a country was on the victorious or the defeated side; more particularly, there would be differences depending upon how much direct destruction a country suffered, whether it was invaded, fought over, occupied, etc. □

Exercise   Reflecting on some of the main points made about the nature of the war in Unit 7, what arguments could be made to support the view that to look for major social reforms and higher living standards as consequences of the war would be quite absurd? ■

Specimen answer   The main argument concerns the enormous destructiveness and cost of the war.
and discussion   Roberts estimates that the war cost the equivalent of eight years' peacetime accumulation of wealth. This doesn't clinch the argument, however. Apart from anything else, some countries suffered much more than others, as I have already hinted. But certainly this major point bears careful thinking about. □

In these three units we shall look in turn at the ten areas of social change introduced in Book I, Unit 1, and discussed in Book I, Unit 5. We start, however, with the question of international, geopolitical and strategic change. In each section it will be necessary to make a distinction between changes taking place during the war, and the long-term consequences which are the major source of contention in the general debate.

You will realize that these units are not divided into three discrete units, although they do, of course, represent three weeks' work. For the purposes of your study time, therefore, you should note that Unit 8 is the equivalent of sections 1–2.2, Unit 9 covers sections 2.3–2.6, and Unit 10 covers sections 2.7–2.10.

Note that sections 1–2.4 are written by Bill Purdue.

1 INTERNATIONAL, GEOPOLITICAL AND STRATEGIC CHANGE

1.1   Geopolitical changes

The First World War was one of the great cataclysms of Europe which divided one epoch from another. Yet this was not quite so, for the change in public opinion of Europe was a more important dividing point. The First World War completed a process started much earlier . . . (George L. Mosse, *The Culture of Western Europe*, 1988)

In the above, somewhat contradictory, sentences Professor Mosse combines two of the well-established views regarding the impact and consequences of World War I: that the war was a great watershed in history, with effects which created a divide between the pre- and post-war worlds; and that the war completed, perhaps speeded up, and, in some versions, was a culmination of pre-existing processes and tendencies.

The test of the 'watershed' may well depend upon the sort of factors we are considering. Professor Mosse was primarily concerned with cultural change, and there is room for considerable debate as to the war's effect upon cultural and, indeed, social developments. When it comes to the physical boundaries of states and to their very existence, it is difficult to question the decisive impact of the war. Whatever other effects World War I may have had, it is certain that the period of the war and its immediate aftermath saw a radical change in the political map of

Europe. The war was more than just the catalyst for such change, for its outcome did much to shape it. Yet, notwithstanding the overriding impact of the war, there are other factors we must consider in assessing the geopolitical changes. They include:

1   the effects of nationalism, particularly the nationalisms of 'those people without history', as Marx dismissed the hitherto largely subject nationalities of East Central Europe who had been busy discovering or inventing their histories before 1914;

2   the ideals and aims of the statesmen of the victorious states who gathered at Paris to make the peace settlement;

3   the effect of the ideological dimension inserted by the Bolshevik Revolution;

4   the changes to the map that were dependent on the outcome of the chaotic struggles and wars which continued in Eastern Europe until 1923.

Let us start with some simple and straightforward exercises which will concentrate our minds on the changes to the map of Europe between 1914 and 1923, a period during which that map can be said to have altered continually.

Exercise What changes to the map of Europe occurred during World War I itself? Consult Maps 4 and 5 in Roberts, pp.601 and 602. ■

Specimen answer and discussion We can distinguish here between the *de facto* map, as areas and regions changed hands with the advances and retreats of armies, and changes to the map which were given some legal form by treaties – even if, as with the provisions of the Treaty of Brest-Litovsk, they were overturned after the war was over.

On the western front only the opening and closing stages of the war saw a war of movement. The result of the virtual stalemate, which began in November 1914 and lasted, despite major offensives, until 1918, was that both sides faced each other along a 400-mile line from the Channel to the Swiss frontier. This left Germany in control of most of Belgium and part of Northern France.

The Italian front, which opened with Italy's entry into the war on the Allied side in May 1915, saw another stalemate and no significant territorial gains for either side as the Italians failed to break the Austrian front along the river Isonzo.

On the eastern front the war was much more mobile, and both sides made sweeping advances at different times; by October 1917, however, the central powers had made enormous gains. Serbia, Montenegro, Albania and Romania had been overrun. With the 'October' Revolution and Lenin's decision to accept peace at almost any price, the central powers were able to dictate the terms of the Treaties of Brest-Litovsk and Bucharest. German troops and Austrian troops occupied vast tracts of what had been Russian territory, and Germany was in a position to encourage the creation of new states – Finland, the Ukrainian Republic and the Baltic States – under her control and to reward her allies, Bulgaria and Austria-Hungary. □

Of course, most of the territorial changes that took place during the course of the war were ephemeral (although, as we shall see, the Treaty of Brest-Litovsk left its mark) and were to be overturned by the final outcome of the war, the defeat of Germany in the west. We need now to take a longer view and consider the redrawing of the map of Europe that took place between 1914 and 1923. This is not just a matter of considering the Versailles Settlement, for much of Eastern Europe was not directly affected by Versailles, and not all the provisions of that settlement were ever put into effect.

Exercise   Look at your *Maps Booklet* and summarize the major differences between Europe in 1914 and in 1923. ∎

Specimen answer   The greatest changes have taken place in East Central and Eastern Europe; in **and discussion**   comparison, the changes in Western Europe are comparatively minor.

The old framework of East Central Europe has disappeared with the erosion of the eastern frontiers of Germany and the western frontiers of Russia, and with the disintegration of the Austro-Hungarian Empire. Austria and Hungary are now separate states and much attenuated. Bulgaria is reduced in size, while Romania has acquired new territory and Serbia has become the nucleus of the new state of Yugoslavia, incorporating territory previously belonging to the Austro-Hungarian Empire together with Montenegro. Much of the non-Russian periphery of the Russian Empire is independent of the Soviet Union. In the wake of the old empires, 'successor' states have appeared: Poland, Czechoslovakia, Finland, Estonia, Latvia and Lithuania. Italy has acquired a modest amount of territory from the old Austro-Hungarian Empire, while Greece has extended its frontier at Bulgaria's expense and, like Italy, gained islands from Turkey. The Ottoman Empire has been replaced by a Turkish Republic, but Turkey retains territory in Europe. In Western Europe France has re-acquired Alsace and Lorraine, Belgium has made small gains, and Germany has ceded part of Schleswig to Denmark.

Such radical changes amounted to a redrawing of the map of Europe only rivalled by the transformation at the end of the Napoleonic Wars. □

This great reconstruction of Europe was not synonymous with the Versailles Settlement, for the Treaties of Versailles, St. Germain, Neuilly, Trianon and Sèvres did not cover all the areas where territory changed hands, and Sèvres (the treaty with Turkey) was never ratified or fully implemented. Russia and the frontiers of Russia and her neighbours were excluded from Versailles. In much of Eastern Europe the boundaries and the very existence of states were decided not by gentlemen in tail-coats at Paris but by the outcome of often confused and little recorded fighting on the ground.

Exercise   How does Roberts (p.321) distinguish between the different processes which made for the general reconstruction of Europe? ∎

Specimen answer   He separates the reconstruction into three processes:
and discussion
1   a series of treaties with defeated nations;

2   the cancellation of Brest-Litovsk and the stabilization of Russia's relations with its neighbours;

3   the settlement of the eastern Mediterranean and Aegean. □

I shall follow Roberts's categories, but it is worth noting at this stage the tremendous difference that the Bolshevik Revolution, the Treaty of Brest-Litovsk and the severance of relations between Russia and her erstwhile allies made to both the dispensations and the scope of a post-war peace settlement. A peace settlement in which Russia ranked among the victorious powers at Paris would undoubtedly have provided for areas in Eastern Europe not covered by the

Versailles Settlement, might have made very different provisions for areas that were covered by it, and would have been in a better position to enforce its decisions on Turkey.

1.2   The Versailles Settlement

World War I and World War II (in the European sphere) can be seen as the hot phases in Europe's Thirty Years' War of the twentieth century, which was fought to decide whether or not Germany was to become the dominant power in Europe. Such a reading not only relegates the characters of particular regimes and the immediate causes of both wars to a secondary importance, but contrasts sharply with the official war aims of the powers. The pursuit of power and natural self-interest were, however, unsuitable for public consumption while states were engaged in a mode of warfare which demanded mass participation and major sacrifices from their populations. Loftier aims had to be found. Thus, although for the Allies World War I was no more a 'war for civilization' than World War II was, in its essential motivation, a 'war against fascism', states became the victims of their own propaganda and were hamstrung both when it came to war short of total victory and to making a rational peace settlement.

The expectations aroused by the feverish propaganda of the Allies in the minds of their electorates were both unrealistic and contradictory: if, on the one hand, the central powers and particularly Germany were peculiarly wicked and culpable, then any settlement should be punitive; but if, on the other hand, the victorious powers were peculiarly virtuous, then a settlement should create a better, more peaceful world that reflected the principles which made those powers so worthy. The actual peace settlement was an unhappy compromise between the pursuit of the interests of the Allied powers, a desire to punish the vanquished, and the furtherance of notions of internationalism, democracy and national self-determination. Such notions gained increased importance with America's entry into the war and were enshrined in President Wilson's Fourteen Points; this document saddled the Allies with a written manifesto of a highly idealistic nature which contrasted with the secret treaties concluded by the European Allies during the course of the war. 'Fourteen Points', exclaimed the French Prime Minister Clemenceau, 'it's a bit much. The Good Lord had only ten!'

Given the underlying purpose of the war, the ideal peace settlement from the viewpoint of the Allies, as they were constituted early in 1917, would have been one which modified the map of Europe as it existed in the mid-nineteenth century. Such a settlement would have expanded the frontiers of Russia and her Balkan allies, retained a weakened Austro-Hungarian Empire, and partially dismembered the German Empire, giving France control of the Rhineland. A secret treaty between France and Russia in March 1917 had been a move in this direction, underwriting Russian control of Poland and providing for French domination of the Rhineland. By 1919 the Russian Revolution, Russia's defeat by Germany, the disintegration of Austria-Hungary and America's entry into the war had radically changed the situation, leaving Clemenceau to press for more limited aims with a weaker hand.

Exercise   1   How does Roberts describe France's aims in 1918?

2   To what extent does Roberts think France succeeded in achieving those aims at the Peace Conference? ■

Specimen answers and discussion

1   Roberts sees security as the French goal and, following from this, a 'determination to wound Germany as deeply and permanently as possible'.

2   He considers the final terms of the Versailles Settlement as a diplomatic defeat for France. □

At first sight the terms which Germany was forced to accept seem harsh enough. The Germans certainly thought so, and liberal opinion in Britain and the United States soon came to feel remorseful about the supposed harshness of the terms. Germany was labelled the guilty party, was forced to pay reparations, and suffered limitations on the size and nature of its armed forces. Germany also lost territory, including all its colonies; Alsace-Lorraine was returned to France; a small amount of territory went to Belgium; part of Schleswig went to Denmark; and in the east, a large tract of territory went to the new Polish state.

But France gained little security. Germany remained substantially intact and potentially strong. As Roberts points out, France had hoped to detach the left bank of the Rhine from Germany, but obtained only the demilitarization of the Rhineland and its occupation for fifteen years as well as possession of the Saar coalfield. It soon became clear that to enforce the Treaty of Versailles France could depend on no one but itself. An Anglo-American guarantee of assistance in the event of an attack by Germany was abandoned by the Americans, and Britain made it clear that it would not bind itself to observe the guarantee unilaterally.

Dr Tony Lentin (an Open University historian, incidentally) has commented on the Treaty of Versailles as follows:

> It was a wise precept of Machiavelli that the victor should either conciliate his enemy or destroy him. The Treaty of Versailles did neither. It did not pacify Germany, still less permanently weaken her, appearances notwithstanding, but left her scourged, humiliated and resentful. It was neither a Wilson peace nor a Clemenceau peace, but a witches' brew concocted of the least palatable ingredients of each, which though highly distasteful to Germany, were by no means fatal. (A. Lentin, *Lloyd George, Woodrow Wilson and the Guilt of Germany*, 1985)

France lacked even the comfort it had enjoyed prior to 1917 of a formidable ally to the east of Germany. Instead of its erstwhile Russian ally, France would be forced to rely upon alliance with the new states of East Central Europe to contain Germany. These states were a poor substitute; they all shared some commitment to their midwife Versailles, but had many quarrels and rivalries among themselves.

As we observed at the beginning of this section, the major changes to the map of Europe were in Central and Eastern Europe. Even if the Allies had wished to preserve the Austro-Hungarian Empire, as perhaps they were still prepared to do in 1917 if the Emperor Charles had been able to break free from Germany and make a separate peace, it was almost certainly too late by 1919. At the same time as German armies had been winning the shooting war in the East, nationalist exiles, with Western historians as their fuglemen, had been winning the propaganda war. In the last month of the war the Habsburg government came out in desperation with a federalist manifesto, but the Empire was being torn apart. The efforts of the exiles and of liberal academics and journalists in the Western capitals inclined Western opinion towards the break-up of the Empire, but, by November 1918, its disintegration was well advanced.

The Allied statesmen were thus already sympathetic to the idea of national self-determination and the setting up of new states in East Central Europe at a time when, as the old order disintegrated, national councils were seeking to pre-empt their decisions. In addition to the principle of self-determination, two other guidelines influenced Versailles, modifying and cutting across it: the desire to punish Germany and its allies, and the need to create buffer states on Germany's eastern frontier after the collapse of Tsarist Russia. All three guidelines can be detected in the Treaty of Versailles itself, the Treaty of St. Germain with Austria, the Treaty of Trianon with Hungary, and the Treaty of Neuilly with Bulgaria.

The attempt to make state boundaries correspond to divisions between nationalities was, of course, foredoomed to failure in East Central Europe, where there was not even a patchwork of nationalities. Nationalities overlapped each other, so that towns might be primarily German and Jewish with a Slavonic hinterland, or one village might be Magyar and the next Croat. Nationalism had not been, nor was it to be, either a rational or a civilizing influence in the region. That the Allies permitted their enthusiasm for national self-determination to be modified by their desire to punish the vanquished central powers and to make the successor states as strong as possible only compounded the problem and ensured that more, not fewer, minorities were created.

Exercise   Can you find examples of where the settlement departed from the principle of self-determination? ■

Specimen answer   A notable example is the treatment accorded to Germans. Austria was forbidden
and discussion   to unite with Germany, regardless of the wishes of its German population. The Sudetenland Germans were incorporated into Czechoslovakia, and the South Tyrol passed to Italy without benefit of plebiscite.

Romania, Czechoslovakia and Yugoslavia swallowed up 1.75 million, 0.75 million and 0.5 million Magyars respectively. □

How were all these territorial changes decided? Who made the final decisions as to which side of a border a particular area or town would go? Here is an extract from the diary of Harold Nicolson, a British diplomat:

> *March 2, Sunday*
> . . . At 5.00 to Quai d'Orsay for sub-committee of Slovak frontiers. We put Lerond in the chair, which is a great help. We begin with Pressburg and secure agreement. Then we get to Grosse Schlutt. French want to give it to the Czechs. The US want to give it to the Magyars. I reserve judgement, saying it depends on whether German Hungary is given to Austria. Then examine frontier from Komorn to Jung. The very devil. The Yanks want to go north along the ethnical line, thus cutting all the railways. We want to go south, keeping the Kassa-Komorn lateral communications, in spite of the fact that this will mean putting some 80,000 Magyars under Czech rule. Eventually a compromise.
>
> The Yanks give way as regards Eipel and we as regards Miskolcz. As for the rest we decide to wait and hear Benes. Dine with Princess Soutzo at the Ritz – a swell affair. Painlevé, Klotz, Bratianu there. Also Marcel Proust and Abel Bonnard. Proust is white, unshaven, grubby, slip-faced.
> (Nicolson, *Peacemaking 1919*, 1933)

Exercise   1   What do you suppose was the real basis of the disagreements in this sub-committee?

2   What factor that I haven't mentioned so far does Nicolson note as having to be taken account of?

3   What term comes to mind to describe these sort of compromises? ■

Specimen answers and discussion   1   The Americans were in this instance the most persistent in wanting to pursue national self-determination, while the French put their influence on the side of making the new Czechoslovakia as big as possible with the most defensible frontiers. The British were more flexible and pragmatic.

2   Communications: roads and railways cut through ethnic boundary lines.

3   'Horse trading' or 'give and take' are the terms that occur to me. The future of Eipel and Miskolcz are decided fairly casually on a 'one for you and one for us' basis. It is striking that the future of Pressburg doesn't seem to have caused any disagreement and yet the decision to give it to Czechoslovakia ignored the fact that the town, with its mixed racial composition, stood amidst a region containing 700,000 Magyars and had been the capital of Hungary during the Turkish occupation of Buda. □

It was over the question of the Polish-German frontiers that the Versailles treaty-makers disagreed most strongly among themselves; it was also one of the most flagrant departures from their principle of national self-determination. No one (save General Smuts) doubted the wisdom of re-establishing a state of Poland after well over a century, but France and the United States on the one hand and Britain on the other disagreed over the extent of the territory to be awarded to it. The report of a commission on the Polish frontiers proposed that many areas which were predominantly German should be given to Poland. France and the USA both supported the most extreme Polish claims. Lloyd George argued that it was folly to place 2,132,000 Germans 'under the control of a people which is of a different religion and which has never proved its capacity for stable self-government throughout its history' (quoted by W. N. Medlicott in *British Foreign Policy since Versailles*, 1940). The exact number of Germans in inter-war Poland is a matter of contention. A. J. P. Taylor has estimated that the German minority was one and a half million (*The Origins of the Second World War*, 1961) but P. Wandycz argues that, *excluding* Danzig, the German population was 585,000 (*'Origins of the Second World War' Reconsidered*, ed. G. Martel, 1986). It was decided that there should be a plebiscite in the disputed region of Upper Silesia and that Danzig should be made a free city, instead of going outright to Poland.

By the time the plebiscite was held in March 1921, France and Poland had concluded a military alliance (in February 1921) and France was determined to strengthen her ally as much as possible. To the chagrin of the French and the Poles, the plebiscite in Upper Silesia resulted in a clear majority for those wishing to be part of Germany. The Polish plebiscite commissioner then resorted to force and, at the head of an irregular army, took over a large part of the region. British troops had been withdrawn and French troops took the Polish side. The Germans organized themselves for resistance and British troops were sent back to Silesia. The French government went so far as to issue a solemn warning to Britain that its attitude threatened a definite rupture between the two countries, which elicited a firm response from the British Foreign Secretary, Lord Curzon. The Silesian question was eventually referred by the Conference of Paris, August 1921, to the League of Nations, and a committee of four – a Brazilian, a Chinese, a Belgian and a Spaniard – arrived at a decision. Poland received about one-third of the territory but about half of the inhabitants and the greater part of the industrial resources.

This crisis illustrates some of the salient features of Versailles and the immediate diplomatic aftermath:

1   It demonstrates the enormous difficulty of securing frontiers in East Central Europe which would correspond with national self-determination. Upper Silesia was a classic case of German towns and villages surrounded by a Slav countryside.

2   It illustrates the way in which the powers, in this instance France and the United States, were prepared to subordinate self-determination to other factors: the desire to punish Germany and keep her weak and the aim of creating strong states to the east of Germany.

3   It shows how Anglo-French relations had deteriorated within a few years of victory. The French, insecure in the absence of British and American guarantees for the settlement, were seeking to build up allies on Germany's eastern frontiers. Britain now favoured a 'normalization' for Germany which would have been made easier if the important industrial areas of Upper Silesia had been returned to Germany.

4   The episode illustrates the dangerous ambitions and inflated great power pretensions of Poland. While Poland faced a threat from Russia on its eastern frontiers, it was not willing to give an inch to Germany on its western frontiers.

5   The outcome could be seen as an example of the smooth working of the League of Nations system, but the League was only called in as a result of Anglo-French compromise, and its decision was only accepted by Germany because of the latter's weak position, which was to be temporary.

The historian H. A. L. Fisher, who was a member of the Lloyd George coalition government, later defended the territorial provisions of the settlement. Despite problems and anomalies he argued (and he was writing in 1935): 'the political map of Europe is drawn more closely than ever before in accordance with the views of the populations concerned' (*A History of Europe*, Vol. III). He did admit that the treaty had 'left sore places'. He could have said that again!

1.3   Eastern Europe

The law of Versailles and of the statesmen who met in Paris did not extend to the greater part of Eastern Europe. Here the post-war map of Europe as it was established by 1923 was the outcome of a series of struggles which were often complex and confused but always bloody. As we have seen, Poles and Germans skirmished in Upper Silesia to decide Poland's western frontier, but its eastern frontiers were decided by a full-scale war with the Soviet Union.

Like Austria-Hungary to the west, two great multinational empires, the Russian and Ottoman Empires, tottered and fell apart in Eastern Europe during 1917 and 1918. Their subject nationalities made their bids for independence, and the successor regimes to the old central authorities, the Soviet Union and the Turkish Republic, rallied and fought back. We will deal first with Russia, the establishment of new national states on its periphery, and the stabilization of Russia's relations with them.

The Soviet Union and Eastern Europe

Germany had won the war on the eastern front only months before being forced to concede victory to the Western powers. The Treaty of Brest-Litovsk, signed on 3 March 1918, was testimony to Germany's overwhelming victory. Roberts refers to Brest-Litovsk as 'an imposed peace – a diktat – in a far truer sense than Versailles', but if this was so, it was largely because Russia was in a far weaker position in March 1918 than Germany was at the time of the armistice.

Brest-Litovsk has the paradoxical quality of a treaty that was formally abrogated within a matter of months, for one of the conditions of the Allies' armistice on 11 November 1918 was the abandonment of Brest-Litovsk, and yet was of lasting importance. It did much to shape the Eastern Europe of the post-war years.

From early in the war the Germans had encouraged nationalism as a weapon against Tsarist Russia, and indeed attached greater hopes to the effects of such nationalisms than to that 'plague bacillus', Lenin, whose return to Russia they facilitated. The Russian state began to disintegrate with the February Revolution, and this disintegration accelerated after the October Revolution. By March 1918, Finland, Russian Poland, Estonia, the Ukraine, Lithuania, Moldavia and Latvia were all claiming independence from Russia, most of them encouraged by Germany. Their chance of success depended upon the continued weakness of Russia and the support of Germany. Brest-Litovsk and its immediate aftermath saw a German hegemony in Eastern Europe under which many of these movements for national independence, but not all, were able to establish themselves securely enough to retain their independence into the 1920s and 1930s.

Exercise   Read Roberts, pp.306–8, and answer the following questions:

1   The acceptance of the terms of Brest-Litovsk was a victory for whose view among the Bolshevik leaders?

2   Which national independence movements had their claims underwritten by the treaty? ■

Specimen answers and discussion   1   It was a victory for the view of Lenin, who was prepared to accept peace at almost any price in order to use time to consolidate power. It is not clear in fact whether there was a realistic alternative. To have waged a revolutionary war as Bukhanin advocated would have required a revolutionary army capable of standing up to the Germans.

2   Roberts mentions that Russia gave up Poland, Lithuania, the Ukraine, the Baltic Provinces and Transcaucasia. It was also agreed that Finland would immediately be cleared of Russian troops. □

As Roberts argues, the Treaties of Brest-Litovsk and Bucharest together brought Germany close to the realization of a *Mitteleuropa*. Despite the recognition of the Ukraine as an independent state, German and Austro-Hungarian armies remained in occupation of the border territories from the Baltic to the Caucasus and occupied the Ukraine, defeating the advancing Bolsheviks.

The events of 1918, prior to the defeat of Germany in the west, seemed to foreshadow the dissolution of Greater Russia. If all the areas which declared themselves independent had succeeded, Russia would indeed have been diminished; as it was, the eventual success of the Bolsheviks in Russia's civil war enabled them to re-establish control over White Russia, the Ukraine, Georgia and

Azerbaijan and Armenia (the Allies sponsored the formation of a single Armenian state out of Russian and Turkish Armenia, a scheme which foundered in 1921 with Turkish recovery under Mustafa Kemal – later Kemal Ataturk – with the aid of a Soviet-Turkish treaty).

The states which did emerge independent from the confused fighting of the years 1918 to 1922 owed their independence in the first place to Germany's triumph in the east. But an independence within a German-dominated *Mitteleuropa*, though no doubt preferable to being part of the Soviet Union, would have been a very qualified independence, and Germany's attitude towards the independence of Poland and the Baltic states was equivocal. Such genuine independence as the smaller states and peoples of Eastern Europe could ever hope to enjoy was dependent, at best, on both their great neighbours being weak and, at second best, on the ability to play one off against the other. Their inter-war independence was a lucky break, depending as it did on Germany's defeat of Russia, the subsequent defeat of Germany by the Western Allies and then on the weakening of Russia by civil war and Poland's victory over Russia in 1920.

The Russo-Polish war of 1920 came at a time when the Bolsheviks were decisively gaining the upper hand in the civil war. Intervention by the allies had largely ceased and, save for Wrangel in the Crimea, there was little left of White Russian resistance. At this point, the Poles, led by Marshal Joseph Pilsudski, negotiated an agreement with the Ukrainians, who were losing their bid for independence, and advanced into Russia. The Poles got as far as Kiev and were then beaten back by a Russian counter-attack which came close to Warsaw in August 1920. Pilsudski then counter-attacked in turn, pushing the Red Army back into Russia. The Treaty of Riga, 18 March 1921, set the Russian-Polish frontier until 1939, placing it much further east than had been suggested by Lord Curzon in 1920. Poland's victory did much to force the Soviet Union to accept the independence of Finland and the Baltic states of Estonia, Latvia and Lithuania, and treaties recognizing their independence were signed in 1921.

Thus was concluded a wonderfully confused period of constant warfare on Russia's borders, a period of topsyturvydom which witnessed British sailors fighting in Latvian trenches alongside German soldiers and the offer by a German Social Democratic government to provide Ludendorff to serve under Foch at the head of a combined Allied-Germany army which would have aided the Poles.

Turkey in Europe

The demise of the Ottoman Empire had been long anticipated, and Turkey's entry into World War I led to a number of secret agreements among the Allies over the final dismemberment of the empire. The ambitions of France and Britain to gain control of large tracts of the Ottoman Empire in the Middle East were to be largely satisfied, but a resurgent Turkish national movement led by Mustafa Kemal (Ataturk) proved capable of defying the diktat of Sèvres, the territorial ambitions of Greece and Italy and an Armenian separatist movement, and was able to preserve not only Anatolia but its last territory in Europe, Eastern Thrace.

By August 1920 an Allied force was occupying the Straits and Constantinople, Greek and Italian troops had landed on Turkish soil, and an independent Armenian Republic had been proclaimed. The Treaty of Sèvres of that month provided for a small and much weakened Turkish state which would have been an insignificant power: as well as losing the Middle Eastern provinces of the Empire and most of the Aegean islands together with the Dodecanese, Turkey was to lose Armenia to an independent state and Eastern Thrace to Greece, while Smyrna and the surrounding area in eastern Anatolia were to be administered by Greece for five years followed by a plebiscite; what remained of Turkey was to enjoy only a qualified independence subject to a commission of representatives of France, Britain and Italy.

The treaty, however, was signed by the discredited government of the Sultan, which was now challenged by the national government of Kemal in Ankara. By a combination of successful generalship and skilful diplomacy, Kemal was able to overturn the least acceptable features of Sèvres. Armenian independence and Greek invasion were smashed by force of arms. A succession of treaties with the Soviet Union, Italy and France settled frontiers and isolated Britain as the only power determined to uphold Sèvres. Although Britain and Turkey came close to war in the Chanak crisis, this crisis was settled by negotiation, and the Treaty of Lausanne of July 1923 considerably revised the provisions of Sèvres.

By the Treaty of Lausanne, Turkey became the only ex-enemy state not required to pay reparations. Turkey regained full control of Smyrna and surrounding Western Anatolia, and of Armenia; the Straits, although demilitarized, were returned to its sovereignty; and with its re-acquisition of Eastern Thrace, Turkey remained in Europe.

Roberts comments that Lausanne was the only 'negotiated, rather than imposed, peace treaty, and it has lasted longer than any of the other post-war settlements'. One reason for this may well have been that the compulsory exchange of Greek and Turkish minorities that accompanied the settlement meant that populations were ruthlessly made to fit frontiers, and the removal of the Greek minorities on the Turkish mainland signalled the end of Greek ambitions for an Aegean empire.

Lausanne settled effectively two questions that had been central to European diplomacy for a century: the question of the control of the Straits, and the question as to whether Turkey would remain in Europe. The demilitarization of the Straits was amended by the Montreux Convention of 1936, when Turkish sovereignty was restored subject to certain restrictions, the most important of which was the closure of the Straits to warships of belligerents in time of war. Turkey remained, albeit marginally, a European power through its possession of Eastern Thrace. This was to be important psychologically to a country undergoing rapid westernization under Ataturk, and was to buttress Turkey's self-image as a secular European state.

1.4   Conclusion

The geopolitical changes that took place in Europe between 1918 and 1923 were, indeed, overwhelming, and their strategic implications incalculable, but to what extent were they attributable to World War I?

Exercise   To what extent do you consider the war was responsible for these great changes to the map of Europe? List other factors which influenced such changes. ■

Specimen answer and discussion   It is undeniable that the war was responsible for both the sweeping nature of change and for many, if not all, of its specific features. The war was responsible for the disintegration of great states and for the changed balance between victorious and defeated nations. The Versailles Settlement was, obviously, the direct outcome of the war.

Other factors are closely associated with the results and effects of the war. There were many national movements in Europe prior to 1914, but the nature of the war gave some of them their opportunity. The Russian Empire may have been unstable, but a successful Bolshevik revolution was an unlikely outcome in 1914. Even the predilection of Versailles for self-determination can in large part be attributed to the course of the war and America's entry into it. □

Nevertheless, the effect of the war on the political geography of much of Eastern Europe can be seen as essentially contextual. It destroyed the old framework, but what replaced it was often due to the success or failure of national movements and armies in that confused period of sporadic warfare which continued up to 1923. Perhaps we should properly conclude, if we suspend our national West European viewpoint, that the wars that took place in Eastern Europe until that date were in fact part of World War I, or at least of Europe's 'Thirty Years' War'.

2 SOCIAL CHANGE

2.1 Social geography

In any consideration of historical change there can be no more basic a variable than population change. The impact of World War I and of events in the years immediately after the war on the numbers, composition and geographical distribution of the European population was considerable.

Wars, inevitably, result in people being killed, but do not necessarily result in a decline in the population. The Great War saw enormous loss of life but no overall decline in Europe's population. The war rather cut back the rate of growth of the European population, cut across long-term patterns of growth, and altered the balance between the sexes and between different age groups.

How many people were killed by the war? The answer is that we don't know precisely. We have to choose between informed estimates and rough guesses whereby we 'give or take' a few million. You should recall our attempt to provide some 'precise' figures in Unit 7.

Exercise   Read Roberts, p.368, on the 'biological cost' of the war, and answer the following question: Why is it so difficult to estimate precisely the biological cost of the war? ■

Specimen answers and discussion   1   Because accurate figures for the numbers killed in the fighting do not exist for all states.

2   Much depends on whether November 1918 is taken as the end of the war or whether we also consider the aftermath in the East.

3   We have to take into account births which would have taken place were it not for the war, as pre-war demographic trends were interrupted by it.

4   We have to take account of deaths that occurred after the fighting ended, in so far as many died earlier than they should have done due to the effects of wounds, malnutrition and diseases which flourished in conditions of social and administrative disarray and famine. □

The inclusion under war losses or costs of deaths due to the Spanish influenza epidemic is somewhat contentious. The Spanish 'flu spread throughout the world, affecting combatant and neutral nations alike. Its impact can only properly be considered part of the war's toll in so far as it may have had a greater effect because of widespread malnutrition in the last year of the war.

One estimate by B. C. Urlanis puts European losses due to the war (including Russian but excluding Turkish losses) at 8,260,000 (quoted in L. A. Kosinsky, *The Population of Europe*, 1970, p.11). This estimate of deaths differs from that of Roberts (p.368), which is taken from W. S. and E. S. Woytinsky's *World Population and Production* (1953). This puts death directly caused by the fighting at nearly 10 million. The difference may be accounted for by the fact that Urlanis did not include Turkish deaths, but it also bears out the point made by Roberts as to the difficulty of precision. The experts disagree, in part because of what they include or don't include as European war deaths and in part because for many countries accurate figures simply do not exist.

Total losses are obviously greater if we consider the fighting which raged before and after World War I itself and look at a longer period, say 1912–23. The First Balkan War began in 1912, and Urlanis estimates the losses of the Balkan Wars as 142,000, including Turkish deaths. The warfare which continued in Eastern Europe until 1923 resulted in hundreds of thousands of deaths. Urlanis estimates deaths due to the fighting in the civil war and the foreign intervention in Russia as some 800,000, but this figure pales beside the figure of twenty million given by Nicholas V. Riasanovsky in his *History of Russia* (1984) as his estimate of total losses due to 'epidemics, starvation, fighting, executions and the general breakdown of the economy' between the October Revolution and the end of the civil war.

Roberts goes on to quote 13 million deaths due to fighting for the period 1914–20 (he takes the figure from M. R. Reinhard and others, *Histoire générale de la population mondiale*, 1968). He concludes that, if we include the losses of potential births in the calculation, we have to think in terms of a 'demographic cost' of between 20 and 24 million people due to World War I. Seeing that his higher figure is only 4 million above that given by Riasanovsky for Russia in the period 1917–21, we have to reconcile ourselves to the fact that even well informed historians can differ widely in their estimates.

The war interrupted a rapid increase in the European population which had been taking place since the eighteenth century. The population had increased from 152 million in 1800 to 296 million in 1900. A glance at Roberts's table (Appendix 1, p.581) will show you how rapid the increase in population was in the first decade of the twentieth century.

You will see from the table, and should remember from the discussion of population in Book I, Unit 5, that the long-term trends in population growth that the war cut across were by no means uniform throughout Europe. The European population was certainly increasing in the late nineteenth and early twentieth centuries, but it was increasing at different rates in different countries.

Roberts doesn't claim more for his table than that the figures give a general picture of comparative population movement. We shall see that the difficulties with it are greater than he implies, but for the moment let us take it at face value and consider what it tells us about population increase *before* 1914.

Exercise   1   Which countries stand out from the table as having particularly high rates of population increase and which as having particularly low rates before World War I?

2   Can you see any broad distinction between categories of European nations? ■

Specimen answers and discussion

1   Romania has a phenomenal rate of increase, trebling its population between 1880 and 1910. Bulgaria registers a 100% increase in the same period, Russia over 50% and Germany just below 50%. The British increase is more modest at around 25%, while France is positively sluggish, expanding by only 5.5% in thirty years.

2   The sharpest increases are in Eastern Europe and the lowest in Western Europe. □

A valid generalization about European population growth up until 1914 is that, although a historically unique surge in population growth was continuing, population growth in the richer northern and western countries was beginning to decrease, while it was accelerating in the poorer eastern and southern countries (see Unit 5). It is often argued that, by the late nineteenth century and early twentieth century, countries that were industrialized and urbanized were exhibiting decreasing birth rates, although the continued decline in the death rate made up for this; largely agricultural societies in Eastern and Southern Europe, on the other hand, had soaring birth rates and an accelerating population increase. Those of you who analysed Roberts's table very closely may have noticed a flaw in this argument. France had a very low rate of population increase and remained a largely rural society – agriculture remained its largest industry and, as late as 1935, more than 55 per cent of the French population lived in villages or very small towns – yet France's birth rate was notoriously low. Norway, too, was a largely rural society with a modest rate of population increase. Rural areas were exhibiting some of the lowest as well as the highest rates of population growth.

The equations of agricultural/rural equals high and industrial/urban equals low birth rates does seem far too simplistic. Historical demographers have pointed out that differences between the birth rates of Western and Eastern Europe (and indeed the rest of the world) go back a long way, with Western Europeans having a late age at marriage and a propensity to match population to resources by adjustment of both the age at marriage and the numbers getting married (H. J. Hajnal, 'European marriage patterns in perspective', in D. V. C. Glass and D. E. C. Eversley (eds), *Population in History: Essays in Historical Demography*, 1965). Some West European agricultural societies adopted birth control as a means of reducing marital fertility as an alternative to and in part a substitute for delayed marriages.

Industrialization and urbanization led at first to an initial increase in the birth rate, which was slackening in the industrialized areas of Western Europe by the end of the nineteenth century. It was in agricultural Eastern Europe, where peasant economies based upon the extended family, within which marriage had traditionally taken place at an early age and children had been seen as a source of wealth, that population increase was accelerating in the early twentieth century.

The evaluation of the effects of World War I on the population figures of individual countries is beset with considerable difficulty and numerous complications. You should, I think, be able to work out what the problems are.

Exercise   Identify the major problems in estimating population increase or decrease due to the war in specific countries. ■

Specimen answer and discussion

1   The redrawing of the map of Europe in the years immediately after the war makes estimation very difficult. States disappeared or were broken up and new states appeared; frontiers changed.

2   There was a series of large migrations, referred to by Roberts, p.369, which redistributed population and changed the pattern of racial and national groups in some areas of Europe.

The United Kingdom was the only combatant country whose frontiers did not change at the end of World War I, although they suffered a contraction in 1921 when the Irish Free State was given separate Dominion status. Frontier changes in Western Europe were modest in comparison to those in Eastern Europe, but France's acquisition of Alsace-Lorraine brought 1.8 million new citizens, and for all continental states the difference between the population figures for 1910 and 1920 in Roberts's Appendix 1 reflect, as well as the birth rates and mortality rates, losses or gains in territory and the exodus or influx of migrants or refugees. □

Exercise   From Roberts's table, which countries appear to have had an absolute decrease in population as a result of World War I? ■

Specimen answer   Only France registers a decline in population in this table for the period 1910–1920. So far so good, but remember the warnings about the difficulty of obtaining accurate figures and the question of the basis of calculation of any figures used. It may well be that Roberts's table rather underestimates the effect of the war. The American demographer, D. Kirk, calculated that Poland, Yugoslavia, Czechoslovakia, Belgium and Romania all had a decrease in population *within the boundaries as they were during the interwar period* (*Europe's Population in the Interwar Years*, 1946). □

Let us consider the cases of some individual countries.

Germany

Here are two sets of figures for German population movement (in millions):

1880	1890	1900	1910	1920	1925
40.2	44.2	50.6	58.5	61.8	
45.2	49.4	56.3	64.9		63.1
			58.4		

The first row of figures are Roberts's, while the second row is taken from B. R. Mitchell's *European Historical Statistics 1750–1970* (1975), p.20. Clearly we have a problem. Mitchell's figures are taken directly from the census returns, and although these are by no means always entirely reliable, the difference between his figures and Roberts's are too great to be accounted for by any exaggeration in the returns, especially as the German Empire was a state noted for its bureaucratic efficiency. The clue to the differences is in the two figures given by Mitchell for 1910, the higher figure being that for the German Empire and the lower figure that for the *post-war* boundaries of Germany with the population they contained in 1910. Thus, although you may be forgiven for having thought that Germany's population had gone up by 1920, despite war casualties (estimated by Roberts at three million, although other sources suggest lower figures), you were in fact comparing figures for Germany with those for Weimar's boundaries. The three million rise in population is accounted for by the arrival of refugees from Germany's lost eastern territories mitigating the effect of war losses.

Russia

As Roberts remarks, even Russia's great losses during the war were not sufficient to prevent the continued growth of its population. One estimate of the numbers of the Russian armed forces killed in the war is 1,650,000 (N. Golovin, *The Russian Army in the World War*, 1934), but of course the number of civilians who died from war-related causes was enormous. As we have seen, the war itself was followed by the death toll of the civil war and the droughts and famines of 1920 and 1921. We have also to take into account the loss of territory, for the USSR lost territory that had been part of the Russian Empire, territory that had contained nearly 28 million people in 1897. Roberts's figure of 153.8 million for 1920 can be compared with the census figure for 1926 of 147 million.

Romania

Romania's apparent increase in population over the period 1910–20 in Roberts's table is entirely due to its acquisition of large tracts of territory after the Balkan Wars and as a result of Versailles. This extra population disguises a probable absolute decrease in population within the pre-war frontiers. Romania's losses during World War I have been estimated at 250,000 or 3.3 per cent of the population (Urlanis) and, using wider criteria, as 1,088 or 14 per cent by D. H. Aldcroft (*From Versailles to Wall Street 1919–1929*, 1977).

Yugoslavia

The Kingdom of the Serbs, Croats and Slovenes, as Yugoslavia was called until 1929, had perhaps the highest war losses of any country. Serbia and Montenegro, which had been overrun during the war, ended up with a population deficit estimated at 31.3 per cent by Aldcroft. The 11.9 million population in 1920 shown in Roberts's table is, of course, the population of the new kingdom, made up not only of Serbia and Montenegro but of Bosnia, Herzegovina, Slovenia, Dalmatia, Croatia and other territory acquired at the end of the war.

France

World War I inevitably had a greater impact on France with its low birth rate than on almost any other European country. Paul Gagnon has succinctly summarized its effects:

> A quarter of all Frenchmen between the ages of 18 and 30 were dead. Six hundred thousand were disabled in body or mind or both. Counting civilian deaths and those unborn because of war, France lost 3 million people. Only the return of Alsace-Lorraine (1.8 million) and immigration enabled her to return to 40 million by 1930. (Paul Gagnon, *France Since 1789*, 1972, p.329)

By 1930 there were over 1.5 million foreign wage-earners in France, mainly Poles, Spaniards, Belgians and Italians.

Britain

Roberts estimates the numbers of British dead at 0.75 million, but as you can see from the illustration opposite from a rather grisly book of photographs, *Cov-*

enants with Death, published by the *Daily Express* in 1934, there have been higher estimates. War losses were not sufficient to prevent the slow growth of the population, which increased by over a million and a half during the decade 1910–20. As with other countries, the fact that emigration ceased during the war years helped to balance war losses.

Greece

Greece is not shown on Roberts's table, but the increase in its population between 1907 (2.3 million) and 1920 (5.0 million) was spectacular and was due to its

'Blood on the Map' (reproduced from Covenants with Death, 1934, London, the Daily Express)

acquisition of new territory in the period. By 1928 the population had expanded to 6.2 million, reflecting not only changes in birth and mortality rates, but also the arrival of more than one million Greeks from Turkey and Thrace after 1922, and the exodus of some 350,000 Muslims (Roberts, p.369).

Clearly there are special difficulties with the successor states of the Austro-Hungarian Empire (the Empire's war dead have been estimated by B. C. Urlanis at 1.1 million or 1.8 per cent of the population) and with the newly created states of East and Central Europe. The lack of continuity, the boundary changes and the migration and exchanges of population make any attempt at estimating the effects of war on the population difficult in the extreme, although, as we have seen, three of them – Poland, Czechoslovakia and Yugoslavia – are among those estimated by D. Kirk as having had an absolute decrease in population.

Exercise   Two further effects of the war, evident in the population structure of every combatant country after the war, can be detected in Table 8–10.1 below. What are they? ■

Table 8–10.1   *Population of countries by sex and age groups (in thousands)*

	Germany 1925		France 1921		United Kingdom 1921		Bulgaria 1920	
	M	F	M	F	M	F	M	F
0–4	2,984	2,887	1,148	1,121	1,632	1,640	253	243
5–9	2,023	1,963	1,507	1,501	1,767	1,752	315	303
10–14	3,134	3,079	1,714	1,699	1,837	1,823	330	312
15–19	3,285	3,258	1,734	1,721	1,728	1,775	271	268
20–24	3,065	3,086	1,410	1,643	1,448	1,703	213	221
25–29	2,468	2,839	1,235	1,556	1,340	1,620	165	178
30–34	2,027	2,553	1,256	1,516	1,281	1,520	138	163
35–39	1,965	2,319	1,227	1,501	1,273	1,472	151	160
40–44	1,853	2,054	1,320	1,444	1,223	1,378	108	117
45–49	1,860	1,936	1,275	1,335	1,162	1,244	95	96
50–54	1,588	1,645	1,137	1,209	971	1,043	87	92
55–59	1,327	1,401	1,021	1,107	782	849	83	71
60–64	1,029	1,137	852	966	601	681	67	70
65–69	740	876	651	774	449	537	51	45
70–74	467	591	736	984	281	376	41	41
75–79	246	338			159	234	21	18
80 and over	135	200	160	265	92	129	28	28

Source: B. R. Mitchell, *European Historical Statistics, 1750–1970*, 1975.

Specimen answer and discussion   World War I resulted in the deaths of far greater numbers of men of fighting age than of any other groups it may have been responsible for. This resulted in (a) an imbalance between the sexes, and (b) a skewing of the age-group profile by the shortfall of men in the age groups who had fought in the war. These imbalances had a continuing impact during the inter-war years. There was a disproportionate number of old people in the population and a large number of unmarried women. At the 1925 German census there were 100 men to every 113 women in the 20–44 age group, while in 1911 the comparable ratio had been 100 to 101. Roberts notes that in 1933 Germany had nearly one million more women than men aged 40–54, while the 1931 census in France revealed a 'surplus' of 728,000 women aged 35–49. Despite high birth rates in the immediate post-war years, the low birth rates of the war years and the shortage of husbands, combined with a trend towards small families in the inter-war years as a whole, meant that the proportion of children in the population of West European countries was disproportionately low. In 1925 the birth rate per 1,000 of European countries varied as follows: Germany 20.8; Italy 28.4; France 19.0; United Kingdom 20.3 (England and Wales 18.3; N. Ireland 22.0; Scotland 21.4); Russia 44.7; Poland 35.4; Romania 35.2; Hungary 28.3; Bulgaria 36.9; Austria 20.6. The pattern of much higher birth rates in Eastern than in Western Europe had become even more pronounced. The overall fall in European emigration and the ending of what Roberts calls the 'Great Resettlement' partially counteracted the effects of falling birth rates in many West European countries (the French indeed came to rely on immigrants to offset a shortage of labour) but added to the problems caused by high birth rates in countries whose economies were in little shape to absorb rapidly rising populations. □

Exercise   What do you think the implications of these demographic changes were for international politics (see Roberts, pp.370–3)? ■

Specimen answer   Size of population is an important though by no means the only factor in determining the military strength of a great power. The enormous population of Russia had always been its great asset and it maintained Russia's great power status even when its cumbersome bureaucracy and backward economy had made it a less 'modern' state than the other great powers of Europe. The French had been conscious throughout the nineteenth century that their low birth rate imperilled the country's military potential and its great power status. Britain, because of its island situation and reliance on naval rather than military might, had been able to adopt a more insouciant attitude towards its birth rate. Germany had enjoyed the best of all worlds since 1870, the second largest population and an industrialized economy, together with an efficient bureaucracy. As regards the two most populous powers, Russia and Germany (see Roberts, p.371), the effects of the war and the demographic trends of the early treaties were to increase Russia's preponderance in population though leaving Germany superior in terms of its economic infrastructure and the education and skills of its labour force. The gap between the military potential of France and Germany had actually increased to France's disadvantage, despite France's victorious position in 1918. □

Exercise   You should read Roberts, pp.371–3, and then answer the following question: What were the reactions of states to the decline or increase in their populations? ■

Specimen answer   Given the implications for military potential, no government, save perhaps the British, could remain unconcerned at the relative decline of its population as against possible rivals. The French were, vainly, to attempt to encourage larger families, to forbid abortion and to discourage birth control. During the inter-war period the totalitarian states were to enjoy some success in encouraging larger families (the Italians hardly needed to, nor did the Russians). It seems doubtful, however, whether such policies had much effect in comparison to the long-term trend for Eastern European populations to speed ahead of their Western counterparts. □

During the nineteenth and early twentieth centuries there had been considerable movement of population. Emigration outside Europe had been the most spectacular example of this, but there had also been movements from country to expanding towns and from backward rural regions to thriving centres of industry and commerce. Such latter movements had affected the balance between regions in individual countries, for example the shift of population to the north in nineteenth-century Britain, and a massive migration from the rural provinces of eastern Germany to Berlin and the industrial regions of the west. After the great shake-up of populations in Eastern and Central Europe in the years immediately after World War I, movement tended to be much more restricted within often smaller national boundaries, although the movement of Italian and Spanish workers into France was an exception to this.

Exercise   Read Roberts, pp.373 and 374, and summarize his conclusions on changes in the distribution of population in the post-war period. ◼

Specimen answer   1   Urbanization continued to increase, but along lines that had already been laid down. It was a matter of the growth of existing cities rather than the creation of new ones. Cities spread out into sprawling conurbations with extensive suburbs. The old industrial area 'running from Manchester across northern France and Belgium, and on across north Germany from the Rhine to Upper Silesia' consolidated its position, and the countries in its swathe became even more different, as regards the balance and the relations between town and country, to Southern and Eastern Europe.

2   In Central, Southern and Eastern Europe large populations in the countryside grew even larger. There was considerable movement into towns, but into relatively small towns with populations of between 20,000 and 100,000. ☐

2.2   Economic performance and theory

The effects of World War I on the European economy were almost all disagreeable. It is possible to find compensatory developments: scientific and technological advances; 'spin-offs' from the wartime production of weapons and armaments which would be utilized by other manufacturers; and the diversification of industries within some national economies. It is very much a matter of interpretation what weight is placed on these spin-offs. Arthur Marwick, for example, has argued for the significance of developments in medicine (DDT), medical psychology ('shell shock'), motorized transport, aircraft, radio valves (in war, for communication with aircraft), electricity as a power source, and new heavy metal industries in Paris (*Britain and the Century of Total War*, 1968). The fact remains that Europe was, both absolutely and relatively, a poorer place in 1919 than it had been in 1914.

To the majority of contemporaries in 1919, the most obvious effects of the war must have been the enormous loss of population and the tremendous physical damage. We have already considered the loss of population due to the war, though not its economic dimension, but the years of warfare had also resulted in the destruction of factories, houses, ships, railway lines, bridges and machinery, and millions of acres of agricultural land were put out of use.

Exercise   Which areas of Europe and which countries do you suppose suffered the most extensive physical devastation? ◼

Specimen answer and discussion

Naturally, the theatres of war received damage from the actual fighting, while some areas that were occupied found their resources pillaged by the occupying power. In many cases the same regions were fought over and then occupied. France and Belgium suffered most in the West, while extensive areas of East and Central Europe were devastated as the eastern front was more mobile. The physical damage to Russia was considerable, exacerbated as it was by policies of 'evacuate and destroy' in front of advancing enemy armies, though such damage was to be exceeded by that caused by the civil war. In relation to its size, however, Serbia probably came off worst. The relative size factor is important, since, though in absolute terms the destruction suffered by countries like Romania and Poland was modest, it involved the loss of a large proportion of their net assets. Those countries which were not fought over – Britain, Germany, Austria and Bulgaria – escaped relatively unscathed in respect of physical damage. □

A few cases will suffice to exemplify the amount of physical damage suffered by the worst hit countries.

Belgium

Nearly all of Belgium was invaded and occupied. D. H. Aldcroft details the damage as follows:

> Some 100,000 houses, equivalent to 6 per cent of the 1914 stock, were destroyed or damaged beyond repair; three-quarters of the railway rolling stock and one-quarter of the fixed stock were destroyed, and by the Armistice only eighty locomotives were in reasonable working order; about half the steel mills were smashed completely and most of the remainder were badly damaged. The position was little better on the land. Over 240,000 acres . . . of land were rendered unfit for cultivation by shelling while the animal population was decimated. One-half of the horned beasts, two-thirds of the swine, one-half of the horses, 1,500 million fowl and 35,000 goats perished or were seized during the course of hostilities. (D. H. Aldcroft, *From Versailles to Wall Street 1919–1929*, 1977, p.19)

Poland

According to Antony Polonsky,

> By 1920 when operations came to an end, 90 per cent of the country had been touched directly by war and 20 per cent the scene of heavy fighting. In consequence 55 per cent of bridges, 63 per cent of railway stations, 48 per cent of locomotives and 18 per cent of buildings had been destroyed. Polish industry had been seriously affected by the requisitioning by the occupying powers. The metallurgical industry of the Kingdom of Poland had ceased production. As late as 1922 only 7 out of the 11 furnaces working in 1914 were in operation. (R. F. Leslie (ed.), *The History of Poland Since 1863*, 1987, p.140)

Poland was primarily an agricultural country. Nearly 11 million acres of land were made unfit for agricultural use, 6 million acres of forest were destroyed, and a vast amount of timber was removed by occupying armies.

The situation in Belgium, France (where the regions laid waste were both important agriculturally and also major industrial centres) and in Serbia (where the economy lay in ruins after the Austro-Hungarian retreat) has to be borne in mind before we join in any criticisms of the demands for reparations as vengeful and short-sighted. Such physical damage was far more economically debilitating than was population loss, despite the fact that the majority of those killed were men between 18 and 45 and that many of them were highly skilled; the inter-war period was to see large-scale industrial unemployment and a surplus of agricultural labour.

Great as the loss of property was, the financial cost of the war to the belligerents was far greater and was spread more evenly, as it fell both upon those countries like Britain and Germany whose territory was not fought over and on those like France and Belgium who were invaded. D. H. Aldcroft has estimated the financial cost as follows:

> The direct cost of the war to all the belligerents amounted to some $260 billion, of which the Allied share accounted for $176 billion. The largest expenditures were incurred by the UK, the United States, Germany, France, Austro-Hungary and Italy in that order. Some idea of the magnitude of the total outlay can be gained from the fact that it represented 6.5 times the sum of all the national debt accumulated in the world from the end of the eighteenth century up to the outbreak of the First World War. (Aldcroft, *From Versailles to Wall St*, p.30)

Just how were such vast sums found? In the stress and urgency of war, financial orthodoxy and peacetime common-sense were thrown to the wind as governments embraced deficit financing (called debt when individuals do it). Even though taxation was increased in every country, no country financed more than 25 per cent of its wartime expenditure from revenue, with the balance being raised from credit of one sort or another. The gold standard was an early victim of the war, the money supply was rapidly expanded with inevitable inflationary consequences, while the respective trade values of currencies altered rapidly.

Germany kept going by relying almost entirely on internal borrowing; France utilized a mixture of internal borrowing, sales of foreign assets and loans from its allies (more than 30 billion francs, mostly from the United States); Britain, although raising far more from revenue than the other European powers, sold some £207 million of dollar investments and another £54 million of sterling, in addition to borrowing £1,027 million from the United States. The British and French financed the Russian war effort to a considerable degree, the British government lending Russia £568 million (Britain lent a total of £1,741 million to its allies). Such loans, together with the 12 billion francs of French investments, were to be a virtual write-off after the Bolshevik Revolution.

Exercise 1   What do you think were the long-term consequences of the financial and monetary policies followed by the European powers for their economic positions in the post-war world?

2   Can you think of any other way in which the war and the economic effort involved in fighting would affect the economic position of the European powers after the war? ■

Specimen answers and discussion 1   The main result of the war as regards Europe's economic importance *vis-à-vis* the rest of the world was that its importance suffered a considerable decline. Britain in particular was to feel the effect of the loss of a considerable proportion of its foreign investments and the burden of its debt to the United States; the impact on the position of sterling and the influence of the City of London was to be considerable.

2   The effect of the war-time economies was to direct production towards the war effort and away from manufacturing for civilian use and for exports. Combined with the physical damage experienced by many countries, this meant that output and exports suffered a reversal during the war. Imports from other parts of the world both of raw materials and manufactured goods increased, and markets for exports were lost.

The European economy was thus in a mess, even if the position of individual countries varied greatly: its financial and trading pre-eminence was gone and its productivity had fallen alarmingly. Inflation was widespread, the relative values of currencies veered drunkenly, while the issue of war loans compounded by the renegation of the Soviet Union was to bedevil international relations. The powers that gained most from all this were the USA and Japan. □

It was not, of course, the war alone that affected the European economy and the performance and future prospects of European status at the end of it. We must take account of the post-war settlement and the aftermath of the war, especially in Eastern Europe.

Exercise   From your reading of Roberts, pp.359–63, what aspects of the post-war settlement do you think adversely affected the European economy and the economies of the European states? ∎

Specimen answer and discussion   1   The dismemberment of the multinational empires, the founding of new states, and the pursuit of the principle of national self-determination all had economic implications. Economic factors and the economic viability of the new states were not, however, uppermost in the minds of the statesmen at Versailles when they made their decisions. Roberts has noted that 'None of the new states except Czechoslovakia had a balanced economic structure.'

2   The reparation terms, which Roberts calls 'the heaviest and most unwise penalties inflicted on Germany.' □

Certainly the new states of Eastern Europe lacked balanced economic structures. The most viable economy was that of Czechoslovakia, the exception mentioned by Roberts; part of the reason for that viability was that the principle of national self-determination was imperfectly applied in the instance of Czechoslovakia. The new political map of East Central Europe cut across trading patterns, communications systems and mutually dependent branches of industries which had grown up in the context of empires which now no longer existed. The new states were poor and heavily dependent on agriculture, while their pasts lay heavily upon them – Poland, for instance, was composed of three parts possessing different systems of law, different customs units and, to begin with, three different currencies; Yugoslavia inherited five different railway systems with four different gauges (Aldcroft, p.28). The co-proprietors of the old Dual Monarchy, Austria and Hungary, were left an undesirable legacy, Austria inheriting a capital city with industrial suburbs along with a largely agricultural country, and Hungary denuded of most its valuable resources.

In attacking reparations Roberts has a great weight of historical opinion on his side. One is tempted to assert that the only aspects of the Versailles Settlement to have stood the test of time are the criticisms of it. But in respect of reparations one has to ask whether the error is supposed to lie in the idea of reparations, in the size of the amount Germany was supposed to pay, or in the size of the payments Germany did in fact make. There was nothing new or surprising in the notion of making the power regarded by the victors as the aggressor pay indemnities. Certainly the sum fixed by the Reparations Commission of $33 billion was, to say the least, dauntingly large, even if compared with Allied war debts of $26.5 billion. Whether the crisis that arose in 1923 over repayments was the result of Germany's not being able to afford to pay or was provoked by Germany to show that it could not afford to pay, is a moot point, but the Dawes Plan set up a much more feasible system of payments. The initial mistake was probably to consider Allied debt repayments and German reparation separately. France, Britain and Italy could hardly be expected both to repay their wartime loans and forgo reparation. Russia owed France and Britain but refused to pay; France, Britain, Italy and Belgium owed the United States and were reluctantly prepared to pay; and each felt that they had the right to expect payment from Germany. David Aldcroft has suggested (*From Versailles to Wall Street*) that it might have been easier to cut out the middle men and make Germany settle with the USA, offsetting the debts and credits to the other Allied powers. In the end a large part of the Allied war debts was never repaid, with America and Britain coming off worst. The Americans recovered only about one-sixth of their loans, while the bulk of German reparation payments were made with American loans which were also never recovered. Britain was the only country to continue debt repayments on a large scale.

The problems that beset the economies of the European states at the beginning of the 1920s were many and varied. We should perhaps start by looking at the victorious Western Allies, as one might expect the economies of the victors to be in the best shape.

Britain

Britain had emerged from the war without serious damage to its manufacturing capacity. By 1920 its productivity level was approaching that of 1913, though it did not fully regain that level until 1923. The war and its effects had two deleterious consequences for the British economy, one serious and the other deeply damaging. There had already been signs before 1914 that Britain was dangerously dependent on a number of heavy and long-established industries such as coal, steel, shipbuilding and cotton textiles. The demand for these products, although high in the immediate post-war years, was to be affected by the lost markets and new competition due to the war, and in the case of coal by the increased use of oil. Of far greater consequence was the shattering of the old international economy in which Britain had performed so well and of which it had been the financial and trading centre.

France

At the end of the war, France appeared in a much worse position than Britain. Part of its territory had been fought over and occupied – 289,000 houses had been destroyed, and three million acres of land rendered unfit for cultivation. France also had enormous debts, both international and internal, and was particularly affected by the loss of all the capital which French governments and individuals had invested in Russia. France had lost 50 per cent of its pre-war purchasing power. The recovery of Alsace and Lorraine with their mineral and industrial assets was, however, an advantage and, of course, much was hoped for as regards reparation.

By the early 1920s France was on the way to a good recovery. In its case the depreciation of its currency may have been a positive benefit, encouraging exports and tourism. The agricultural sector may have been both large and old-fashioned, but it did mean that France had a more balanced economy than other Western European powers and wasn't very dependent on imports. The patchy nature of its industrialization before 1914 meant that it was able to concentrate on developing modern metallurgical and chemical industries. By 1924 production had climbed back to pre-war levels and French gold reserves were high.

Belgium

We have already mentioned the devastation suffered by Belgium. Recovery was remarkably swift. By 1924 most of the spoilt agricultural land was back in use, and agricultural production stood at about the 1913 level. The destruction of war provided an opportunity for a complete rebuilding along modern lines of the iron and steel industry, and by the mid 1920s industrial production was above the pre-war level.

Italy

Of all the European allied powers Italy appeared to have emerged from the war with its economy in the best shape, if its performance in the immediate post-war years is anything to go by. Italy was to experience continuous industrial expansion up to 1926, and by 1922 industrial production was some 13 per cent above 1913. Progress was especially marked in iron and steel products, the manufacture of rayon and the expansion of the merchant fleet. This period of comparative prosperity was, however, based upon a number of short-lived favourable factors, among them the temporary weakness of its neighbours France and Germany.

Magnanimity in victory may be both an elevated virtue and often of long-term utility to the victors, but it is not particularly common. The victorious powers of 1918 were not notably magnanimous, though it is possible to argue that if they had wanted to prevent Germany's revival, they should have been a great deal harsher than they were. Certainly Germany, its economy and therefore its population, suffered in the immediate post-war world.

Germany

As measures of the damage wrought by the war upon the Germany economy, one can cite the figures that in 1919 the general level of industrial production was about 38 per cent of what it had been in 1913, and that agriculture was also badly affected, with grain production some 30 per cent below pre-war levels in 1920. The latter fall in production was partly due to the loss of territory to the east, which had been largely rural, but Germany remained a country with a large proportion of its workforce engaged in agriculture – nearly 10 million or 30 per cent in 1925.

Some of Germany's post-war economic problems were self-inflicted: the roots of its massive post-war inflation were to be found in the way it had financed the war by internal borrowing, while industrial production was handicapped by the way the maintenance of machinery had been neglected during the war years. Revolution, strikes, the loss of territory, the problems of demobilization and reparations were all to exacerbate the problems of the economy, as were the optimistic plans for expansion and the wildly generous social welfare arrangements of the early Weimar governments. With other Central and East European economies in as bad or a worse state, export potential was limited.

Historians, given time, will find advantages in almost every disaster, as they will detect the seeds of ruin in every success, and many historians have recently pointed to the benefits of the post-war German inflation. There were indeed some advantages in inflation: not only did it permit the painless (for the government) repayment of war debts, but it also helped exports and employment and may well have aided the socially egalitarian aims of governments. It was, however, the disadvantages – the destruction of savings and capital, together with the general loss of faith in currency – which were seared on the collective German memory.

Central and Eastern Europe

The destruction wrought by the war in an area which had seen mobile warfare and the effects of a territorial settlement which had paid little attention to economic considerations, left East and Central Europe in a state of chaos and poverty. As we have seen, Austria was left as a small, largely agricultural economy, with a capital city out of all proportion to the country's size. The bulk of the industry of the old Empire had been located in what became Czechoslovakia, while Hungary, to a lesser extent, inherited an industrialized economy. The economy of the empire was parcelled out between the successor states in a way which left industries separated from their raw materials and which severed trading and communication links. Austria, Hungary and Poland all endured the inflation of their currencies, and economic pride led almost all East European states to attempt to maintain the value of their currencies at a higher rate than their economic position warranted.

Perhaps the main problem for all East and Central Europe was agriculture. Even in Czechoslovakia agriculture was backward, while everywhere the rural population was increasing rapidly. Land reform was called for in all states of the region, but the type of reform instituted (taking land away from large estates and giving it to peasant proprietors) was a reform for political and social, rather than economic, goals. The large estates had not on the whole been efficient, but the smaller holdings which resulted from reform were often less so.

As in the case of Germany, one can see some advantages in the widespread inflation of the immediate post-war years. It aided the initial industrial recovery of Austria, Hungary and Poland, but it was a feverish and weakly based expansion which in the longer term resulted in excess capacity.

A general tendency in Central and Eastern Europe was towards economic nationalism and protectionism, which were later to become characteristic of the world economy in the inter-war period.

Russia

Roberts comments that 'Russia has, for our purpose, an almost independent economic history during these years.' Beset by civil war, national rebellions, war with Poland, and foreign intervention on top of the devastation of World War I, that history was inevitably one of chaos, falling production and widespread famine. One estimate is that the total output of mines and factories fell in 1921 to 20 per cent of the pre-war level, and that cultivated land had fallen to 67 per cent of the pre-war acreage, with a harvest yield 37 per cent of that of 1913 (Riasanovsky, *History of Russia*, 1984, p.488). Recovery only began with the end of the fighting and the inauguration of Lenin's New Economic Policy in place of war communism.

Corporatism and the challenge to the market economy

The widespread dismay in business circles at the outbreak of war in 1914 (see Book I, Unit 2) was justified by events. Not only had the war destroyed factories, disrupted trade and distorted patterns of production, but it had dealt body blows to the old world economy and to previous assumptions as to the limitations of the state's role in economic as in social life. If the all-powerful state is best symbolized by the industrial-military complex headed by Ludendorff in Germany during 1917 and much of 1918, it is also discernible in the war economy headed by Lloyd George.

The new pretensions of the state were not to be easily blown away by peace. If one reaction in 1918 was to return to normal and re-establish the ground rules of 1914, another was to use the power of the state for national directives in peace, as it had been used in war. The social and economic problems and divisions of the post-war societies could be dissolved or ameliorated by the buttressing of the power and role of the state and its attendant ministries, commissions and experts in a number of ways: as planner, as conciliator, and as umpire. The 'common sense' of a contemporary 'progressivism' that ranged over Left and Right invested enormous capital in the role of the state. Collectivism might be the *raison d'être* of the Soviet Union, and corporatism was soon to become the official philosophy of Mussolini's Italy, but in Britain, France and Germany a collectivist or corporatist tendency can be detected.

In Britain the Lloyd George Coalition began with an enthusiasm for 'reconstruction' that gained support from Liberal and Conservative members alike and was seen as involving the government in economic planning, in such social initiatives as house-building and the co-ordination of the insurance and medical services, and in intervention in employer–employee relations via Joint Industrial Councils. If the damage wrought by the war to the economy and society was one reason for this corporatist tendency, another was the new power of the trades unions, which had been given greater stature by their involvement in wartime government. Keith Middlemas has argued in *Politics in Industrial Society* (1979) that influential politicians came to believe that tripartite arrangements between the state, organized labour and employers' organizations were necessary in order to deal with or head off industrial conflict. What had merely been interest groups (the Trades Union Congress and the National Conference of Employers' Organizations) 'crossed the political threshold and became part of the extended state'. Middlemas is careful to distinguish this development as leading to a system with a 'corporate bias' rather than a corporate state.

The more statist initiatives of the Lloyd George Coalition lost popularity as the fortunes of the Coalition waned, and with the fall of the Coalition one can see the end of a period of flirtation with corporatism. The peak of this corporate tendency had come with the National Industrial Conference in 1919, which had made sweeping proposals regarding wages, working hours, the state development of new industry and a permanent National Industry Council. What remained, apart from Whitley Councils, local wage boards and a penchant for Royal Commissions, were a considerable widening of the perceived responsibility of government in matters industrial, a tendency to treat organized labour and organized employers as estates of the realm, and an influential but oppositional view, shared by such diverse politicians as Lloyd George, Sir Oswald Mosley, John Strachey and Harold Macmillan, that government, in partnership with industry, should plan and direct the economy.

The liberal market economy, like liberal democracy, had never been so firmly established in Imperial Germany as in Britain, and the series of compromises between Right and Left, between civil authority and the army, and between employers and unions which characterized Weimar Germany, moved the German economy and society a long way towards corporatism. In November 1918 an agreement was reached between leading German employers headed by Hugo Stinnes and trades union leaders led by Carl Legien, which, as well as giving workers an eight-hour day and other concessions, recognized the unions as the legitimate bargaining representatives of the workers and provided workers' committees in industry to supervise collective bargaining agreements. Weimar had an economic and a social constitution, as well as a political constitution, and the Stinnes–Legien agreement can be seen as a cornerstone of the former. Germany in the early 1920s was a society in which the state figured very prominently in social and economic affairs and in which not only were employers and workers highly organized, but they came together in the *Zentralarbeitsgemeinschaft* (ZAG, the Central Association of Employers and Employees).

Exercise   I would now like you to read document II.2 in *Documents 1*, the 'Programme of the Union of Economic Interests' adopted on 7 April 1919. What does this programme of an employers' organization tell us of the attitudes of French employers towards such questions as the role of the state in economic life and co-operation with trades unions? ■

Specimen answer   The document begins with what seems a trenchant defence of property and private enterprise and opposition to state control of industries and services. Further points, however, suggest that the employers do see a considerable role for the state and foresee industry co-operating with various interest groups and workers' organizations. There are calls for harmonization, co-operation and organization rather than for economic freedom. Training and education should be organized (presumably to suit industry's needs); the state should play a major social role, taking account of the needs of different regions and their economies. □

Discussion   The tone of the document does not exude confidence. One does not feel that here is a group of employers confident that they can flourish and make profits in a world of market forces. Rather this is a call for the co-ordination of a national effort.

The immediate socio-economic background to the document was of widespread social unrest. Early in 1919 the Chamber and Senate had passed laws on the eight-hour day and on official recognition of collective bargaining, but strikes and demonstrations continued during the spring, and both the Socialist Party and the unions were split between reformers and revolutionaries.

The document is not, however, representative of the attitudes of French employers as a whole. Many, among them the most powerful, were far from ready to accommodate the demands of unions or to accept limitations on their freedom of action.

There *was* a challenge to the principles of the market economy in most post-war Western societies – a challenge based on the growth of government powers during the war, the problems of reconstruction and demobilization, and the increased strength of socialist parties and trades unions. Greater governmental responsibility for economic and social matters and a more influential position for trades unions were to remain features of most Western societies during the 1920s, but within a few years of the war Britain, France and even Germany were demonstrably once more free market economies.

We will conclude this section by returning to the wider picture of the European economy as a whole and, indeed, to the world economy of which Europe had been the centre before 1914 and of which it continued to be an important part.

Exercise   I would like you to read D. H. Aldcroft's introduction to his book *From Versailles to Wall Street* (1987 edition) in the *Offprints Booklet*. In this introduction he discusses two alternative interpretations of the main effect of World War I on the international economy. What are they? ■

Specimen answer   1   The war had a decisive impact and effectively destroyed the old international
and discussion   economy which had developed during the nineteenth century. Without the war the world economy would have continued on much the same lines as formerly.

2   The war did knock the world economy off course, but, after a period of recovery and readjustment, economies reverted to their previous practice and direction. Aldcroft is, of course, looking ahead, beyond the period of painful post-war recovery we have been concerned with, to the depression that began in 1929. That is the subject of Book III, Unit 15, but it puts into a larger perspective the question of the degree to which Europe had recovered from the war by the early 1920s. □

What cannot be denied is that the European economy and the individual economies of the European states emerged much weakened from the war. Extra European markets were lost, some never to be regained; the United States and Japan improved their productivity and their trading position; and Europe's, and particularly Britain's, position as the financial and trading centre of the world economy was never to be recovered. The balance of economic power swung away from Europe.

2.3   Social structure

Assessment of the effects of World War I upon European society and the social structure is made complicated, to say the least, by sweeping and widely differing views as to the nature of the pre-war society. The titles of two books to which you are introduced in this course point to one controversy: Arno J. Mayer's *The Persistence of the Old Regime* (1981) and Charles S. Maier's *Recasting Bourgeois Europe* (1975). Clearly, if an aristocratic *ancien régime* persisted up until 1914, then a 'bourgeois' Europe could not have been *recast* after the war. (You have already been introduced to *The Persistence of the Old Regime* in earlier units, and *Recasting Bourgeois Europe* will be discussed in Book III, Units 14 and 15. For the moment it is sufficient to say that Maier's central argument is that after a post-war crisis in which socialist and revolutionary elements threatened the existing order of 'bourgeois' Europe, governments and establishments rallied and adopted policies which skilfully maintained the essential features of pre-war society.)

Considering the ubiquity of monarchies, the prevalence of great landed estates, and the wealth and prestige of great aristocratic families in Edwardian Europe, it may seem to you a trifle odd that Arno J. Mayer's thesis – that monarchies, aristocracies and landed wealth retained the greater part of political power and social influence – should be seen as startling and even 'revisionist'. As Arthur Marwick has already pointed out in Book I (Unit 4), F. M. L. Thompson (*English Landed Society in the Nineteenth Century*, 1963) described the influential position of the landed aristocracy in pre-1914 Britain some time ago, and that thesis has recently been reinforced by J. V. Beckett (*The Aristocracy in England 1660–1914*, 1988). Both Thompson and Beckett have challenged the historical timetable that comes from the penchant of Whiggish or Marxist historians for the 'new' and from their discounting of continuity. Such 'progressive' historians have tended to find the dissolution of *anciens régimes* and the emergence of modernizing or revolutionary forces in almost every century and have perceived in the nineteenth century industrializing or modernizing waves sweeping all before them.

We should remember from Unit 4 that Mayer's book lies within a sectarian historiographical tradition and, indeed, the Mayer–Maier controversy is within that tradition. It is a tradition at once materialistic, teleological and loosely Marxist, which starts with a theory of historical development that finds 'meaning' in history via economic change and class conflict; their divergence is about the timescale of a scenario rather than about the scenario itself. Maier is, of course, much closer to Marx's view that aristocratic society was finished as early as 1848, while Mayer attempts to account for the 'failure' of the 'bourgeoisie' to do its 'historic duty'. For both, whether a society can be termed 'bourgeois' or aristocratic/old regime is the most vital of all questions, for almost all else follows from it, as if to have the name was to possess the essence. Those who take a more empirical view of class terminology and who see class structure as an aspect, rather than a definition, of a society may, nevertheless, still accept the importance of the question as to how far it was changed by World War I, along with the other delineating characteristics of and divisions within European society. Such other characteristics and divisions – religious, national and cultural – could, confusingly, both cut across and contribute to social stratification.

Whether we can generalize to much effect about *a* European society or social structure is questionable. Albania, at the end of World War I, consisted of a million or so inhabitants who were divided between the tribal Ghegs in the north and the semi-feudally organized southern Tosks. Things were, obviously, very different in Surrey. If we take any general list of social groups or classes, such as Arthur Marwick's list in Book I, Unit 4 (p. 147), and look for those groups in every European state, it becomes apparent that, in the social structure of individual states, there are gaps. We find, for instance, that there is no peasantry in Britain (save perhaps in the north of Scotland), no aristocracy in Serbia or Bulgaria, and little in the way of industrial working classes in much of Eastern Europe. It is usually, therefore, considered necessary to classify European societies in sub-groups, and the usual divides are between East and West, wealthy and poor, industrialized and largely agricultural, or rural and urbanized societies. There is only a rough and ready correlation between these divides, and one may question whether, for instance, the religious division is not as important as any of them; the vitality of Catholicism in contrast to Greater Russian Orthodoxy as a socio-political force is difficult to explain in economic or class terms.

One important division, which makes it difficult to disentangle this section from section 2.4 on national cohesion, is between those, mainly Western, societies where we can consider social structure as separate from racial or national composition, and those where national identity and social position remained inextricably intertwined. Thus in Lat ia the nobility was German, merchants were Germans or Jews, and the peasantry was Latvian, while in Slovakia the nobility was Magyar, the merchants usually Germans or Jews (or Jewish-German) and the peasantry Slovak. The importance of the Jews in the social structure of many European societies, as indeed in the cultural and economic life of these societies, cannot be underestimated. In Romania, for instance, Jews were, by themselves, almost what Marxists call the bourgeoisie: they were the merchants, the manufacturers, the agents of landowners who were mortgaged to them, the professionals and, to a great extent, the intelligentsia. Norman Stone, in *Europe Transformed 1878–1919* (1983), has argued that in secularized Calvinism and secularized Judaism we find the roots of modernity in both its economic and cultural forms.

Thus there were considerable variations both before and after the war between the social structures of different European societies (Unit 4 discussed in some detail the pre-1914 social structures). Such differences could be found within states as well as between them. Unit 4 emphasized the disparity between North and South Italy, while the Austro-Hungarian Empire encompassed a number of diverse societies. The Italian North-South divide was still apparent in 1920, as indeed it still is today, while even the successor states to Austria-Hungary exhibited internal variations (Czechoslovakia, for instance, had in Bohemia one of the most industrialized areas of Central Europe and contained not only a large number of industrial workers but considerable middle-class sectors, while in the province of Ruthenia, the peasantry made up the great proportion of society).

As with other aspects of the question of the impact of the war, in dealing with social structure we have not only to decide whether change took place at all between 1914 and, say, 1921, but, if there was change, whether that change was due to the war. An ancillary question, even if we accept that change took place in a particular society and it was due to the war, is whether it was due to the nature of warfare as experienced between 1914 and 1918 (or 1921) or to the special outcome of the war for that particular society (i.e. was it on the winning or the losing side?)

Exercise Can you think of reasons why World War I *could* have affected the social structures of European societies? ■

Specimen answer and discussion 1 In the first place, the social and economic pressures of the war on the societies which engaged in it were enormous. Vast numbers volunteered or were conscripted for the armies of the combatant states and, as we have seen, the death toll was considerable. The economies of the states lost their peacetime direction as they were abruptly harnessed to the war effort; wartime needs and shortages altered patterns of supply and demand. Such developments could affect the relative positions and advantages of different sections of society.

2 The impact of defeat in war would have a destabilizing effect on the political structures of the defeated states and, in so far as political and social leadership were intertwined, a destabilizing social result. It could (as it did) lead to the

break-up of states, with immense social implications, and to revolutions with overt social aims.

As you will have realized, the specimen answer above corresponds to my previous distinction between changes due to the nature of the war which could affect all participants, and changes due to the losing of the war. In their attempt to enlist mass support, governments gave their war aims a quasi-ideological dimension and invested more in the necessity of victory than would have been wise if defeat had ever been considered possible. The implications of defeat were momentous. □

But *did* the war have much of a long-term effect upon social structures? As Arthur Marwick has pointed out in the introduction to these units, many recent studies by historians have tended to deny that the war had any significant long-term effects in the way of social change. Such a denial appears more credible for Western than for Eastern and Central Europe (the massive transfer of population between Greece and Turkey seems, for instance, to be a fundamental type of social change), but we need, in any case, to be clear what we mean by change to the social structure. Do we mean that whole sectors of society disappeared or that sectors changed place in the pecking order? Do we, more modestly, mean that although the social order remained similar in its gradations, the relative power and influence of different social groups changed? While recognizing the distinction, I shall assume that both sorts of change may be counted as changes to the social structure.

Exercise   Can you think of a particular social group, structure or class (I'm not too worried about which terms you prefer, although I'll probably slip into class terminology as it is most current in everyday language) that appears to have lost ground as a result of the war? ■

Specimen answer and discussion   Aristocracies do seem to stand out as the social groups which suffered a diminution in political influence, economic position and social standing across Europe.

I suppose that, if we thought of royalty as a class – and if not a class it is certainly something of a caste – we could have even more definitely plumped for it. The kings certainly departed, if only because so many of the most powerful monarchs were on the losing side (one can, of course, see the Tsar of Russia as a ruler whose country lost the war, even if his allies subsequently won it). But if we define aristocrats as those whose families own great landed estates and who are usually, but not always, titled, then it does seem clear that to a greater or lesser extent, and whether in countries that won the war or lost it, World War I was a disaster for aristocrats.

     The demise of aristocracy was most obvious in Russia, where the war ended in revolution, and death or exile was the fate of so many aristocrats. It was obvious, too, in parts of Central and Eastern Europe, where many aristocrats, especially if their nationalities were different to those dominant in the new states, lost all or the greater part of their estates. Prince Lichnowsky (German ambassador in 1914) found that with the new frontiers his estates were now just inside the Czech borders. He thought, wrongly, that the Allies had arranged this deliberately. Even in Britain a case can be made for a major decline in aristocratic wealth and influence as a result of the war. □

Exercise   What factors do you think may have contributed to a weakening of the position of aristocracies? ∎

Specimen answer and discussion

1   The position of many aristocracies was intimately bound up with that of the monarchies and governments that had gone to war in 1914. When under the impact of defeat monarchies and governments fell, the position and influence of aristocracies declined.

2   In many areas of East and Central Europe aristocracies were of a different nationality to the peasantry, and with the creation of new national states, they lost their land and position.

3   Demand for land reform grew among the peasantries of East and Central Europe, encouraged by promises made by governments and national movements. Such a development threatened the economic position of aristocrats.

As regards point (1), it is clear that the German aristocracy lost ground in 1918. It has been argued that, as the aristocracy depended for its wealth upon agriculture, it was in any case in a long-term decline, a decline that would have been accelerated by the agricultural depression after 1870 had it not been checked

> by the ossification of Wilhelmine society – partly due to military influence – and by the constant political, economic and ideological support which the landed gentry received from the Wilhelmine state. The collapse of the state in the revolution of 1918–19 did not remove altogether the gentry's influence, but rather restricted it to certain areas – to Westphalia, Pomerania and East Prussia – and narrowed its focus even more than before the war to the representation of sectorial economic interests. (Michael Geyer, 'Professionals and Junkers: German re-armament and politics in the Weimar Republic', 1981).

According to Roberts (p.375), land reform in East and Central Europe resulted in the redistribution of some 60 million acres from great estates to the peasantry. In Russia, of course, a more drastic change took place by which peasants gained or seized the land of the great estates only to lose it again when the collectivization policy was imposed some years later. Outside Russia, by far the greatest absolute amount of land was redistributed in Romania, and the greatest percentage of land in the Baltic states. It is noteworthy that in Latvia and Estonia the landowners were German and in Lithuania Polish. In general the confiscation of land was highest in the areas where the aristocracy was not of the nationality of the new state. Thus in Romania landowners were allowed to retain most land in the *Regat*, where they were Romanian, and least in Transylvania and Bukovina, where they were respectively Magyar and Russian. In Czechoslovakia, too, landowners from the national minorities such as the Magyar landlords in Slovakia were discriminated against.

The number of aristocrats killed in battle was relatively higher than the proportion for other sections of the population. The following quotation from Trevor Wilson is instructive for British death rates:

> That numbers of the officer class were drawn disproportionately from the upper ranks of society may be inferred from statistics comparing the death rate for mobilised men as a whole with that for men from various élite institutions. For mobilised men *in toto*, the death rate was 12 per cent. For students from Oxford and Cambridge who served in the war it was,

respectively, 19 and 18 per cent. For members of the peerage it was 19 per cent. (Wilson, *The Myriad Faces of War*, 1986)

It seems likely that the disproportion would have been true for other European armies, and would have had an effect on the vitality of aristocracies in the post-war years. In a country like Britain, which had death duties, it could also have profound economic consequences for aristocratic families. □

So far so good (and so Mayer); a picture seems to be emerging of a definite decline in the position of the upper echelon of the social structure, but there are important *caveats*. So far as Western Europe is concerned it is debatable whether we can see the aristocracy and those possessed of great industrial and financial fortunes as distinct before or after 1914. The pristine images of aristocratic and 'capitalist' may seem clear enough, but theories of an 'embourgeoised aristocracy', an 'aristocraticized bourgeoisie' or a general symbiosis between aristocracy and upper middle class suggest all is not quite so distinct after all. We probably need to distinguish between lesser landowners or gentry who, entirely dependent upon incomes from land or salaries as army officers, had for long been in straitened circumstances, and those great landowners whose incomes were supplemented by mineral royalties or who, like the Dukes of Westminster, owned urban land. A word commonly used to describe the wealthiest sections of society in Edwardian Europe is plutocracy, and plutocracy and aristocracy had in many instances become intertwined. American heiresses had married into the European aristocracies; the Krupps, von Thyssens, Devonports and Northcliffs acquired titles, as did Bismarck's Jewish banker, Bleichroder; Lord Rosebery married a Rothschild, while Sir Ernest Cassel's grand-daughter was to marry the future Earl Mountbatten. Perhaps we should conclude that so far as aristocracy dependent purely upon birth and land ownership was concerned, the Great War dealt it, as it did monarchy, a severe blow, and that certain symbols of aristocratic life, like the great London town houses, disappeared soon after its end. The decline of European agriculture had arguably been eroding its position for long enough, but the war precipitated a more rapid decline. The wealthiest strata of European society, however, continued to have aristocratic connections, titles and aspirations. In Poland, where large and medium landowners continued to occupy a strong position in agriculture, leading industrialists sought country estates for the prestige they gained from them; however impoverished the individual, a claim to belong to the lesser gentry still conferred social status.

If the war hastened the decline of those sections of the upper classes who most closely fitted the profile of aristocrats and gentry, it may well have increased mobility into the upper classes. Certainly, fortunes were made by those who manufactured and organized supplies for the war effort. The notion of 'hard-faced men who had done well out of the war' is, of course, something of a caricature: no doubt most profits were honestly earned out of the provision of services necessary to the war effort, and if it is true that some failed to take advantage of war-time opportunities, then they behaved little differently to other sectors such as trade unionists in key industries. Nevertheless, a philanthropic gesture, such as that of Stanley Baldwin, who gave a substantial part of his fortune to the nation in recognition that much of it came from war profits, was rare, while there are many well publicized examples of those who emerged from the war with fortunes made by questionable means. In Britain, Italy and France and even in defeated Germany, financial and manufacturing wealth not only survived the war but was often increased by it. Wartime corporatism also brought manufacturers closer to and often into governments, increasing influence and prestige as well as wealth. There were both winners and losers. Smaller manufacturers and businessmen whose affairs were not related to the war effort found their position diminished by restrictions, labour shortages and increased taxation, while the war was disastrous for those who lived on fixed incomes or relied upon rents. Many, especially French, investors lost heavily from the collapse of Tsarist Russia and the Austro-Hungarian monarchy. If the wartime and post-war inflation in Germany and other Central European states can be seen as benefiting the working classes (see section 2.2), then it also worked to the advantage of landowners who were able to pay off their mortgages and industrialists who paid off their loans and turned inflated profits into new factories.

It is especially difficult to generalize about the effects of the war upon the middle classes. As you know from Unit 4, this group can be broken down into numerous sub-sections, with little in common save that they were in the middle. The profile of this middle group, and indeed its wealth, also changes considerably

This cartoon from the German satirical magazine Simplicissimus *(16 April 1918) represents the* Mittelstand *as squeezed between the upper class (note the baronial castle) and labour. (Bildarchiv Preussischer Kulturbesitz, Berlin)*

as we go across Europe. The steady expansion of the middle classes is a feature of modern European history, but in Eastern Europe they were less numerous and, as we have seen, often consisted of nationalities different to the majority nationality of the new states.

Overall, however, it would appear that the war had a deleterious effect on most members of the middle classes, though the effect was for the most part short-lived. Like the aristocracy, the middle classes suffered disproportionate losses from war deaths, not just because the proportion killed was greater than for the working classes or peasantries, but because many of the middle classes had tended to have smaller families than other social groups, so that the number of middle-class families who lost their only or both of their sons was particularly high. There was no clear divide between upper middle class and upper class, so that the effects we noted above of increased taxation and a decline in rental income and fixed income penetrated well down into the middle classes. The salaried middle classes found that salaries tended to lag behind wages and prices in the wartime and immediate post-war economies. Wartime and post-war inflation, especially in Central Europe, destroyed middle-class savings. Craftsmen and shopkeepers suffered from the general decline in middle-class spending power, though where, as in Britain, working-class spending power increased, manufacturers and retailers were able to find new customers among those who could now afford to buy better clothes and food and modest luxuries.

As we move towards Eastern Europe it becomes apparent that West European generalizations about social structure and the war's effect upon it are difficult to substantiate. I would like you to read the following extract from a chapter by Antony Polonsky in *The History of Poland since 1863*, edited by R. F. Leslie, which describes the social structure of the urban areas of the new Poland:

> Industrialists and capitalists, who with their dependants numbered about 260,000 persons, did not play an important part in social life. Industry was not highly developed. Indeed, industry and commerce gave employment to a larger number of Germans and Jews which excited prejudice against them, but industrialists were able to exert pressure on the government through the Central Union of Polish Industry, Mining, Trade and Finance, commonly known as 'Leviathan'. The absence of a strong native bourgeoisie explains the role of the intelligentsia, which embraced a far wider group than it did in Western Europe and totalled 1.4 million persons in urban society. *Swiat pojec*, a popular pre-war encyclopaedia, defined the intelligentsia as follows: 'The intelligentsia in the sociological sense of the term is a social stratum made up those possessing academic higher education. Typical representatives of the intelligentsia . . . are professors, doctors, literary figures, etc. The social position of the intelligentsia does not mean that its members have a rigidly defined social or ideological position. Members of the intelligentsia can identify with the most varied social and political trends. In fact, they occupy the leading role in all political groupings.' Membership of the intelligentsia was not in fact to be identified strictly with the possession of a high school diploma. It was more important that a man's manners should be those of the educated classes and that he should have some familiarity with the humanities. In spite of many differences of income and status the intelligentsia had a markedly strong feeling of solidarity and responsibility. Descended from *szlachta* [minor gentry] who had migrated to the towns in the 1870s and 1880s, they saw their careers as an alternative to a way of life which had collapsed. The intelligentsia saw themselves as representatives of the

nation, the keepers of its conscience and its directing force. A post in the service of the state enjoyed great prestige, while a certain disdain for trade and industry led some to develop pretensions to wide cultural interests. Respect for culture and knowledge was often that of the dilettante and not of the specialist. An overproduction of 'literary intellectuals' had much to do with the right-wing radicalism prevalent in the universities.

There were other significant urban groups, 1.3 million people deriving their livelihood from trade. Petty trade was primitive, but it was adapted to existing conditions of economic development. The government tried without much success to replace private tradesmen with peasant co-operatives. Trade was concentrated in Jewish hands. In 1921 62.9 per cent of persons employed in trade and industry were Jews, but of those 88.9 per cent were engaged in retail trades. It is difficult to estimate the number of people owning handicraft workshops, because many were not registered with the authorities. The figure of 1.1 million for such workers and their families is therefore hypothetical. Most workshops were small, often employing only members of the owner's family. Many were owned by Jews, especially in tailoring, leather work, baking and bookbinding. Jews were correspondingly not numerous in heavy industry. Industrial workers and their families amounted to 4.6 million. Of these 1.8 million were employed in handicrafts or cottage industries, while 2.8 million worked in heavy industry and mining. Standards of living varied widely among the working class. Workers in government monopolies were among the better-off enjoying higher wages and relative security. Unskilled workers were often very poor as were those employed in cottage industries, especially in and around Lodz, Bialystok and Bielsko-Biala. The majority of industrial workers were Poles, but many skilled workmen in Upper Silesia and Lodz were German. In common with other under-developed countries, industrial workers in Poland were better-off than the peasantry.

Exercise   Which features of the social structure of urban society in Poland strike you as being markedly different to most West European societies? ■

Specimen answer and discussion   1   The degree to which nationality and occupation are intertwined and the degree to which so many of the social groups we would put within the middle classes are not made up of Poles. Germans and Jews are prominent in industry and commerce, while trade is concentrated in Jewish hands.

2   The concept of an 'intelligentsia' and the size of this group. The intelligentsia is unknown in Britain, and while the French and Italians are fond of the notion of 'intellectuals', they confine this to a fairly small group, including academics, writers, etc.

What was true of Poland was also true for much of East and Central Europe. Several factors accounted for the lack of commercial and industrial middle classes of the national majorities. The diversity of races and nationalities and the history of conquests, partitions and alien regimes had contributed to a class-ethnic or occupation-ethnic correlation. Racial or religious cohesion and the laws against Jews engaging in many occupations had resulted in a high degree of specialization for the Jewish community, while the urban world of Eastern and Central Europe had experienced something of a German hegemony. Industrialization had usually come from a conscious state initiative and from outside local society rather than in response to local conditions and demands. □

A feature of Eastern Europe after the war was the existence of a larger number of arts and, to some extent, law graduates than state jobs or the private sector could properly absorb. This chronically dissatisfied sector was to be a source of political instability.

In much of East and Central Europe the main effect of the war so far as middle-class groups who did not belong to the national minorities were concerned was discrimination, if not disappropriation. In many instances the ambitions of those members of the national majorities who via the educational system rose out of the peasantries were directed towards the state bureaucracies or to becoming army officers, rather than towards industry or commerce. The lack of substantial middle classes involved in manufacturing and trade was to be a major handicap to many Central and East European countries in the inter-war years; it was a problem that had been made worse by the formation of new national states, with the consequent diminution of the security of the minority middle-class sectors and the disinclination of the national minorities to take their place.

Exercise   Which sectors of European society do you think might have gained most from the war? ■

Specimen answer and discussion   The industrial working classes in Western Europe and the peasantry of East and parts of Central Europe did appear in the immediate post-war period to have made gains.

So far as the industrial working classes are concerned, it has been argued (Arthur Marwick, *The Deluge*, 1965) that one effect of total war is that groups whose support for the war effort is crucial will achieve gains in influence and in standards of living. For Britain, there is considerable evidence of an increase in working-class living standards. Trevor Wilson (*The Myriad Faces of War*) quotes A. L. Bowley to the effect that 'the proportion in poverty in 1924 was little more than half that in 1913', and concludes that 'although the size of the cake was not greater in 1924 than in 1913, the better-off were getting marginally less of it at the later date and the worse-off marginally more'.

Trades unions representing workers in key industries were able to ensure that their members did better than most of the population in keeping their wages in step with inflation, while wartime corporations saw labour leaders consulted by government and participating in government. Bernard Waites (an Open University colleague) has argued that distinctions between skilled and unskilled working men were eroded by the wartime experience ('The effect of the First World War on class and status in England 1910–20', 1976).

In both Italy and France there were pointers towards greater trades union influences and working-class militancy at the end of the war. Socialism flourished in the major Italian industrial centres, namely Milan, Turin and Genoa, which had grown rapidly during the war. By 1919 large groups of industrial workers had gained the eight-hour day, while the membership of the Socialist Party had grown fourfold since 1914 to 200,000 members. In France the action of the Chamber of Deputies and the Senate in passing laws for the eight-hour day and giving recognition to the results of collective bargaining failed to stem a wave of strikes and demonstrations. French workers made few of the strides of their British counterparts in increasing their standard of living: the dislocation to industry caused by occupation and the fighting (the areas occupied and fought over included some of the most industrialized regions of France) ensured a general lowering of living standards; taxes were not, as in Britain, increased; and the short-lived post-war inflation brought French workers no advantages.

In Germany there appeared to be major advances for the industrial working classes. The early years of the Weimar Republic saw increased co-operation between industry and the trade unions, the establishment of the eight-hour day, increased welfare provision, and an increase in taxation with distributive effects. As we have seen, it has been claimed that the inflation which began during the war and reached its zenith in 1923 had positive advantages for urban workers.

As regards the peasantry, Norman Stone has argued that, 'By 1906, a movement that had nothing at all to do with traditional politics was under way: the mobilisation of backward peasant Europe' (*Europe Transformed*, p.127). The war may have accelerated such a mobilization, as wartime service in armies brought more of the peasantry into contact with the world of the towns, with their superior living standards and raised new ambitions. The emergence of new national states gave the peasants of the national majorities opportunities to press their demands for land reform and for greater influence in government. Within existing states like Bulgaria or Romania, peasant parties were to be a major feature of inter-war politics. In countries with little in the way of aristocracies and where the peasantry constituted the mass of the population, as in Yugoslavia and Bulgaria, it appeared that the potential for the social and political dominance of the peasantry and peasant/agrarian parties was strong.

In Russia the fall in living standards for almost everyone that resulted from famine, drought, revolution and civil war makes it difficult to argue that any class had improved its position in an absolute sense. The industrial working classes now had a government that was in theory their dictatorship, while, prior to collectivization, the peasantry could hope to retain their increased holdings and in better times reap some benefit from them. The strata above proletariat and peasantry had largely been removed and replaced by a new party bureaucracy, though the New Economic Policy marked a temporary retardation of the process.

The effects of the war upon the European social structure looked less considerable when viewed from the mid rather than the early 1920s. While the European economy and largely the individual economies were depressed, stagnant or had not returned to the production levels of 1914, there does appear to have been both a turbulent political situation in which working-class, socialist or peasant parties were able to maximize their influence, and a time in which diminished economic rewards were distributed in a more egalitarian fashion. By the mid 1920s, in a more successful economic environment, the erosion of different standards of living between middle classes and working classes appears to have been halted and perhaps reversed: the effects of unemployment were felt more severely by workers, while deflation favoured those on salaries and fixed incomes rather than wage-earners. It was not that workers started to get poorer; indeed, all in work were getting richer, and in many countries the unemployed were better provided for than they had been in 1914. However, the better-off began once more to get richer faster. At the same time the threat from millenarian socialist parties largely receded, and reformist socialist parties found themselves with an often enhanced (compared to 1914) but rarely dominant place in refashioned political systems. The German economy, for instance, can be seen as going back to normal in late 1923 with the end of inflation due to the revalued currency, the Rentenmark, and the abrogation of the eight-hour day in December. □

A 'recasting of a bourgeois Europe' or a return to normal economic and social life – according to taste – had taken place. So far as Western Europe was concerned, the effects of the war, its dislocating effects, the shortages and its emergencies, had resulted in the classes being temporarily squeezed together in a concertina effect, but in the longer term, perhaps because what Arthur Marwick has called 'structural factors' triumphed over the cataclysm of war, the social structure of West European society reasserted the social pattern and the process of change discernible before 1914. This is not to deny that the war may have speeded up changes to the social structure discernible before 1914, nor that there were distinct differences between the pre-war and post-war societies. In Eastern Europe it can be argued that the changes were greater, but they owed more to the force of nationalism and to the national/political, geopolitical changes consequent upon the post-war settlement than to social forces. The relative position of the East European peasantry was enhanced by the removal of minority aristocracies and the political control over towns, merchants and bureaucracies that resulted from national rather than social revolution. Yet even where land reform was greatest, and it was rarely sweeping, the position of the peasantries of Eastern Europe in the context of increasing populations and declining agricultural incomes, represented an empty inheritance, although a less invidious one than that of their Russian equivalent.

2.4   National cohesion

It is significant that it was the League of *Nations* that was established by the Treaty of Versailles and not a League of *States*. Although 'nation' can be defined as a people under the same government and inhabiting the same country, our use of the word tends to be coloured by its other meaning of a people belonging to the same ethnological family and speaking the same language. The word 'state' sits rather more happily on a multinational empire like Austria-Hungary than does 'nation'; a subject could be loyal to and even patriotic about the Empire, but he (or she) could not be a nationalistic Austro-Hungarian, though he could be a Hungarian, a German or a Czech nationalist. The term League of Nations was thus in harmony with the importance attached by the Versailles Settlement to nationalism and the principle of national self-determination.

Nationalism, whether regarded as a 'natural' force or a conscious political and social philosophy (see Units 3 and 5), is the joker in the pack of modern history. It has cohabited with every other 'ism', with socialism, liberalism, conservatism and even monarchism, yet it cuts across all of them. Many historians, while accepting its importance, have seen nationalism as a rather disreputable intruder in the modern world, atavistic in its attachment to blood and soil, but it is a creation of the modern world, flourishing in the context of industrialization, secularization and democracy. It can be argued that World War I's most fundamental consequence was that national identity became paramount as the basis for the existence of states.

A common ethnic origin is far from the only, and is not always the preponderant, criterion of national identity. Language, common traditions, common interests and religion can both buttress ethnic considerations and override them. Thus new senses of national identity can develop which are composites of other identities or independent of them. Thus, for example, a sense of British nationality grew from the mid eighteenth century; a Belgian identity has survived uneasily despite language/national divisions; similarly, but with greater longevity, there is the linguistic and religious patchwork that is Switzerland; conversely, Pan Slavism foundered on the rocks of diverse national traditions, religions and alphabets. Whatever the factors that contribute to a sense of national identity, it can be said that from the late eighteenth century the nation state embodying it has become progressively the most common and the most cohesive form of state.

Exercise   What factors other than ethnic identity do you consider bound together the citizens of the states of Europe in 1914? ■

Specimen answer   1   The subjects of monarchies could feel loyalty to monarchy and dynasty.
and discussion   2   Citizens and subjects could identify with the political and cultural values their states appeared to embody and with the past achievements and history of states. French Republicans could then feel loyalty to the Republic, while all French people could identify with France.

3   States were economic as well as political units, and economic self-interest could be a cohesive force.

Such factors could merge with a pride in ethnic identity to create national identities, but they could also be separate from it and an alternative to it. □

Of the forces making for cohesion within states in the world before the war, the national and the monarchical principles were by far the most important; the former had increased in importance during the nineteenth century while the latter had waned. Monarchism nevertheless remained an important force for stability in *ancien régime* Europe. Nationalism and monarchism could appear opposed, with monarchical legitimacy seeming cosmopolitan in contrast to nationalism; thus in Austria-Hungary, for example, it provided a focus for unity above competing nationalities. The blood relationship of the royal families of Europe made them supra-national; as Queen Victoria wrote, 'a freedom from all national preju- dices . . . is very important in Princes' (H. Nicolson, *King George V*, 1952, p. 14). In practice the relationship between nationalism and monarchism had been some- what confused: the self-consciously national states that had emerged in the Balkans had, with the exception of Serbia and Montenegro, chosen to be ruled by German kings, while the Emperors of Germany and Russia synthesized legitimism with nationalism.

Exercise   From the knowledge you have acquired in the course so far, say what effect you think the outbreak of hostilities had upon the cohesion of the European states. ■

Specimen answer   The war fanned nationalism in nation states and was, in the long run, to give
and discussion   national movements in multinational states their opportunity. In the short run, however, the multinational empires – Austria-Hungary, Russia and the Ottoman Empire – stood up better to the strain of war than an emphasis upon their pre-war national problems might have led us to expect. The effect of the war upon Austria-Hungary confirms Arthur Marwick's comment in Book I, Unit 5 that in 1914 'the monarchy was managing to hold together its disparate nationalities.' Austro-Hungarian armies remained loyal until the last months of the war.

If the war gave national movements in East and Central Europe their oppor- tunities, it was not immediately apparent what those opportunities were, for they depended upon whether the Allied or the central powers would eventually win the war. Should, for instance, Polish nationalists support the war effort of the central powers and hope for an Austro-Polish or German solution to their national aspirations, or should they support Russia, hoping for a better deal from that quarter? The war was, of course, ultimately fatal to the Austro-Hungarian Empire, and it detached western regions from Russia – developments which were to the benefit of Polish, Czech, Serbian, Lithuanian, Latvian, Finnish and Estonian national ambitions. ☐

Exercise Going beyond the war itself and also considering the effects of the Versailles Settlement and the continuing warfare in Eastern Europe until 1921, what do you see as the overall effect of the war upon national or state cohesion? ■

Specimen answer and discussion

1   It increased the number of European states, giving Europe many more miles of frontiers.

2   National or ethnic identity became more than ever before the main basis for the existence of states.

3   It dealt a mortal blow to the principle of monarchical legitimacy.

Roberts comments that Versailles saw 'the end of a century-long struggle between legitimacy and nationalism, which won its greatest triumph at Versailles'. ☐

It is perhaps paradoxical that Woodrow Wilson, the President of a state engaged in an unremitting effort to weld a new sense of national identity binding diverse ethnic groups, should have supported so unswervingly the notion of national self-determination. The concept can, of course, be seen as a democratic one and, indeed, plebiscites were held in many areas, but democracy, whatever other admirable features it may have, does not by itself provide for the rights of minorities, and if Versailles turned minorities into nations, it created new minorities. Far from each national group being cosily nestled in its own national box, the post-war settlement created as many new minorities as it satisfied old ones, and all the guarantees for the linguistic, cultural and religious rights of minorities that were to be provided by the League of Nations were to prove worthless. In East and Central Europe the new nationalism penetrated deeper down the social scale than in the past; nationalism became a matter for peasants as well as professors, and in doing so became far less tolerant of minorities.

Exercise What do you think were the main threats to the national cohesion of the European states in the post-war period? ■

Specimen answer and discussion

1   Even though most states were now national states, the main threat to their national cohesion came from nationalism – the nationalisms of their minorities and of their neighbours. Most states in East and Central Europe had hostile minorities to contend with and frontier disputes with neighbouring states.

2   A further threat to national cohesion was ideology. Socialism was ostensibly international and claimed that class divisions ran across natural frontiers, though, as we have seen, in 1914 most socialists and the great majority of the working classes rallied to national banners. The Soviet Union was from the beginning equivocal on the issue of international revolution: on the one hand it sought to export it, setting up the Comintern or Third (Communist) International to this end, but, on the other hand, it sought to retain control of as much of Tsarist Russia as possible, maintaining, after the adoption of the policy of 'socialism in one

country', near normal relationships with other states. Fascism was a nationalist ideology, seeing the nation rather than class as the dynamic historical force, so it presented in principle less of a threat to the cohesion of states, though in practice fascist parties could be divisive and gain support from fascists in other countries.

3   Religion could be a divisive factor, particularly in those parts of Eastern and Central Europe where the divide between the Orthodox and the Catholic Churches ran within a new state. Croatian and to some extent Slovenian separatism was fanned by Catholicism within the new Yugoslavia. That this phenomenon was not confined to East and Central Europe is, of course, demonstrated by the religious dimensions of the Irish problem. Bavarian separatism in Germany had much to do with the Catholic south's suspicion of a Protestant Prussian hegemony. Even Islam was a potential problem in Albania, Yugoslavia and Eastern Russia. □

Western Europe

The major powers of Western Europe were, on the whole, nationally cohesive, and their cohesion had been strengthened by the experience of war, even though Germany and Italy had only short histories as national states.

Exercise   Which power do you think was the most firmly and solidly cohesive? ■

Specimen answer and discussion   France would seem the favourite from a number of points of view. It had a long history as a national state, was a highly centralized state, had a cohesive common culture, and no major separatist problems. It was, therefore, a nationally cohesive country, and its eventual victory after four years of war in which a portion of its territory had been fought over and occupied, further cemented such cohesion. French nationalism had always been as much cultural as racial and, as an imperial power, France had tended to have Roman aspirations, feeling that colonies could be assimilated and become truly French. Thus Algeria was considered to be part of metropolitan France.

However, the re-integration of Alsace and Lorraine, part of the German Empire since 1871, proved surprisingly difficult. Although the great majority in the provinces welcomed their reunification with France, the effects of nearly half a century of German rule were not to be swept away. The re-incorporation of the provinces was accompanied by friction between French officials and the local population, and the desire of the Radical government of Herriot to extend all the anti-clerical legislation passed in France between 1871 and 1914 provoked strong resistance among the large number of devout Catholics, who under German rule had had close associations with the German Catholic Central Party. Herriot was forced to withdraw his proposals, but the incident left a legacy of discontent and unrest. □

Britain also emerged from the war with the strong sense of British identity that had developed in the nineteenth century having been heightened. One effect of the wartime experience was that, as a result of the war effort of the dominions, British public opinion was extremely conscious of the Empire and felt little empathy with Europe. It is a measure of wartime patriotic fervour that the royal family was forced to sever its German links. In the atmosphere of 1917 the German connections of the ruling dynasty were, increasingly, an embarrassment. Told of H. G. Wells's charge that the court was 'uninspiring and alien', George V retorted:

'I may be uninspiring but I'll be damned if I'm an alien.' The inauguration of the House of Windsor and the dropping of their German titles by the junior members of the royal family completed the family's anglicization and was a blow to the cosmopolitan traditions of royalty. As Count Albrecht von Montgelas commented, 'The true royal tradition died on that day in 1917 when, for a mere war, King George changed his name' (Kenneth Rose, *King George V*, 1983, p.174).

The great exception to the cohesiveness of the United Kingdom was, of course, Ireland, where the outbreak of war had interrupted a crisis over Home Rule that had seen unionists and nationalists facing each other in armed intransigence, and a Liberal government faced with the refusal of both northern unionists and the Conservative and Unionist Party to accept the passage of the Home Rule Bill. The outlines of the future settlement, which was reached in 1921 and which provided for an Irish Free State with dominion status and kept Northern Ireland within the union, were already discernible in 1914. However, the settlement was to be preceded by the Easter rebellion in Dublin in 1916 and by a long and bloody campaign against the IRA in the years 1919–21, and was to be succeeded by an even bloodier civil war in the south.

A unified German state was less than fifty years old at the end of World War I. In fact, the German Empire had not been a full unitary state, for the old Bismarckian structure had recognized the existence of individual states within it which had retained their identity as kingdoms or duchies. The particularism of individual states had remained a force, albeit overlaid by a strong and fervent German nationalism. The possibility of breaking up Germany and replacing it with a number of smaller states was one that occurred to the Allied powers during both the First and Second World Wars.

The Weimar Republic was more of a unitary state than the Empire had been. Many of the prerogatives of the old states were abolished: they had to have republican governments, the *Reich* government assumed the power of direct taxation over all citizens, and central government controlled the army. But the *Länder*, as the states became, continued to have considerable powers: they controlled education, the police and the process of law. The existence of the *Länder* gave a weapon to separatists or to those who simply wished to defy the will of the *Reich* government.

In 1923 the French gave support to separatists in the Rhineland who were encouraged to declare an independent Rhineland Republic (there was an earlier attempt at this in 1919), and supported a Palatinate Republic which was reorganized by the Rhineland Commission in January 1924. Neither of these Republics lasted for more than a few months, as there was little real support for them. The events in Bavaria in 1923 were more serious and drew on a more significant vein of separatist sentiment. In fact, two elements came together: national right-wing movements under the leadership of Hitler's National Socialist Party, and conservative Bavarian separatists who wished to regain Bavaria's previous more independent status. One must not, however, exaggerate threats to the national cohesion of Germany. Regional pride, a suspicion of Prussia and Berlin, and a nostalgia for separate cultural and political traditions coexisted with German national feeling.

Italy, too, was politically a recent creation and economically and socially a less homogeneous entity than Germany, but, despite the continuing disparity between north and south, Italian cohesion can be said to have increased during the war years. Italian territorial ambitions, if fully satisfied, would have impaired such cohesion; even as it was, the more modest gains made by Italy in 1919 (the frontier on the Brenner and Istria) and the later seizure of Fiume brought into the Italian state discontented German and Slav areas on its periphery.

Central and Eastern Europe

It was clearly in Central and Eastern Europe where there was such a multiplicity of overlapping national and ethnic groups that threats to national cohesion were greatest. As we have seen, Versailles attempted to provide for the principle of national self-determination but vitiated this by its parallel preoccupations with rewarding victors and providing against a German revival. Further east, frontiers were settled and states established after years of continued warfare. It was something of a paradox that the more national aspirations were satisfied, the greater were the problems of national cohesion for the expanded nation states. For a state to fulfil its national ambitions was to be saddled with greater numbers of hostile minorities. After 1918 Bulgaria and Hungary were cohesive states largely because they came out of the war and the peace settlement diminished in size (and bursting with a desire for revenge), while Czechoslovakia had endemic racial problems largely because the most grandiose plans of Czech patriots had been fulfilled. The diplomatic success of Romania and the diplomatic and military success of the new Poland had extended frontiers well beyond areas that were homogeneously Romanian or Polish. As we have seen in section 2.3, almost all East and Central European states inherited from pasts characterized by successive conquests, important social elements that were not of the majority nationality. Thus in Finland the aristocracy was Swedish, and in Slovakia, Magyar, while the divide between town and country in many states was characterized by German and/or Jewish predominance in towns which were surrounded by a Slav (or Latvian or Lithuanian) countryside.

A specific example will have to suffice to illustrate the ethnic and social mix that existed especially in frontier areas. We have already come across Bratislava in section 1, where we saw how it was given to Czechoslovakia by the peace settlement. Here are some passages from a traveller's account of it in 1933, although the account was not written until many decades later. Patrick Leigh Fermor walked across Europe to Constantinople, and in his book *A Time of Gifts* (1977) described his experiences. His companion on this stage of his travels was Austrian:

> His family lived in Prague and, like many Austrians at the break-up of the Empire, they had found themselves citizens of the new-born Republic, tied there beyond uprooting by old commitments; in this case a family bank. Hans helped to run the branch of an associate establishment in Bratislava – or Pressburg, as he still firmly called it, just as ex-Hungarians stubbornly clung to Pozony . . .

Fermor describes three different drinking places:

> a lively drinking hell with the Magyar word VENDEGLÖ printed in large letters across the frontpane and [I] bumped into a trio of Hungarian farmers . . . rigorous, angular-faced, dark-clad and dark-glanced men with black moustaches tipped down at the corners of their mouths. Their white shirts were buttoned at the throat. They wore low-crowned black hats with narrow brims and high boots of shiny black leather with a Hessian notch at

the knee . . . My next call, only a few doors away, was a similar haunt of sawdust and spilt liquor and spit, but this time, KRCMA was daubed over the window. All was Slav within. The tow-haired Slovaks drinking there were dressed in conical fleece hats and patched sheepskin jerkins with the matted wool turned inwards . . . I singled out one of the many Jewish coffee houses . . . conversing and arguing and contracting business round an archipelago of tables, the dark-clad customers thronged the place to bursting point. (These marble squares did duty as improvised offices in thousands of cafés all through Central Europe and the Balkans and the Levant). The minor hubbub of Magyar and Slovak was outnumbered by voices speaking German, pronounced in the Austrian way . . . But quite often the talk was in Yiddish. (Fermor, *A Time of Gifts*, 1977, pp.213–20)

These extracts from Fermor's account of his impressions of Bratislava bring out several important facets of life not only in Bratislava but in much of Central Europe: the legacy of Austria-Hungary was to be found in the importance of Germans in banking and trade; the Jews were similarly important in all branches of finance and commerce; the different nationalities not only lived separate social lives but they dressed differently; and different languages were to be encountered at every turn. These were formidable obstacles in the way of national cohesion.

The constitution of the Czechoslovakian state declared the Republic to be a 'Czechoslovak national state', recognizing only Czechoslovaks and, in Ruthenia, Ruthenes as *Staatsvölker*, which made the other inhabitants Germans, Magyars and Jews – not peoples of the state, but minorities. The concept of Czechoslovaks, as opposed to Czechs and Slovaks, was itself denied by many Slovaks, who saw it as a device to submerge Slovak identity.

In the new Kingdom of the Serbs, Croats and Slovenes (Yugoslavia in 1929) from the beginning there was antipathy from the Croats towards Serbian hegemony, and Croatian separatism was fuelled by Croatia's different religion, different alphabet and distinct traditions, as well as by Serbian arrogance. The new state had many minorities: 'some half-million each of Germans, Magyars and Albanians, a quarter of a million Roumanians and the half-million Macedonian Slavs, many of them strongly Bulgarophile' (Macartney and Palmer, *Independent Eastern Europe*, 1962, p.172). Macartney and Palmer comment that Yugoslavia's 'reasonable measure of social stability and an absence of social conflict . . . only threw into greater relief the intractability of the Serb-Croat-Slovene problem' (p.219).

By contrast, the rump of a great empire that was Austria was now fairly homogeneous nationally – a German state that was forbidden to unite with Germany – but divided socially and economically between the former capital of the Empire, Vienna, and the largely rural provinces. Vienna, which possessed about a third of the population of the new state, was dominated politically by the Social Democratic Party, while provincial Austria tended to be conservative and Catholic.

Along with Czechoslovakia and Yugoslavia, Romania and Poland were the great winners of the post-war settlements. Poland was a far from nationally homogeneous state. The census of 1921, which almost certainly exaggerated the number of Poles, counted some nine million non-Polish citizens out of a population of 27 million: four million Ukrainians, over two million Jews, a million White Russians, a million Germans, and a quarter of a million 'others', chiefly Czechs and Lithuanians. In fact there may well have been over three million Jews and over five million Ukrainians. Nor were the Poles themselves completely united, as ex-Russian, ex-German and ex-Austrian Poles had different outlooks and traditions. Romania's new territories diluted its homogeneity, for in the ex-Hungarian provinces there was a bare majority of Romanians over Hungarians and Germans, while in Bukovina the north was purely Ukrainian; in Bessarabia the Romanians, although the largest single national group, made up less than half the population, and in Southern Dobruja the population was largely Bulgarian (figures taken from Macartney and Palmer).

The Soviet Union remained, like the Tsarist Empire it succeeded, a multi-racial and multinational state dominated by Greater Russia. The Finns, the Latvians, the Lithuanians, the Estonians and the Poles had made good their bids for national independence, while others like the Ukrainians had failed. The constitutional arrangement of a union of republics could be seen as a recognition of national diversity, but real power lay in the central control of the Communist Party; that firm control would disguise and hold down separatist tendencies as firmly as the Tsarist governments had done.

Not only were the states of East and Central Europe not nationally homogeneous or cohesive, but territorial disputes and conflicting ambitions between neighbours ensured that national minorities and their treatment would become the pawns of national rivalries. Sandwiched between the great powers of Germany and the USSR and faced with the revisionist ambitions of Bulgaria and Hungary, the powers that had benefited from Versailles and the aftermath of World War I were almost universally divided against each other by territorial disputes. The only exceptions were Finland and the Baltic states, who had no differences with each other, although Lithuania and Poland had a bitter dispute over Vilna. Czechoslovakia, Romania and Yugoslavia had minor differences with each other, although these paled when set beside the ambitions of Bulgaria and Hungary to reclaim their *irredenta* or lost territories. But in the hostility between Poland and Czechoslovakia over Teschen, two of the new powers of Central Europe had a major dispute. People did not, unfortunately, fit frontiers.

You should note that the following sections 2.5–2.10 are written by Arthur Marwick.

2.5   Social reform and welfare policies

In Section 1 you read about the geopolitical settlement of Europe made through the Treaty of Versailles and other treaties and arrangements. One unprecedented and unique part of the Treaty of Versailles was Part XIII, which was entirely devoted to the welfare of labour and the setting up of an International Labour Office. The preamble to Part XIII declared that 'universal peace' was dependent on 'social justice', and called among other things for a maximum working week, the prevention of unemployment, a living wage, protection against sickness, the protection of children, young people and women, and provision for old age and injury (see document II.3). At the end of the war, and in the early 1920s, many countries passed important (or important-sounding) Acts within the realm of social reform and welfare policy (see Table 8–10.2 on pp.98–100 below). That there were such provisions in the Treaty of Versailles and such legislation in the years immediately after the war does not automatically establish that (to use what is in any case a naive and unsatisfactory phrase) 'the war brought social reform'; but neither can they be ignored. They establish a *prima facie* case for at least examining the potential relationship between war and changes in social welfare. In looking at these post-war developments towards the end of this section, we shall have to consider (a) how far they were simply continuations of trends apparent before the war, and (b) how far, on the other hand, they were brought about by particular post-war pressures which had little to do with the war itself. But we will also have to ask why such developments came together, concentrated in a short space of time close to the war, and not spread over a much longer period of time. First, however, I want to consider developments during the period of the war itself.

Exercise   On a common-sense basis, in the light of what you already know about the nature of the war, it would be possible to argue

1   that certain aspects of the war made certain forms of social welfare action essential; and

2   that, on the contrary, certain other aspects of the war made social welfare policies extremely unlikely, if not impossible.

Write down the main points in support of both arguments. ■

Specimen answer   1   The mobilization of large numbers of husbands and fathers, the disruptions to
and discussion   family and business life, and the very high risk of injury and death on the various fronts, created a pressing need for separation allowances, pensions, disability payments, etc. From one point of view these can simply be seen as governments merely meeting their barest obligations (often in an extremely stingy way) rather than real advances in social welfare; from another point of view they can be seen as precedents leading to more comprehensive developments as the war progressed and in the post-war period. In fact, in different countries and at different times, developments were sometimes very much of the first type, sometimes inclining towards the second.

2   The very destructiveness of the war, the immense stress it placed on resources, particularly of the less developed countries, very much ran against the setting aside of funds for social welfare.

With regard to the likelihood of social reform, other arguments have been advanced, and you have my heartiest congratulations if you thought of throwing them in here. These arguments (which are closely interrelated), based on the notion of *participation* which you encountered in Book I, Unit 1, are:

(a)   that in this total war, this war of entire peoples, governments needed to buy the support of their subjects, or keep their morale up, by granting social reforms; and

(b)   that because they were so necessary to a successful war effort, ordinary people, and particularly those organized in trades unions, were able to force governments to make concessions in the realm of welfare. □

Now, general considerations about the different nature of the different societies, and about the different impact of the war on different societies, again come into play. Where a country was completely conquered, there would be no need for the conquering government to grant social welfare to the conquered people, nor would that people be in any position to demand reforms. More critically with regard to the major societies, none of which, of course, was conquered or totally invaded, there is the question of whether government was autocratic or constitutional; more subtly, but more crucially, there is the question of how strong the forces of pluralism and democracy really were. For example, although Italy was technically a constitutional country, it was much easier for the Italian government to impose a kind of military dictatorship over much of the country than it would have been for the British or French governments to do this. Fascinating cases are provided by Germany and Austria-Hungary. In Germany there was, as we know, a very strong autocratic tradition, but there was also a strong labour movement which could exact concessions from the German government. In Austria-Hungary, however, there was much less successful resistance to the form of military dictatorship that was widely imposed to facilitate the waging of war. It is, in my view, wrong to argue either that total war necessarily increases dictatorship, or, on the contrary, that total war necessarily increases the powers of labour. In 'society at war', there are pressures and processes not present in 'society not at war', but how these work themselves out depends on the nature of the individual societies and the nature of the impact of the war. It is also the case that autocracy can be strengthened during certain parts of the war, then give way in other parts of it; above all there is the question of what happens at the very end of the war.

Exercise   From what you already know about the way the war impinged on different countries and about the economic strengths of different countries, compile a table, listing on the left-hand side of the page those countries which would be least likely and able to 'indulge' in welfare legislation during the war, and on the right-hand side of the page those countries where you would expect the most in the way of welfare legislation, putting the least likely at the top of each column and the most likely at the bottom. ■

Specimen answer   Serbia   Italy
and discussion   Romania   France
                      Turkey   Germany
                      Bulgaria   United Kingdom
                      Russia
                      Austria-Hungary

Remember we are discussing the war period itself, so that the critical factors are the economic strength of the country as it was before the war (and perhaps also the extent to which it already had a tradition favourable to social reform, which might result in your quite properly putting Germany after the United Kingdom), and the extent to which it suffered occupation, invasion, and direct damage; we are not concerned here with whether the country eventually emerged on the victorious or defeated side. The exact positions for Austria-Hungary and Italy are highly problematic. You may quite reasonably have put them in reverse positions to my own, or perhaps both in the left-hand column, or even both in the right-hand column. This is simply a preliminary exercise concerned with broad-brush general principles.

For the purposes of this discussion we can ignore all the countries before Bulgaria. Serbia and Romania were effectively overrun and conquered by Austrian and German forces; as long as it survived, the Imperial Turkish regime was not amenable to pressures for social reform. □

Bulgaria

Bulgaria, for the war period, was in effect a kind of client state of the Germans, and thus was protected from the devastation and economic deprivation which affected surrounding countries. Prior to the war, as we have seen, Bulgarian politicians and publicists, as part of the attempt to bring Bulgaria within the ambit of European civilization, were advocating social reforms of the type to be found, for example, in Italy. Georges T. Danaïllow, in his standard work *Les effets de la guerre en Bulgarie* (1932) follows the argument that the pressures and sacrifices of war, the desire to reward soldiers and their families, led to these pre-war aspirations being turned into practice, though not, it has to be said, on a very substantial scale. The main piece of legislation was the introduction in March 1915 of social insurance, but this was limited to workers in transport and public works. Largely as a direct development from the need to treat wounded soldiers, there was an improvement in medical provision, partly in association with the Red Cross, which was greatly assisted by the presence in Bulgaria of German doctors.

Russia

Given the nature of the regime, the backwardness and inefficiencies of Russian society, and, from the very start, the direct impingement of military events, such minimal legislation as already existed, for instance protecting women and children from night work, was rescinded. Even if it had had the will, the state did not have the means to persevere with anything effective in the way of price controls, rent controls, rationing, or the procurement and distribution of food and fuel. Sporadic and entirely counter-productive rationing schemes were introduced, but a project for the procurement of coal at fixed prices, together with planned distribution, was abandoned in the face of the opposition of mine owners and industrialists who declared it an unwarranted infringement of freedom of enterprise. Out of sheer necessity, the autocracy did, reluctantly, have to allow a place in the organization of the home front to what are usually referred to as 'voluntary organizations', that is to say the unions of town councils and unions of village councils (*zemstvos*) which were established by patriotically minded middle-class citizens, and also the War Industries Committees, likewise mainly the product of voluntary action by middle-class individuals; through this *participation*, such groups were in a position to press for egalitarian social reforms. In the *Duma* the Progressive bloc called in particular for reforms which would give the peasants civic rights on a par with those of other classes. Workers' representatives on the War Industries Committees put forward claims for comprehensive social legislation, including the eight-hour day and land for the peasants. All such initiatives failed.

The interrelationship between the needs and pressures of war and the first Russian Revolution of February 1917 is discussed in Units 11–13. One implication of this revolution was that the claims just discussed were, in theory at least, recognized. The new government enacted the eight-hour day, a minimum wage, and nominal pay rises averaging 50 per cent. On 11 May, Kerensky, as Minister of War, produced his Declaration of Soldiers' Rights, which met some of the major grievances that had been rumbling throughout the war. The Provisional Government's last Agrarian Bill aimed to set aside reserves of land for the peasants, though with all kinds of qualifications and exceptions. The Tsarist regime had been unable to meet the levels of organization and efficiency required in 'society at war' and had collapsed. The Provisional Government did enact significant measures of social legislation, but in face of the continuing high costs of war and continuing inefficiencies within Russian society, they were largely a dead letter. What happened was the second revolution and the conclusion of peace, as we shall see later.

Austria-Hungary

As you learned in the discussion of national cohesion (section 2.4), not only did the experience of war offer opportunities for the minority nationalities to express their disaffection from the Empire, but the pressure and demands of war provoked an increasing split between Austria and Hungary themselves. In addition, then, to the autocratic nature of the regime, these developments have to be taken into account in any discussion of the possibilities of social policy. Austria-Hungary provides, in virulent form, a classic mix of the following:

1   existing welfare legislation being forced into abeyance because of the demands and destructiveness of war;

2   new legislation, which might be described as 'dire straits legislation', being introduced to try to mitigate some of the worst privations brought on by the circumstances of war, but which was decreasingly effective, and which scarcely brought standards back to what they had been before the war; and

3   legislation, generally more theoretical than practical, related to the general need to reorganize society in order to meet the exigencies of war, and even plans for social reconstruction after the war.

The first point is exemplified by the legislation governing the employment of women and children, which was largely ignored. As a consequence, and for other reasons as well, children were deprived of schooling, their teachers having been conscripted and their schools having been taken over for use as hospitals and for other military uses (by 1918 nearly two hundred had been thus taken over). With regard to the second point, both price controls and rent controls were introduced, but proved increasingly ineffective: in fact, because of desperate food shortages people had to shop on the black market, where prices were grossly inflated. By the War Service Act of 1913, within the Austro-Hungarian autocracy everything, if deemed necessary, could be put at the disposal of the military apparatus. Thus, throughout the war, factories and mines were placed under military supervision, and everywhere workers were subject to military regimentation: 'the discipline of the barracks was transplanted to the factory' (A. J. May, *The Passing of the Hapsburg Monarchy 1914–1918*, 1966). Thus the opportunities for labour to exploit the need which their country had for them were greatly curtailed; the need for the authorities to buy their support was scarcely felt. The third point is best illustrated by the setting up in March 1917 of a Commission for War and Transition Economics, which included representatives of commerce and distribution, delegates from the Chambers of Commerce and labour, and representatives of the workers' organizations. The secretariat to this Commission was called the General Commissariat for War and Transition Economics, headed by a general Commissary. 'Because', in the words of David Mitrany in *The Effect of the War in South-Eastern Europe* (1936), 'of the great importance which questions of social policy were bound to acquire, especially in connection with unemployment, the chief of the social section in the Ministry of Trade acted as assistant to the General Commissary.' In other words, the organization and the personnel for social planning were there: because of the actual destructiveness and privations of war, not a lot was actually accomplished. Governmental initiatives apart, we do find that in the hectic, but sometimes stimulating, new circumstances of 'society at war', various other initiatives develop – people, for instance, are congregated in new ways, they become interested for the first time in national and international problems. At any rate, A. J. May, in his *The Passing of the Hapsburg Monarchy*, singles out adult education as a flourishing development in wartime Austria.

Italy

In entering the war, Italy made a decisive break from its autocratic allies, Germany and Austria, and threw in its lot with the democratic Entente. In the excitements of war, and conflicts over whether or not Italy should have remained neutral, the always highly coloured rhetoric of Italian parliamentarianism became greatly inflated. Italian politicians and publicists liked to believe that their society was organized very differently from that of Austria-Hungary. Yet, in face of the exigencies of war, substantial areas of Italy, including many factories, were placed under military rule. Thus, as in Austria-Hungary, there were severe limits on the extent to which labour could try to exploit the national need for its services. Italy was a poor country, desperately dependent, particularly for such basics as grain and coal, on imports. Thus there were no surpluses with which to fund welfare benefits. Nonetheless, the history of social welfare during the actual period of hostilities did differ significantly from the one we have just been looking at. Principally, Italian governments, to a greater extent than their Austrian counterparts, felt the need to impose collaboration between employers and employees in securing the materials of war, and also felt the need to preserve some show of democratic forms. Of the two major developments while the war was actually being waged, the first concerned one of the most traditional of all aspects of social legislation, and the other, arguably, worked very much to the disadvantage of working men. Compulsory workmen's compensation was very much a late nineteenth-century idea. In Italy in August 1917 this provision was extended to agricultural labourers. The other main development was in the realm of compulsory arbitration for industrial disputes. Beginning with regulation 1377 of 22 August 1915, the new compulsory arbitration system started in factories and workshops designated as being subject to the rules governing industrial mobilization. Similar procedures were introduced in factories within the even more strictly governed 'war zones' – the term was an elastic one, and Turin, an important industrial centre but quite far from the war front, was declared a war zone in the autumn of 1917. For most of the war the regulations taken together generally served to limit the bargaining power which the workers otherwise might have had, though the comprehensive decree 1672 of 13 October 1918 which universalized the system of compulsory arbitration probably operated less unfairly towards the workers. To satisfy the demands of the munitions industries for labour there was a great influx of population into the cities of the northwest, producing all kinds of sanitary, health, housing and overcrowding problems. Remedies were called for, though not usually immediately implemented.

As in other countries, claims and plans for social reform were articulated in time of war more clearly than they had been in time of peace. Some sense of what the country owed to those who waged war on its behalf (and recognition too of the new assertiveness and confidence of peasants forced out of their traditional ways by the upheaval of war) is to be found in the promise made by Prime Minister Salandra in 1916 that peasant soldiers would be granted land of their own on their return from the war. During the war the Italian Socialist Party and the Italian trades unions were brought into much closer co-operation than ever before, and together, in the last stages of the war, they were making claims for the eight-hour day. Inclining more to the workers than the employers in this case, the government had advised the adoption of grievance committees, though stopping far short of legalizing these; there was considerable resistance from employers.

France

French workers were free of the kind of direct military control which obtained in Italy. On the whole, it seems that they benefited from the compulsory arbitration and conciliation schemes which the government introduced in January 1917. In the same month minimum wage rates were established in all of the industries involved in direct government contracts. From practically the start of the war (5 August 1914) the French, in a highly practical way, introduced a system of fairly generous separation allowances, so that soldiers' wives might maintain themselves and their children. Schemes of public assistance, mainly in the form of the distribution of free meals, were also instituted.

In August 1914, in a development similar to those we have noted in other countries, French labour inspectors were instructed to interpret existing factory regulations less stringently in order that production might be increased. But as it became clear that employers, under the plea of national interest, were grossly abusing their employees, overworking them and evading safety regulations, it became necessary for the government to take much stronger action. Thus, through the exigencies of war, new regulations which gave French employees greater protection than ever before were introduced in 1915 and 1916. Furthermore, the problem of unemployment in the early days, together with the influx of refugees, forced the government to increase its provision of pensions.

Germany

Our understanding of what happened inside Germany during the First World War was enormously advanced by the pioneering study, published over twenty years ago, by the American historian Gerald Feldman, entitled *Army, Industry and Labor in Germany 1914–1918* (1966). Feldman pointed out that it was just at the time of apparently intensified military control of the domestic economy, the time of the regime of Hindenberg and Ludendorff and the introduction of the Hindenberg programme in 1916, that organized labour was able to insist on substantial concessions for itself. The Hindenberg programme, in the words of Professor Wolfgang Mommsen,

> envisaged the total mobilisation of all human as well as material resources for war production regardless of the economic consequences or the social costs which this would bring, in order to maximise the production of war materials and raise the recruitment levels once again. But this programme could no longer be implemented without the cooperation of the trade unions. So the trade unions were now officially acknowledged as an equal partner of the government in implementing these new stringent regulations intended to push the German war effort up to hitherto unknown levels. The unions succeeded in having those stipulations in the new legislation eliminated which restricted the free choice of the employer, that is to say the exploitation of the opportunities of a favourable labour market on the part of the workforce. It had become a widespread practice to change employers frequently in order to enhance one's wages, in particular in the engineering industries. Certainly neither the employers' nor the military authorities' attitude to the trade unions changed in substance; the old distrust of working-class organisations continued to rule labour relations even now. But the first step toward social partnership had been achieved. Henceforth the trade unions had to be consulted and indeed were given substantial influence in all legislation affecting wage

and price policies. This certainly must have had a positive effect on the material well-being of the industrial workforce. (Wolfgang Mommsen, 'The social consequences of World War I: the case of Germany', 1988, pp.33–4)

Exercise   You should now read the extract from *Army, Industry and Labor* by Gerald Feldman, up to 'Epilogue', in the Course Reader. Do you get the impression that the 'industrial workforce' as a whole made substantial gains? Explain your answer. ■

Specimen answer and discussion   Feldman does speak of gains for organized labour, but the general impression I derive (however, read him carefully and make up your own mind) is of deals done by the union leaders which often had little concrete benefit for ordinary workers. □

Great Britain

With respect to legislation actually enacted and welfare plans taken to their advanced stage, more was achieved in Britain during the war than in any of the other countries studied. Britain already had the unemployment insurance and health insurance schemes established in the 1911 Act, which came into operation in the year before the outbreak of war. Because Britain only had a small professional army, army pensions were very much a private, rather than a government, responsibility. A number of piecemeal developments were enforced by the war emergency. Then, in late 1916, a new Act, concerned as much with the disruptions and flux in domestic employment as with the military situation, extended the 1911 unemployment insurance provisions to cover all persons employed in trades relating to the war effort. On 26 February 1917 a more generous schedule of war disablement and widowhood pensions was introduced. Throughout 1917 discussions proceeded on the issues of education reform, housing reform, and the establishment of health reforms through the creation of a new Ministry of Health (formed in part out of the old Local Government Board). The education proposals were put before the House of Commons in August 1917, and the Act passed into law in the summer of 1918, some months before the end of the war. A universal minimum leaving age of 14 was to be enforced, and there were to be compulsory day continuation schools for those aged between 14 and 18 not undergoing suitable alternative instruction. All fees in public elementary schools were to be abolished. In a particular expression of the general concern for health, a Maternity and Child Welfare Act was passed just before the war ended. Under its provisions local authorities were to establish Mothers' Welfare Clinics (see document II.4 in *Documents 1*).

Exercise   Why was there more in the way of social reform and welfare planning in Britain than in the other countries we have discussed? ■

Specimen answer and discussion   This was due to a combination of factors, I would suggest. Britain was both a wealthier country than France, or even Germany, and while Britain's human losses were horrific enough, the cost of waging war high, and times of desperate crisis far from unknown, it suffered nothing like the deprivation of basic foodstuffs of Germany, nor the direct destruction of France. Britain had the most developed labour movement of all of the European countries, and, despite censorship and other wartime restrictions, the most open society during the war period, when discussion of problems of social reconstruction could carry on quite freely. More than that, Britain was a very unified society, and there was both a genuine feeling among the powerful and the wealthy that those who were contributing to national survival deserved to benefit, and a relatively dispassionate atmosphere in which to discuss remedies. In short, the various factors which earlier I suggested could make for social reform were at their strongest in Britain, whereas the negative factors which I referred to at the same time were at their weakest. □

Post-war social legislation

Even the Balkan countries shared in the burst of social legislation which marked the immediate post-war years. There, and in several other countries, an obvious consideration is the change in regime at the end of the war: democratic republics in Germany and Austria, the Bolshevik regime in Russia, and so on.

Exercise 1   Look at the information contained in Table 8–10.2 below. What point could be made in support of the argument that a change of regime was certainly not a sufficient reason for social reform in the post-war period?

2   On the basis of discoveries we have made so far in this section, what argument could be advanced to link post-war social change with the war?

3   Can you think of any other general arguments linking post-war social change to the war? ■

Specimen answer and discussion 1   Social reform also took place in countries, such as Britain, France and Italy, where there was no change in regime.

2   Social reform, albeit often of a very limited and sometimes rather hollow character, was already taking place during the war. It could be argued that the post-war reforms were simply a culmination of this trend, coming to fruition once the negative circumstances of war had been removed.

3   There are the points already made about the desire to reward those who had supported the nation in its hour of need, and the arguments about labour being in a strong position to exact rewards. There is also the even more general argument that there was a feeling that this horrific war must result in a better world, and that social reforms were a concrete expression of that feeling. With regard to the reforms associated with a change in regime, it is of course legitimate to link these very changes in regime to the circumstances of war. □

Exercise 1   What arguments would you put forward if you wanted to argue that these social reforms were not primarily associated with the war?

2   There is another argument which could be used (mentioned in my discussion of Aim 1 in Unit 1), which draws attention to certain countries not so far mentioned in this unit. What is that? ■

Specimen answer and discussion 1   It could be pointed out that social reforms were already taking place before the war. It could be argued that they were due to the politicians and parties which came into power in the post-war years, and that election results and the detailed developments of politics had little or nothing to do with the war. It could be argued that the reforms were primarily aimed at new developments taking place in the post-war years, rather than anything to do with the war – for example,

Table 8–10.2 Major welfare legislation in Europe from c.1880 to c.1930

Country	Legislation	19th century 1887–1894	Up to 1913	1914–18	1919–26	After 1926
Austria	Workmen's compensation	1887–1894		Extended Dec 1917		Extended 1928
	Holidays with pay (workers)				1919	
	Compulsory unemployment insurance				1920	
	Poor relief written into state constitution				1920	
	Housing Act (state subsidies)				1921	
	Holidays with pay (salaried workers)				1920–23	
	Social Insurance Act				1926	
Belgium	Workers' housing, cheap mortgage loans	1889				
	Workmen's compensation		1903		Extended 1926	
	National Society for Cheap Houses and Dwellings				1919	
	Employers' equalization funds for family allowances				1919	
	Workers' compulsory old-age widows and orphans insurance				1924	
Bulgaria	Social Insurance Act (accident, sickness, maternity, invalidity, and old-age insurance)				1924	
Czecho-slovakia	Workmen's compensation (old Austrian Act)	1887			Amended 1919, 1921	
	Holidays with pay (miners)				1921	
	Cheap dwellings legislation				1921–24	
	Social insurance (sickness, invalidity, old age, and widows and orphans insurance)				1924	
	Family allowances (state officials and teachers)				1924	
	Holidays with pay (employers in general)				1925	

Table 8–10.2 *Major welfare legislation in Europe from c.1880 to c.1930 (contd.)*

Country	Legislation	19th century	Up to 1913	1914–18	1919–26	After 1926
France	Advances for cheap dwellings	1894				
	Workmen's compensation (industrial accidents)	1898		Extended July 1914	Extended 1922, 1923	
	Assistance for large families		1913			
	National unemployment fund			20 August 1914		
	Compulsory old-age, widows and orphans insurance			February 1914		
	Employers' equalization funds for family allowances			1918		
	Workmen's compensation				1919	
	Central Committee for Family Allowances				1921	
	Extension of advances for cheap dwellings; Housing Act				1922	
	Encouragement for large families				1923	
	General compulsory social insurance					1928
Germany	Sickness Insurance Act	1883				
	Workmen's compensation (accident insurance scheme)	1884				
	Workers' invalidity and old-age insurance	1889				
	Widows & orphans insurance		1911			
	Family allowances (at employees' expense)				1921–24	
	Public assistance				1924	
	Workmen's compensation (occupational diseases)				1925	
	Compulsory unemployment insurance					1927
Italy	Housing Act		1903			
	Workmen's compensation (compulsory insurance)		1904	Extended 1918	Extended 1921, 1926	
	Workmen's compensation (for agricultural workers)			1917		
	Compulsory insurance for invalidity and old age, legislative decree				30th Dec 1919	

Table 8–10.2 *Major welfare legislation in Europe from c.1880 to c.1930 (contd.)*

Country	Legislation	19th century	Up to 1913	1914–18	1919–26	After 1926
Russia	Social assistance proclaimed			12 November 1917		
	Maternity & welfare services				1920	
	Social insurance; labour code (includes holidays with pay)			30 April 1918	1922	
United Kingdom	Workmen's compensation	1897				
	School meals		1906			
	Old-age pensions		1908			
	National health insurance		1911			
	Unemployment insurance (selected trades only)		1911		Universal for working class 1920, Extended 1924	
	Maternity and Child Welfare Service, Notification of Births (Extension) Act			1915		
	Maternity & Child Welfare Act			1918		
	Housing Act (state subsidies)				1919	
	Establishment of Ministry of Health				1919	
	Contributory old-age pensions				1925	
Yugoslavia	Social Insurance Act (accident, sickness, maternity, compulsory insurance)				1922	

depression and unemployment. It could be argued that limited social reforms are a characteristic of a certain phase in the development of modern society which was coming about whether or not there was a war. On a totally different track, it could be argued that in fact the social reforms were of a very limited character and that therefore, even if they are in some way related to the war, they are so trivial as not to count in any general argument about the war being related to significant social change.

2   The argument that the neutral countries (e.g. Denmark, Sweden, the Nether-lands and Spain) have, without being involved in the war, gone through social changes very similar to those I have been discussing. It is a good point, and I shall take it up at the end of these units. ☐

2.6   Material conditions

Exercise   Given what you already know about World War I, would you expect living standards generally to rise or fall over the war period, or would you expect them to rise in some cases and fall in others? Write a few sentences elaborating and explaining your answer. ■

Specimen answer and discussion   Given the destructiveness of war, one would expect living standards overall to go down, though once again this would be much more pronounced in countries which were directly devastated than in those which were not. As is well known, ordinary soldiers are not well paid (though, for the destitute, if they were fit enough to be considered for active service, the army might well have supplied a level of subsistence above what they previously enjoyed). Within that broad picture, however, one might well expect living standards for certain individuals and groups to go up. Certain industrial workers in Germany, as we saw, were considered essential to the national war effort, and one might expect this also to be true of other groups of workers in other countries. As food shortages developed, those who continued to work on the land might well have hoped to cash in (this effect could be completely cancelled out if governments simply requisitioned food supplies, or if all the able-bodied workers in a family were in fact conscripted into the army). Above all (I hope you thought of this one) there would be opportunities (as Bill Purdue has already pointed out in section 2.3) for munitions manufac-turers, army suppliers, etc. to make vast profits. On the other hand, for the ordinary fee- and salary-earning middle class, high wartime taxation might well have a deleterious effect.

I hope you thought of at least some of these points. You see how, taking what you already know about the war and applying a little common sense, you can come up with some sensible general answers. Of course, that is not enough in historical study. We need to go on now and acquire some precise information so that we can see which countries and which groups did worst during the war and which did best, and to see, particularly, where there were long-term changes in living standards as a result of the war experience. ☐

It is very hard, in fact, to find accurate, usable statistics. Wages, or more accurately wage rates, usually refer to a specific unit of work – an hourly wage, say, or a wage for a 'normal' week's work. There is a distinction between money wages and 'real' wages. Money wages are what are actually paid without regard to whether the value of money has changed. Since war conditions involved high rates of inflation, tables of money wages are not usually very helpful. Real wages take account of changes in the value of money (inflation is the problem in wartime) and thus give a more genuine indication of what could actually be bought. There is also a distinction between wages and earnings. Earnings take into account such factors as overtime. In one sense, therefore, if we want to know how well people were really doing, we need to know their real earnings. On the other hand, real earnings might conceal very long hours being worked which, in turn, we might regard as representing a reduction in living standards. Sometimes whole families did better than in peacetime in the sense that *more* members of the family managed to find employment; however, just as often the main wage-earner was serving at the front.

Exercise   What conclusions can you draw from Table 8–10.3 about the war's effect on real incomes? What other information would you like to have? ∎

Table 8–10.3   *Real wages for Germany and Britain, 1915–18 (1914 = 100)*

	Germany	Britain
1915	96	86
1916	87	80
1917	79	75
1918	77	85

Specimen answer and discussion   The table is confined to Germany and Britain. It would be useful to know what happened after the war (in fact British workers gained some substantial rises, German workers on the whole did not). It would be useful to have information on earnings as well as wages. The table overall suggests a decline in real wages in both countries during the war. German workers did better to begin with, then in the later stages fell behind, while British workers finished relatively strongly. ☐

One must always bear in mind that for most of the belligerents the war lasted for rather more than four years. For some groups conditions could be bad at one point in time, better at another. Very generally (and subject to much qualification in detail) the beginning of the war was marked by severe upsets and dislocations, over quickly in some spheres, but lasting until 1915 in others, which tended to create unemployment and loss of earnings. Then there could be a period in which some benefit came to hitherto downtrodden groups as they were sucked into various aspects of the war effort and in which key workers (for instance coal-miners) could make genuine gains. As the war continued, sheer physical scarcities and rampant inflation generally wiped out any gains, while inflicting increasing hardship in most sectors of society. The entire 'timetable' (I use quotation marks because I am employing a highly dangerous metaphor – but the blander word 'process' could be just as misleading) was severely impacted in Russia (and the even less fortunate countries of South-East Europe), so that upsets and dislocations merged with scarcities and inflation without there ever being a period in which any group had much chance to make gains. In Britain it worked out much more slowly and evenly, so that even at the end of the war some working-class groups still had earnings which kept them ahead of inflation.

Exercise So far I have made much of the differential effects of invasion and direct devastation. Neither Germany nor Austria-Hungary suffered more than relatively minor incursions (by Russia) on their territories prior to the armistice in November 1918. Yet there is a general geopolitical and strategic factor which meant that Germany and Austria-Hungary, and all the Central and East European countries, were at a disadvantage compared with France, Britain, and even Italy, in access to necessary foodstuffs and war materials. What is this factor? If you are puzzled, look briefly at Map 3 in the *Maps Booklet*. ■

Specimen answer and discussion The Central and Eastern powers were 'closed in' and thus fairly easily blockaded, and so cut off from access to potential overseas suppliers. Above all (and, of course, this was also a political factor, since the United States supported the Western powers and joined them in 1917) they did not have access to American supplies. □

Exercise Which of the three Western countries would you expect to be best off, and which worst off? Explain why. ■

Specimen answer and discussion Britain was best off, because it had the greatest overseas possessions and connections, the biggest merchant fleet, and the biggest navy. Italy was worst off, as a poor country with few overseas possessions, no Atlantic ports, and no great merchant fleet or navy; supplies from its allies had to come through the Mediterranean, or over the Alps. □

Now, having set up some broad comparative principles, I am going to give quick sketches of living conditions during the war in the various major countries.

Russia

From very early on unskilled labour was brought into the burgeoning war industries, but workers were often forced to take pay lower than the previously going rates and to work compulsory overtime. While there was more work for women and children, restrictions on night work, for example, were lifted, as we have already noted. For a short time skilled workers generally did well, but from the beginning of 1915 inflation wiped out any gains they made: by the second half of 1916 prices were at three times the level of 1913. As happened in so many countries (for instance Italy) there was terrible overcrowding in the towns, rents were high, and there were long queues for food and fuel. Sporadic attempts at rationing in the autumn of 1916 did not bring any sugar into the shops, but simply drove up black market prices. The rationing of flour and bread, introduced in Moscow on 20 February 1917, caused panic buying and further shortages. Poor nutrition and the upheavals of war meant that many parts of the country were afflicted by epidemics of scurvy and typhus. By October 1917 the price of bread was nearly three times the pre-war price, and the real wage of the unskilled worker had fallen by 57 per cent. The Provisional Government deliberately doubled the fixed grain price in the hope of stimulating deliveries; the result was that the actual market price rose by a further 75 per cent on top of the official price. The question of living standards is of importance in itself, but, naturally, it also relates to more dramatic political developments. As Hans Rogger sums up, 'shortages, black markets, and speculation grew apace and with them class hatreds and cleavages' (*Russia in the Age of Modernisation and Revolution 1881–1917*, 1983, p.281).

The Balkans

I am now going to give you an encapsulated account (from 1929) of one of the Balkan countries, leaving out the name of the people and the country, in the hope that you may be able to fill these in for yourselves.

> The most vivid picture left by the War in the memory of the _____ is not of a cemetery of a blood-stained battlefield, although _____ had given a formidable number of victims and had been the scene of the fiercest fighting. The most clear-cut impression of the _____ campaign is the motley, pitiful spectacle of the 'bejaniwa', the endless, disorderly flight of fugitives muffled to the eyes, old men, women, children, on foot or in wooden carts patiently drawn by emaciated and exhausted oxen, driving in front of them some cattle and carrying on their backs or under their arms some chattels, the number and importance of which grew less with every stage of this removal which was always beginning again and never coming to an end. In short, the outstanding event of the _____ war is not a great battle such as Verdun, but the Great Retreat, that retreat which led the _____ into exile through Albania – the last after so many others following on each advance of the enemy.

Exercise   Fill in the blanks in the above quotation. ■

Specimen answer and discussion   Serbs, Serbia, Serbian, Serbian, Serbs. Romania would not have been a bad guess (Bulgaria, remember, being on the German side, was not invaded), but I think you already have enough information, together with the reference to Albania, to make it clear that the country is Serbia. Whenever one is tempted to talk of the social gains resulting from the experience of war (as one may very properly do in certain instances) it is important to remember such extremes of suffering and deprivation as this. (The quotation is from Dragolioub Yovanovitch, *Les effets économiques et sociaux de la guerre en Serbie*, Paris, 1929, p.28). □

Exercise   From what you already know about the basic differences between Austria and Hungary (geography, natural resources), in which of the two kingdoms do you think suffering and deprivation were greatest during the war? ■

Specimen answer and discussion   The basic difference is that Austria was more industrialized and more densely populated, while Hungary was more agricultural. The implications are not necessarily straightforward. To begin with, people in Austria seemed to benefit from Austria's greater industrial power, but as the war wore on (and this is the basic answer I am looking for) the balance swung to Hungary (because it could produce basic foodstuffs, while Austria had increasing difficulty in importing them). When Hungary closed its frontiers to Austria (this development could be used in support of the argument that wars put great stress upon contrived or 'artificial' political arrangements), making the transfer of food impossible, the differences sharpened. □

I have suggested that in some respects war can be likened to natural disaster. The presence of war, of course, does not rule out the possibility of real natural disasters. In Central Europe, the harvest of 1917 was a particularly poor one (the war probably had a marginal, though not determining, effect in so far as it created great shortages of fertilizers, etc.)

From Austria come some of the most striking statistics of the destruction of war, and some of the most telling tales of its deprivations. In 1917–18 total production was down to 67 per cent of that of 1910; national income was down to 69 per cent. For even the most prized workers, inflation far outstripped wages (even in Austria there were signs of the participation effect: to begin with men called up for military service, but continuing in their jobs, received only soldiers' pay; this had to be changed in July 1916 when they were again given the going civilian rate). By 1917–18 it was impossible for most people to light or heat their rooms, street lighting was totally inadequate, and the trams stopped in the early evening. For a brief time it was almost better to be in the army, because food rations were more adequate there. But by the summer of 1918 there was real hunger in the army, and uniforms were in rags. One unit possessed uniforms only for men in the front line, so that men in reserve wore only underclothes. To save clothing materials it was recommended to civilians that their dead should be buried naked. Attempts were made to extract fats from horse-chestnuts and rats. Iron tyres were substituted for rubber ones, with no great benefit to road surfaces.

Our understanding of the sufferings inflicted on civilians in Austria, Germany and Belgium has been greatly increased by the series of specialist essays published in *The Upheaval of War: Family, Work and Welfare in Europe, 1914–1918* (1989), edited by Richard Wall and Jay Winter. Reinhard Sieder, in his chapter on 'Working-class family life in Vienna', makes effective use of interviews with men and women who were children during the war. These children had to queue throughout the freezing winter nights for potatoes, dripping or horsemeat, had to go begging for bread and for milk, had to go miles foraging for branches to burn. The chapter by Peter Scholliers and Frank Daelemans on 'Standards of living and standards of health in wartime Belgium' indicates that (apart from Serbia and possibly other parts of Eastern Europe) the people of Belgium underwent the most terrible of deprivations. They, of course, did not participate in the war effort: they were simply occupied, and brutally exploited, by the Germans.

Germany

Up till the armistice, conditions were never as bad in Germany as they were in Austria. They became substantially worse with the 'turnip winter' of 1917, when because of the shortage of potatoes and grain, turnips became a staple foodstuff. Deprivation was very serious by the summer of 1918. The salaried middle class probably suffered most. Relatively, skilled workers did quite well, though in absolute terms their living conditions probably declined from what they had been in pre-war days. Some industrialists made immense profits.

Exercise   Turn to document II.5 in *Documents 1*, 'Memorandum of the Neukölln Municipal Council' (Neukölln is a suburb of Berlin), and read the entire document. You will find, I think, that it gives a graphic impression of chaos, discontent, near-starvation, and illegality. Concentrate now on the section beginning 'This panorama . . .' to '. . . alleviating popular discontent', and answer the following questions:

1   The official system is clearly very inefficient. What phrase does the Neukölln Town Council use to describe it?

2   What crime are suppliers committing?

3   What illegality are town councils being led into? ∎

Specimen answers   1   'A mixed system of regulated and unregulated trade'.

and discussion   2   Extortion.

3   Breaking the maximum prices laid down by the government in order to feed their own people. □

Italy

You have already acquired some understanding of the different positive and negative factors that affected Germany and Italy. Italy could import in a way that Germany could not, but on the other hand it had had, unlike Germany, a long-standing need to import both wheat and coal. The relatively greater deprivation suffered in Italy is, I think, well expressed in the cost of living indices. Taking 1913 as 100, prices in 1918 were at 228 in Germany, and at 264 in Italy. Italy was subject to particularly severe disruption at the beginning of the war, when hundreds of thousands of workers who had followed the normal pattern of immigration returned in haste to the homeland, thus greatly swelling unemployment. At certain points in the war some districts were totally without bread for days on end. Real wages (1913 = 100) dropped steadily to 64.6 in 1918.

France

For those in the occupied zones, conditions were about as bad as could be found anywhere else in Europe, but for France as a whole living conditions during the war were second only to those in Britain, and it is possible that in some rural areas standards of life, or at least of food consumption, were higher than anywhere among equivalent classes in Britain. Jean Jacques Becker, in an important study which is essentially built up from a series of local studies based on reports on the war situation deposited in local archives by leading local personalities, has written that, at the outset of war, 'The income of many rural families did not fall appreciably with the departure of the men; in the urban working-class, by contrast, it was enough for the breadwinner to be called up for the family income to disappear.' However, he then points out that separation allowances, a moratorium on the payment of rents, the fact that there was one mouth less to feed, all helped to keep living standards at least to acceptable levels (Jean Jacques Becker, *The Great War and the French People*, 1985; see p.21 in particular, and chapter 1 in general).

Documents II.6 and II.7 in *Documents 1* provide further detail on living conditions in France during the war. However, a few quotations from Becker relating to various parts of France show that while there were upsets, truly serious deprivation of the Austrian type did not really exist:

> Fresh food supplies did pose many problems in rural areas, as a few examples show: thus in August 1918, at Plouha, people had to queue for an hour to obtain 'a chunk of hard bread, black and indigestible not even fit for the beasts'. There was a bread shortage at the same time at Paimpol. 'People queue outside the bakers for hours on end.' At Ploubazalnec, bread was scarce in June 1918, and at times customers had to queue for half a day outside the baker's door, but potatoes never ran short. Some items such as sugar, paraffin or chocolate could be difficult to obtain at times, but most agreed that supplies of essential foodstuffs were almost normal. As one witness put it, no single product was ever totally unobtainable. (p.119)

Does that mean that there were no more poor people? The records often make this claim, while not holding that everyone had become rich. To use an expression of the time, 'pauperism had disappeared'. Few or no families were in want, said one reporter; most of the poor had received relief. There were no truly indigent families left in the commune, no needy people during the war. The schoolmaster of Yvignac was not alone in thinking that while there was certainly adversity, there was, on the whole, little financial hardship. (pp.122–3)

In rural areas, it might make a difference whether you were a peasant paying out wages, or a labourer receiving them. Sometimes the very rise in wages meant that casual labourers couldn't get jobs, because employers couldn't pay them.

. . . the shortage of hands had evidently increased the cost of labour. In one commune, domestics who had been paid 250 francs for six months received 400 francs at the beginning of 1916, while labourers were paid 2.50 to 3.00 francs a day, plus their keep. 'Agriculture, which had suffered little during the first year of the war, suffers a great deal now.' The number of uncultivated fields increased, in one commune by at least a quarter, and the harvest of 1916 was judged to be two-thirds of a good normal harvest, the yield having dropped even further for lack of fertilizer. (p.126)

. . . some casual labourers did find it difficult to obtain work, not for lack of vacancies, but because of the very high wages that all hands now fetched. As for local government officials, they had to face inflation with salaries that scarcely altered. (p.129)

United Kingdom

All three of the most authoritative recent commentators on the British experience during World War I, Jay Winter, Bernard Waites and Alastair Reid, are agreed that for the working class as a whole living standards rose during World War I, and that the rise was particularly significant for those at the bottom end – those who fell into the residuum of pre-war times (J. M. Winter, *The Great War and the British People*, 1986; Bernard Waites, *A Class Society at War: England 1914–18*, 1988; and Alastair Reid, 'World War I and the working class in Britain', in Arthur Marwick (ed.) *Total War and Social Change*, 1988). Shortages of various commodities affected all classes in some degree, but as far as real income is concerned, no single class suffered seriously from the war. Older middle-class interests may have suffered marginally: there was a considerable expansion in white-collar jobs, which presumably meant that there was recruitment from the working class. Some landed families suffered severely from paying death duties several times as members of the family were killed at the front, and tenant farmers as a whole did relatively well compared with landowners.

After the war

Immediately after the armistice, as the victorious powers kept up a blockade of the defeated enemies until definitive peace treaties were signed, conditions got seriously worse in these countries. But what I now want to consider are the longer-term effects. During the interwar years, real wages did eventually begin to rise at least slightly almost everywhere. But was this not due to long-term structural (i.e. economic and technological) change rather than to the war?

We have to add in the value of social benefits, then deduct the disadvantages of unemployment.

The equation is a complex one. My general answer would be that everywhere there were *relative* gains for the working class (if *in employment*), but often, because of the severely damaged economies discussed by Bill Purdue in section 2.2, actual wages were lower than they had been before the war, and where there was protracted unemployment, conditions of the severest deprivation existed. Wartime participation played a part in strengthening the hands of the workers, and in places wartime demand played a part in stimulating new industries. But, Britain apart, real gains are not generally apparent till the end of the 1920s, so weight must clearly be given to longer-term trends.

2.7   Customs and behaviour

Exercise   1   Is it reasonable to expect that there would be changes in customs and behaviour due to the war experience? Answer either way, and give reasons for your answer.

2   In which countries – relatively developed ones like Britain, France and Germany, or relatively undeveloped ones like the Balkan countries – do you think there was more possibility for change in customs and behaviour, whether brought about by the war or not? Give reasons for your answer. ■

Specimen answer   1   The argument for expecting change in customs and behaviour would be based
and discussion   on the upheavals of war, the disruptions to normal patterns of behaviour – the movement, for example, of women into new activities – all the features, in short, of 'society at war' not present in 'society not at war'. The argument against would maintain that customs and behaviour are determined by long-term economic and industrial developments, by national traditions, etc.

2   This question could also very reasonably be answered in two opposite ways. If it is argued that customs and behaviour depend on economic, and particularly technological, development – as, for instance, the development of a mass consumer society, or of films, gramophone records and radio – then one would expect the most striking developments (whether related to the war or not) to take place in the more advanced countries. On the other hand, it could be argued that since the more advanced countries already had many of the aspects we associate with twentieth-century lifestyles, it would be in the backward countries that far more scope for extensive change ('catching-up', as it were) was to be found.

What I am going to suggest is that in both types of country there are, of course, long-term forces making for change in customs and behaviour, but that such forces are more apparent in the advanced countries; that within the context of long-term change, the war did indeed have identifiable effects in both sorts of country; that limited but important changes, which can be related to the war experience, are apparent in the developed countries, but that, given their relative level of backwardness, the really striking shake-up, as it were, comes in the less developed countries, where the cataclysmic effect of war was felt most strongly.

There is no absolute end to the argument as between the effects of war and the effects of longer-term trends. My argument with regard to the less developed countries would essentially be that because of the disruptions of war, because of the way individuals were projected into new situations and brought into contact with foreign influences, predominantly peasant societies began to adopt some of the customs of urban societies. Now one could immediately argue that there was, in any case, a long-term trend towards urbanization, and that this would have happened at some time anyway. So we come back to the point that when talking about the influence of war we are talking about how things came about at the precise time and in the precise way that they did. To derive a general idea of the sorts of changes taking place in a peasant society over the war period, I want you to read document II.10, which is an extract from a book written in the late 1920s by the Yugoslav historian we have already quoted, Yovanovitch, for the Carnegie series on the social and economic history of the war. □

Exercise   1   Putting together all the information you have on this document, assess its value, its strengths and weaknesses, and its reliability for the historian as a primary source for the effects of World War I on peasant society.

2   For your own use (I am giving no specimen answer for this one) note down the main changes identified in the document. ■

Specimen answer   You might well query first of all whether this can properly be described as a **and discussion**   primary source. It is, as I have made clear, an account written by a historian ten years after the war. However, it is written by a Serbian Yugoslav with direct, intimate knowledge of his own society. Much of the style of the book (though it might be difficult for you to determine that on the basis of this extract and the one I quoted earlier) is in the form of direct personal testimony. But the crucial point which I hope you got was the date, which shows that this is an account written up later. That, in one sense, is a weakness, yet on the other hand one could regard this favourably as the mature reflections of someone who has had time to see the changes of the war period working themselves out. Remember, though, that the author is a Yugoslav with direct experience of the society he is describing; but he is an academic, and therefore might be a little detached from the realities of peasant society. As a historian writing about social and economic effects of the war he might be inclined to exaggerate. I think myself that his account is a little too precise and cut and dried, in an academic way. Nevertheless, I think we have to see this as a valuable, and on the whole reliable, account of someone who knows what he is talking about. It refers, of course, specifically to Serbia, and in that sense cannot be taken as an ideal source for other peasant societies. However, within the limits to which we have to work on this course, I think we could say that this source gives us a fair idea of the sorts of changes in East European peasant mentalities that were brought about by the cataclysmic upheavals of World War I. □

When it comes to questions of possible changes in customs and behaviour in the more developed countries we find that there are overlaps with two of our other headings, popular culture, and women and the family. Let me list here the main areas that I think would be worth exploring:

1   sexual attitudes and behaviour, and the roles of women;

2   respect for authority, religious observance, etc.;

3   recreational activities: cinemas, public dance halls, radio, etc.;

4   fashion, dress, etc.

It is in this very subject area of customs and behaviour that film and other cultural artefacts have great importance as sources. In briefly developing these three points I am going to confine myself to a few further generalizations, and one exercise based on film material.

Sexual attitudes and behaviour, and the roles of women

It is not unreasonable to postulate, and there is a fair amount of supporting evidence, that the frantic conditions of war, the disturbances to family life, the taking of young men out of the home environment, and the doom-laden partings of sweethearts, led to a loosening of traditional constraints upon sexual behaviour. A Royal Commission on Venereal Diseases had been set up in Britain just before the war; but in the general wartime atmosphere of national crisis, of the need to face realities, to call a spade a spade, the whole subject was discussed much more openly than it would have been in pre-war days when the Commission reported in 1916. There was also much frank discussion of the plight of unmarried girls, pregnant by soldier boyfriends serving at the front. From the later nineteenth century onwards, contraceptives had been quite widely used within respectable middle-class marriages; during the war working-class soldiers were issued with them as protection against venereal diseases. I think it would be reasonable to say that the upheavals of World War I brought quite a sudden and widespread diffusion of contraceptive methods throughout the main countries engaged in warfare. But we must not underestimate the continuing power of traditional delicacies and sensitivities: contraception was still a topic that could not be publicly talked about.

As I have had to keep stressing, it is very difficult to establish whether certain things which happened during, or at the end of, the war could only have happened because of the war, or would have happened anyway. My own view is that the new wartime frankness (relative, of course) *helped* to make possible the publication in March 1918 of *Married Love* (subtitled *A New Contribution to the Solution of Sex Difficulties*) by Marie Stopes, *and* definitely provided the circumstances in which the book was sold and circulated widely; indeed, it was a best-seller. Such was the response from readers that by November 1918 Stopes published another best-seller, *Wise Parenthood*, which concentrated on the question of birth control, only briefly discussed in *Married Love*.

During 1923 Marie Stopes achieved celebrity (and notoriety) when she brought a libel action against a Catholic doctor: sales of *Married Love* practically doubled, from 241,000 to 406,000. Now the new (relative) openness about sexuality joined hands with a significant new recreational activity of the time: the British film company, Samuelson's, invited Marie Stopes to collaborate in the making of a fairly traditional little romantic story which, however, was to be entitled *Married Love* and would contain elements of causes close to Marie Stopes's heart, the advocacy of eugenics (that is to say, creating a fitter race) and birth control. Not altogether surprisingly, the film ran into various censorship difficulties: some cuts were insisted upon, and the title had to be changed to *Maisie's Marriage*, but it did have a successful commercial distribution. *Maisie's Marriage* was, naturally, a silent film, so much of the message is carried in the printed captions or 'intertitles'. The opening caption reads:

> Not ours to preach nor yet to point a moral – yet if, in the unfolding of our story, the thought that comforts, helps or guides, then are our efforts doubly paid.

We start off in Maisie's horribly deprived family background:

> The Burrows family live in Slumland but their prototypes dwell in all our cities – wherever our artificial civilization has planted its weeds, where the struggle for existence is hard and ruthless and a narrow dogma of our disciplined beliefs turn life and the joys of living into meaningless phrases.

Maisie is courted by a fireman, Dick Reading, but, fearing the endless pregnancies which have destroyed her mother, Maisie rejects him, though he has brought to her 'dim tremulous thoughts of waking womanhood'. Maisie is thrown out of her slum home by her brutish father, attempts suicide by jumping into the River Thames, is rescued, but gaoled for the crime of attempted suicide. She becomes a maidservant in the family of Mr Sterling, her rescuer. From Mrs Sterling, who has three lovely children, Maisie learns that she can enjoy married love without the fearful consequences which had driven her apart from Dick. Maisie, alone in the house with the Sterling children, is visited by her degenerate brother, seeking to extort money from her. Fire breaks out, and Maisie is rescued by fireman Dick. Happily reunited, Maisie and Dick get married, with a guard of honour provided by Dick's colleagues.

Exercise   I want you now to watch item 8 on video-cassette 1, which is the sequence from *Maisie's Marriage* in which Mrs Sterling makes her revelation to Maisie. When you have viewed this clip, answer the following questions:

1   How clear do you find the explanation of contraception?

2   What conclusions do you draw about public attitudes towards contraception?

3   Apart from the fact that the sequence is perhaps as much about eugenics as contraception, what other, totally different message do you receive from this sequence?

4   What, finally, is the significance of the film with respect to changing customs and behaviour? ■

Specimen answers   1   The explanation is extremely obscure. One could scarcely be surprised that
and discussion   British people, or many of them, continued to be extremely muddled in their ideas about sex. One wonders if young men went around dreading that young ladies might suddenly produce a pair of secateurs.

2   Obviously public standards demanded the utmost delicacy and restraint in the discussion of this topic to the point of complete obscurity.

3   The other message, surely, is of romantic love, but, in all the circumstances, particularly the association with Marie Stopes, it is romantic love in which sexuality is very strongly stressed.

4   The film is significant in that it is broaching the topic of birth control, and broaching it through film, itself a symbol of cultural change. Perhaps more importantly, it strongly, if obliquely, focuses on the physical aspect of romantic love. □

With regard to the roles of women, wartime necessity meant large numbers of women being projected into entirely new experiences. James McMillan, who is generally hostile to the idea that the war had any significant effects on the position of French women, does accept that unchaperoned French young women were subjected in hospital work and elsewhere to experiences from which they would have been completely shielded in pre-war years. Generally, in the new situation of war, the institution of the chaperone had to be dropped.

Respect for authority, religious observance, etc.

Traditional close-knit communities were disrupted by the war, with young men going out into the big, wide and often irreligious world. Pastors and clerics did their cause little good by enlisting God and religion in support of their own country's military effort. The very havoc of war made many doubt the existence of God. True, there was a long-term trend away from religion, yet the war was significant in bringing together in concentrated form a whole complex of reasons for rejecting religion.

Recreational activities

The era of the erection of huge custom-built cinemas was during the immediate post-war years. During the war cinema had been exploited by governments for patriotic purposes and thus tended to gain respectable middle-class, in addition to the previous working-class, audiences. The immediate post-war years were also the era of erecting large public dance halls. The notion of the public, as distinct from the private, dance, gained respectability during the war when so many young female war workers were, as never before, out in public on their own. The new rhythms upon which the newly popular dances were based originated in America before the war, but as with cinema and so many other developments, it was the conditions of war which gave them wider currency in Europe.

Here I have been speaking largely of cultural change. When it comes to radio, the crucial development was a commercial and technological one – the enormous expansion in the production of radio valves in order to meet the needs of wartime aviation. This capacity having been created, there had to be an outlet, and that outlet came in the form of general broadcasting of news and entertainment.

Fashion and dress

Let's approach dress, etc. with an exercise.

Exercise   1   What would be the best source for seeing how dress changed between the pre-war and the post-war years?

2   What were the most striking changes (a) for women, and (b) for men? ■

Specimen answers   1   Fashion items in the press might be an obvious answer, but I think the best
and discussion   source would be film material, for that shows what people actually wore, rather than what fashion writers said people ought to wear.

2   (a) For women the most obvious change was the advent of the short skirt. Now, once again it is true that fashion was changing, and dress lengths were very slightly shortening in the period after 1905 (associated particularly with the French designer Paul Poiret). Nonetheless both shortage of materials and the need for freedom of movement among women engaged in war work, were important developments during the war. I believe also that post-war fashion can be seen very much as representing the desire to make a break from the bad old restrictive stuffy world, and to put a particular emphasis on youth as the only hope for the future.

(b) For men there was a move towards informality (though, as with birth control, this is not to be exaggerated).

2.8   Women and the family

This is the area in which the debates over the effects of war on society have raged most furiously. Feminist historians have generally taken the line that women's position in society did not change very much anyway, and that where it did this was due either to long-term economic and technological trends, or to the militant activism of women themselves, or both. There are three points here of very great weight, which deserve your full consideration. I am going to make the case (which you are entirely free to reject, particularly if you do some more reading on your own) that there were some changes in the role and status of women, and that the particular way in which these changes came about, and the timing of them, can be attributed to the war experience.

What is not in doubt is that, while the war was being waged, the enlistment of large numbers of men in the various armies meant that women took on new kinds of employment, or entered into paid employment for the first time. Two points pressed by those who argue that the war had no significant positive effects on the status of women, must be considered:

1   How permanent were these changes in employment? In general, the statistics show (see Table 8–10.4 and Figure 8–10.1, which apply to Britain) that while there was a considerable expansion in women's employment during the war years, once the war was over the figures were not very different from those of pre-war years (this is not universally true, since, as we shall see, there was permanent expansion in certain countries, for example France). The general conclusion must therefore be that, as far as working-class employment was concerned, there were not (apart from the exceptions) significant changes for women. However, the figures do suggest that in certain important professional occupations, from which women had very largely been excluded before the war, there were long-term changes, particularly in the legal profession, accountancy, and medicine. The actual numbers involved, of course, are small, and it is very much a matter of personal assessment what weight one gives to them.

Table 8–10.4   *Some broad census data (England and Wales only)*

	Total Population	Total females	Over 10 years	Total females occupied	married	widowed	Females per 1,000 males	Females per 1,000 males in age group 20–45
1901	32,527,843	16,799,230	13,189,585	4,171,751	917,509		1,068	
1911	36,070,492	18,624,884	14,357,113 Over 12 years	4,830,734	680,191	411,011	1,068	1,095
1921	37,886,699	19,811,460	15,699,805 Over 14 years	5,065,332	693,034	425,981	1,096	1,172
1931	39,952,377	20,819,367	16,419,894	5,606,043	896,702	389,187	1,088	

Source: Arthur Marwick, *Women at War 1914–1918*, 1977, Table 1, p.166.

2   The second point can be phrased in two rather different ways:

(a)   How different was this employment of women in wartime? Those who argue against the war's having any significance, point out that industrial

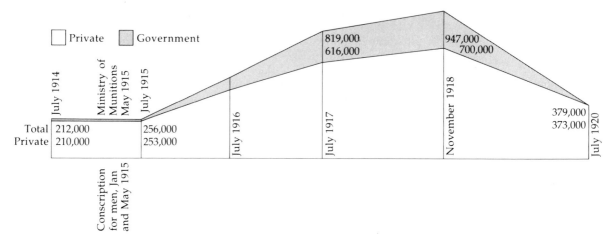

Figure 8–10.1   *Women in munitions (metal and chemical trades) Great Britain and Ireland,*
private and government factories
Source: Arthur Marwick, *Women at War 1914–1918*, 1977, Table 2, p. 166.

drudgery had been the lot of many women since at least the onset of industrialization.

(b)   Economic and technological change was leading anyway to the employment
of women: at most the war was simply an exaggeration of this trend, and in so far
as it did continue in the post-war years it was part of that trend, and unrelated to
the war.

These are arguments I want you to bear in mind in looking at some of the
evidence.

More generally, the point is made that the basic relationships between men and
women did not change, the family continued to be regarded as a fundamental
institution, and women's role as child-bearer and child-rearer continued to be
stressed. This is undoubtedly true. The argument really centres on whether
within that unchanging framework, women did also have a greater role outside
the home, did expect some sharing of roles within the home, did value themselves
more highly, and were prepared to speak up for themselves more than formerly.
Some feminists have joined with historians such as myself in arguing that
working in new situations and supporting the national effort in wartime did raise
women's consciousness, and made them more prepared to speak up for themselves. This is a further point I would like you to keep in mind as you look at some
of the primary and secondary sources.

When the word 'emancipation' was used in the late nineteenth century and
early twentieth century, it referred to the question of political rights: an emanci-
pated woman was a woman who had the vote. Nowadays 'emancipation' means
something much wider. Much of the argument over the effects of World War I
arises from people using this word in two different ways: the usage of people who
actually lived through World War I, and the usage of people today. In almost all of
the European countries women were granted the vote at the end of the war or,
more usually, in the first year of peace. There does seem to be an association with
the war, but again arguments have been made that the war was irrelevant, or even
held up something that was coming anyway. James McMillan, very understandably, makes much of the fact that French women did not get the vote at the end of

the First World War. The debate here is very much concerned with the significance or otherwise of *participation* in wartime. Those who see little value in the general line of argument would maintain that women were simply exploited while the rulers of the day needed them for the war effort, then cast back into their former roles as soon as the war ended. The fact that women in many countries did get the vote at the end of the war cannot, of course, be gainsaid, and here the arguments would be that essentially the winning of the vote was part of a long-term trend and that, anyway, as the example of France shows, participation in war certainly did not automatically guarantee the winning of the vote. For myself, I would say that upholders of that line of argument do then have to explain why the vote came in most countries in 1918, 1919, or 1920, rather than in, say, 1928 or 1938.

Another possible line of argument, for some countries at least, is that votes for women essentially came as part of the radical change in regime associated with the various revolutions in Eastern and Central Europe. I suppose that argument could be combined with the one that in Britain (where manifestly there was no revolution) there was a very fully developed pro-suffrage movement which had already achieved majorities in the House of Commons and the Lords. The distinguished British historian, Martin Pugh, has argued in several books that, but for the war, women in Britain would have got the vote sooner, and that it would not have been limited to women over thirty. Of course, whatever line one follows in the general debate, one could not possibly avoid recognizing the horror and tragedy of war for men, women and children: a vote gained might coincide with a husband or son lost. In the rest of this section I propose not to say much about Central and Eastern Europe, which will be discussed much more thoroughly in Units 11–13. What I want you to do now is to read some secondary and some primary material, and also look at some film evidence, and then draw out some conclusions with respect to the points of debate outlined above.

Exercise After completing the reading/viewing itemized below, and recalling also any points I have already made regarding the role and behaviour of women, note down:

1   what the source is, how useful and reliable you take it to be, and what peculiar features it has;

2   how far the source supports the general view that the war did bring positive changes in the role and status of women, and how far it supports the opposite. ■

Extract (a): The extract below by James McMillan.

> With the end of the war in sight, the prospects of the French feminist movement looked auspicious. Thanks to women's contribution to the war effort (and here of course feminists had been well to the fore) it was widely expected that fitting recognition would take the form of legislation to introduce the female suffrage, which, as we have seen, had become the movement's main demand in the years before 1914. A typical prediction was that of Gaston Rageot: 'Among all the novelties which this war, disrupting the old world to create a better one, will provoke, the most striking, perhaps, and the most lasting, will be furnished by the advent of women to national life.'
>
> In like manner, the socialist deputy Bracke wrote that all the arguments used against women's suffrage collapsed in the face of their wartime

achievements. Naturally the feminists themselves looked forward to the imminent realisation of their hopes. Marguerite Durand, in a front page article in *L'Oeuvre*, stated the case for a new deal for women in the post-war period. Suzanne Grinberg, female barrister and feminist, after sounding out the views of a number of parliamentarians in 1917, was optimistic about the chances of a bill to introduce women's suffrage. Even opponents of votes for women were moved to advocate the suffrage for widows and female relations of those who had fallen in battle (an idea first suggested by the novelist and prophet of integral nationalism Maurice Barrès).

These forecasts of an impending feminist victory appeared to be vindicated in May 1919, when the Chamber of Deputies debated the question of women's suffrage. Time and again in the course of the deliberations politicians of all parties returned to the theme that women were entitled to the vote as a reward for their endeavours on the home front, 'a gesture of justice and recognition', Jules Siegfried called it. The turning point in the debate was a speech by the ex-socialist and former prime minister René Viviani, who eloquently summed up all the principal arguments in favour of women's emancipation, stressing their war record, their special talent for solving moral and social problems, and the example of other countries which increasingly recognised the political rights of women. To his call for the immediate introduction of suffrage equality for women, the Chamber of Deputies responded by voting in favour of the bill by a majority of 344 to 97. The feminist lobby was jubilant. Lucie Colliard, one of the militant schoolteachers persecuted under the Clemenceau régime for anti-war activities, spoke for many when she wrote: 'At last we are going to have it, this ballot paper desired for such a long time. For the old gentlemen of the Senate, led by the sound arguments and eloquence of Louis Marin, will not dare to do less than their colleagues in the Chamber.'

Unfortunately for the feminists, however, all the celebrations proved premature. The 'old gentlemen of the Senate' did indeed do less than their colleagues in the Chamber. Having procrastinated until November 1922 before debating the bill passed by the Chamber, the senators threw it out by the narrow margin of 156 votes to 134. Their discussions allowed most of the hoary arguments against women's suffrage to be aired. Some members took the view that the bill would undermine the already dwindling powers of the husband and head of the family; others claimed that women neither wanted the vote nor had any talent for politics. But the crucial argument against the bill was put by its *rapporteur* in the Senate, Alexandre Bérard, when he objected that it invited clerical rule and was likely to imperil republican institutions. For the remainder of the Third Republic's lifetime, the spectre of clericalism was raised by aged senators of the Radical-Socialist party to defeat further attempts to achieve the political enfranchisement of women. A bill sponsored by the right-wing deputy Louis Marin to give women the vote in municipal elections was passed by the Chamber but thrown out by the Senate in 1927. In 1928, the senators passed a resolution to have no further debates on the subject of women's suffrage. In 1931 the deputies again carried a suffrage bill (by 319 votes to 1) without producing any change of heart in the Senate. If the issue of women's suffrage is any criterion, it is difficult to sustain the thesis that the First World War destroyed 'all the old arguments about women's proper place in the community'. . . .

Certainly, then, the climate of public opinion in France as a whole was not conducive to the easy passage of a parliamentary bill introducing women's suffrage. On the other hand, it would be a mistake to exaggerate the extent to which the principal demand of the feminists had to yield to the force of anti-feminist pressure at the grass-roots. Public opinion was not so exercised by the spectre of votes for women that the enactment of the female suffrage bill was simply unthinkable. It is hardly sufficient to argue, as the anti-feminists did, that women were not entitled to the vote because there was no popular clamour for it. After all, when universal male suffrage was introduced in 1848 this was not in response to any widespread agitation among the majority of the male population. Similarly, no militant suffrage campaign was to precede the extension of the franchise to French women in 1945. Had women received the vote in 1919 – as seemed a distinct possibility – it is scarcely to be imagined that millions of Frenchwomen would have been so horrified as to have removed themselves from the electoral roll.

On the contrary, if the results of mock ballots in the national press can be trusted, thousands of women revealed a positive desire to vote. On the model of the poll conducted by *Le Journal* in 1914, *Excelsior* obtained 34,952 ballot papers in response to their mock election among women in Paris and the department of the Seine in 1919. *L'Oeuvre*, now under the direction of Gustave Téry, who had earlier been responsible for the *Journal* ballot and who opened his pages to feminist contributors such as Jane Misme and Maria Vérone (he was also vice president of the LFDF), organised a ballot of a slightly different kind to try to gauge how the female vote in a Parisian constituency would have affected the eventual outcome of the elections in 1919. Over 12,000 women voted, though had their votes counted the *Bloc National* would still have come out on top. In 1922, *Le Journal* itself held another referendum among its female readers in which some 224,155 women declared themselves in favour of the suffrage with only 1288 against. Even if these polls should be construed essentially as publicity stunts on the part of enterprising press barons to try to increase sales among women, they furnish evidence nevertheless that women's suffrage was a cause which enjoyed not inconsiderable support in public opinion. As an enterprise, the female suffrage campaign was no more doomed to failure in France than it was predestined for success in Britain and America. If votes for women did not become a reality in France after the First World War, this was only partly because of its limited appeal to the majority of Frenchmen and Frenchwomen. More fundamental to the defeat of women's suffrage was the attitude of the male political establishment and the weakness of the feminist movement itself. (James E. McMillan, *Housewife or Harlot*, 1981, pp.178–9, 181–2)

Extract (b):   The article on 'Italian peasant women' by Anna Bravo in the Course Reader.

Extract (c):   Document II.11 *in Documents 1*, extracts from the journal of Brand Whitlock.

Extract (d):   The extract from *A Day in the Life of a Munition Worker*, item 7 on video-cassette 1.

Extract (e):   Document II.12, the newspaper report on British servants, 1919.

Extract (f):   Document II.3, the various extracts from the Treaty of Versailles.

Specimen answers and discussion   Before giving answers with respect to the texts that I have asked you to look at, the point that I thought you might have picked up from earlier reading in these units is the one about changes in customs, dress, etc., with regard to peasant women in Serbia.

Extract (a)   1   This is from an authoritative secondary source, the standard work in English on French women between the late nineteenth century and the outbreak of World War I. Although I have not printed the footnotes, I hope that you perceived that this account is very rigorously based on the primary sources – the references are to the official reports of the French Chamber of Deputies and Senate, and to other contemporary materials. However, we have to be aware that James McMillan has been one of the leading figures in taking up opposition to my own published views that the First World War did bring some measurable changes in the role and status of women. You would have no means of knowing this, but the phrase about the war destroying 'all the old arguments about women's proper place in the community', which McMillan rightly criticizes, is, I am sorry to say, from one of my own books. Indeed, McMillan lets me off lightly, since I actually wrote of 'the total destruction of all the old arguments about women's proper place in the community'. This is a salutory warning about the dangers in historical writing of such exaggerated, absolutist, closed statements. (I would still argue that the circumstances of war made many of the old arguments seem very silly to the overwhelming majority of thinking people – the votes in the Chamber of Deputies quoted by McMillan demonstrate this; but the war, of course, didn't suddenly wipe out all the fuddy-duddies, as the Senate votes show).

2   Wittingly, this extract presents strong ammunition for the case that the war did nothing to help the position of women; if you accept McMillan's arguments in the matter, please do not be in any way swayed by my own comments. I would argue that the very fact that there were substantial majorities in the Chamber of Deputies (which was much more closely in touch with grassroots opinion) shows that attitudes towards women had changed, even if the actual granting of the vote eluded them. Still more important, perhaps, is the evidence that women them-selves did want the vote. We have no direct pre-war material to compare this with, but it is a fact that votes for women was not the burning issue in pre-war France that it had been in Britain. I also noted the argument put forward by the opponents of women's suffrage that it would weaken the already dwindling powers of the husband. This suggests to me that the war experience, where women ran the businesses, the farms, etc., had indeed, irrespective of any legislation, changed the balance of power within the family unit.

Extract (b)   1   This is a secondary source, a learned article, but almost entirely based on one type of primary material, oral interviews. I have to say that it did strike me as slightly peculiar that a researcher working in the 1970s should be able to interview people about experiences which took place sixty years earlier. I know from my own experience of collecting written testimony from British women who lived through the First World War that they often get things wrong (many actually believed that they were conscripted into the war effort, though in fact, as you know, there was no conscription of women then). Nevertheless, I find the evidence impressive, and it is in fact congruent with what we know (not a lot!) from other types of source material.

2   Overall, the article does give an impression of positive long-term changes being brought about in the lives of Italian peasant women by the war, though clearly there were losses as well as gains. The first point is the general one of the massive disruption to normal patterns of life brought about by the war (the massive call to arms, the material difficulties, the increased interference of the state in the fabric of daily life). There was a change in the work balance, and an

ending to the traditional division of labour (much of this, of course, was temporary, but one does get the definite impression of some changes enduring). Women took work in factories, even as far afield as France, and ended the tradition where such work ended at marriage. Here we have a crucial point, often ignored by those in the James McMillan camp, and one which will come up again with respect to World War II: it is true that women did factory work before the First World War, but we have to look closely at what happens with respect to *married* women. Mothers worked in fields, while daughters looked after children, sometimes for several families; in part, of course, this may also be seen as reinforcing traditional roles. That comment might also apply to the instances of women making their own butter and bread, but the new 'managerial' tasks brought about by rationing certainly were of a new order. Even more critical in this 'managerial' development was the part women had to play in the new complicated relationships with the state authorities. Bravo's summing up is well worth full quotation:

> The women's lives, previously restricted to the house and community, were now filled with new tasks: going to government offices, discussing with local administrators and officials, travelling as far as provincial capitals to follow through these extended chores. Thus greater contact was established with the outside world, with new places, with a new environment of different experiences, with the public sphere of life. The women now had a direct relationship with the activities of a state authority which they also identified as responsible for the war.

Here we begin to go off into a slightly different point, that of women's part in a 'more general estrangement from the state' and 'peasant societies' opposition to the war'. We then come to a point which is being increasingly recognized in studies of war and women, the change in 'mentalities', the growth of 'self-realization' (as Bravo puts it), a new self-confidence, which I personally see as crucial in the changed role and status of women that I perceive in the post-war years. With regard to relations between the sexes, Bravo seems to identify one gain and one loss: women's sexuality was now, Bravo says, less restricted and less orthodox (echoes of my discussion of Marie Stopes), but on the other hand their productive and reproductive power, and their role as sexual objects was perhaps intensified. I have already broached the question of whether war brought changes in sexual morality: Bravo's evidence gives a very definite negative for this type of community. Bravo gives a very balanced conclusion (which indeed you may well feel to be more McMillanite than Marwickian):

> A venthole had been opened, which could not be wholly closed; and a good many wives continued to exercise their new-found expertise in dealing with state officials, now on behalf of their husbands. But, within the community, old roles were resumed, and the women forced back into traditional peasant silence, leaving the men to monopolise the claim to war honours.

Extract (c)   1   This is a diary, usually a very valuable type of primary source. However, we have to note that though the subject is the behaviour of Belgian women, the author of the account is an American male. Nevertheless, I can't think of any reason as to why his testimony should be false, and there is indeed corroborating official and other material on the new roles and activities of Belgian women. There is the peculiarity that Belgium at this time was occupied by the Germans, but clearly the women, like other civilians, very sensibly believed that only through hard work would Belgian society be kept together, and the conditions of desperate deprivation be in any way mitigated.

2   This definitely is evidence of changed activities and attitudes of women during the war. It tells us nothing about activities after the war, but in so far as it refers to attitudes, that might indicate a more enduring change (that is how I would argue, anyway).

Extract (d)   1   This is a documentary silent film – in fact a propaganda film made by the Ministry of Information. The purpose of the film was to show what women were already doing, and to encourage more of them to do it. There may be some artificiality in having just one woman going through every process in the making of a shell, but I think in general the film does give an authentic sense of the kind of work women were undertaking.

2   The extract certainly tells us nothing about what happened to women after the war, but it is solid, if not wildly exciting, evidence of the sort of wartime tasks taken on by women.

Extract (e)   1   This is a newspaper report, a type of primary source often treated with great suspicion by historians. However, while editorial matter must be treated with great caution as an indication of that mysterious entity 'public opinion', straight reporting of this sort is extremely useful to the historian.

2   What the document convincingly demonstrates, I believe, is the new assertiveness and self-confidence which women showed in the *post-war* years, but which was derived from the new experiences of war. The document, of course, does not *prove* that connection, but in the light of other evidence (you'd have to consult some of the secondary authorities here), it does seem to me a reasonable deduction to make.

Extract (f)   1   This is a public document of record, an international treaty. It is an indisputable authority as to what was agreed between the signatories. It does not, of course, tell us what was actually carried out. In certain respects it will be an expression of aspiration, rather than reality. But aspiration is in itself an important topic for historians to study. We are concerned, among other things, with whether aspirations changed between pre-war and post-war days.

2   There are three references to women, which taken together remind me of Dr Neil Wynn's remark about the effect of the First World War on American women (a remark which I think has general applicability): 'women made two steps forward and one step backward'. You will see in the seventh clause of Article 427 that the principle is agreed 'that men and women should receive equal remuneration for work of equal value'; one has to comment that it was an aspiration rather than a reality, but nonetheless the setting of an international standard is a gain. You will have noted in Annex 4 to Article 88 that in the plebiscite women are to have the vote as well as men. However, 'the step backwards' is contained in Article 91, where on the question of opting for Belgian or German nationality, 'Option by a husband will cover his wife'. ☐

With regard to family life in general, we have already noted instances of welfare legislation, institution of family allowances, and so on. These on the whole did improve the quality of material life within the family, though it could be argued

'If only there was women's conscription! Then perhaps the marriageable age would also be put back to 50.' This cartoon from the German satirical magazine Simplicissimus *(28 November 1916) refers to the Auxiliary Service Bill; it shows the extreme sexism of the time. (Bildarchiv Preussischer Kulturbesitz, Berlin)*

that all of this legislation served to reinforce the traditional image and role of women. But to keep things fully in perspective, I want you to finish this section by turning to the *Offprints Booklet* and reading 'The German nation's obligations to the heroes' widows of World War I' by Karin Hausen, from *Behind the Lines: Gender and the Two World Wars*, edited by Higonnet, Jenson, Michel and Weitz, 1987.

2.9 High and popular culture

High culture

It would be salutary to start off by re-reading the article by Josipovici in the Course Reader (it was first referred to in Book I). No historian worth his or her salt would ever dream of denying that the new modes characteristic of modernism which predominate in high culture in the twentieth century were already being practised before World War I. The debate is over whether the war was essentially irrelevant to developments in high culture, or whether it helped to give greater acceptability to the new modes and brought a fairly definite end (I must be careful not to exaggerate, or be absolutist or closed) to the spirit of optimism and belief in rational progress which had still characterized much high culture. For a discussion of these points with regard to the visual arts and music, you will need to turn to your audio-cassettes.

Exercise Listen to part 1 of audio-cassette 1, noting down answers to the questions asked on the cassette. ■

Exercise Now listen to part 1 of audio-cassette 2 and write down answers to the questions asked there. ■

You will have noted that both of these cassettes are presented by me, and you may wish to be on guard against my views on the consequences of war. More than this, you may have been struck by the fact that when a historian attempts to generalize in a brief space about matters of high culture, he or she runs the risk of sounding like one of the Sunday colour supplements, or possibly even a candidate for 'Pseuds' Corner' in *Private Eye*. You may feel that I have failed to negotiate that risk successfully. Thus, in order to pose the terms of debate over war's effects on literature, I am going to give you a selection of quotations from other academic authors. You could also remind yourself of the quotation from Gibson which I presented in section 2.1 of Book I, Unit 4.

The first quotation is the conclusion to John Cruickshank's *Variations on Catastrophe* (1982), which is a study of war's effects on various French literary figures:

We noted in the very first chapter of this study that many men in 1914 looked forward to a war as a potential form of moral transformation for society, or as a means of release from the social constrictions of peacetime attitudes and morals. But we also saw that, in the end, technological warfare appeared to an increasing number of participants as nothing other than a peculiarly dramatic and condensed image of the new industrial society . . . The war appeared to dramatize and to intensify social alienation. The hierarchies associated with an increasingly industrial and urban civilization were never quite the same again. After 1918 they were to be increasingly challenged.

At a different though relevant level . . . war also seemed to destroy a number of the old moral certainties. The contrast between the home front and the battlefront itself bred scepticism and suspicion. Furthermore, the propagandist exploitation and simplification of government and resounding moral absolutes left them meaningless and generally repellent. Moral indifference and moral relativism followed. The 'années folles' of the 1920s seem an inevitable consequence. We are in the world of E. M. Forster's 'everything exists, nothing has value' . . .

It would certainly be wrong to suggest that the Great War was the sole and initiating cause of the trends just mentioned. But it indicated awareness of them and probably accelerated them. Without the Great War there would not have been so rapid a growth in philosophical nihilism, social dissent, ethical relativism, and the contending political ideologies of fascism and communism. These doubts were widely experienced as a crisis within the mind and spirit of twentieth-century man. They were seen as part and parcel of a new emergency of which the war was an external manifestation. George A. Panishas implies too direct a causal connection when he describes such things as 'the legacy of the Great War'. But he describes very accurately the postwar state of affairs – and a state of affairs which the Great War helped to dramatize and confirm – when he writes of 'the alienation, the meaninglessness, the cynicism, the hate, the despair, the confusion, the suspicion, the fear, the doubt that possesses modern man even in the midst of his triumphs in science and technology.' It was after 1918 that modern man set out again 'in search of a soul'. The direction which this search was to take was affected in a fundamental way by the catastrophe of 1914–18.

My second quotation is from Barrie Cadwallader's introduction to his *Crisis of the European Mind: A Study of André Malraux and Drieu La Rochelle* (1981):

> The work is a political study of the *crise de l'esprit* suffered by André Malraux, Pierre Drieu La Rochelle and a number of other French intellectuals in the aftermath of World War I; a crisis born of the devastation of war and exacerbated by fears that the European age of world history was nearing its end. Many, including Drieu and Henri Massis, felt that if Europe remained in the state of division with which she had been satisfied, not only would her role in the world continue to shrink but the day would soon come when she would lose control over her own destiny. Europe thus became, for both men, a task at once magnificent and necessary. It was to the past, and specifically to the 'calm and full harmonies of the Middle Ages' (Drieu La Rochelle, *Drôle de voyage*, 1931, p.20) that they and many others now turned for a judgment on the present and an inspiration for the future.

My third quotation is from *German Novels on the First World War and Their Ideological Implications, 1918–1933* (1982) by Martin Travers:

> Some novels advance explicitly political interpretations of the war. Adam Scharrer, for example, in his *Vaterlandslose Gesellen*, tries to show that the professional and ideological differences that separated the ordinary soldier from his officer reflected the conflict of class interests endemic within 'capitalist' society as a whole and devotes much of his novel to an analysis of the industrial and party-political nature of that conflict. A similar kind of overtly political stance is noticeable in certain writers from the extreme Right, in, for example, Ernst Jünger, Franz Schauwecker or Josef Magnus Wehner. Although such writers were not concerned with the socio-economic determinants of the war, they were nevertheless fully aware of the political heritage left by the First World War, and did all they could to exploit that legacy in their own writings.
>
> It is, in fact, the unique perspective evident in the work of many of these nationalist authors, a strange mixture of historical observation and myth-poetical vision, that points to the second way literary text can engage with political issues. For these exponents of nationalist ideology, the war was not so much a definable historical event as a meeting place for the transcendental values of comradeship, self-sacrifice and leadership: the war, in short, was a *symbol* of that kind of personal and social ethics that the Weimar Republic was felt to negate, both in its theory and practice of parliamentary politics. For a writer of war fiction to deny one or all of these values was, irrespective of his conscious or explicit political goals, tantamount to a counter-offensive against this nationalist interpretation of war.
>
> It is this fact which explains the controversy that surrounded the publication of E. M. Remarque's *Im Westen nichts Neues* [*All Quiet on the Western Front*] in 1929. If one approaches Remarque's work within the

framework of traditional literary criticism or with the dogmatic expectations of the cruder type of Marxist methodology, the political reception of this apparently most 'apolitical' of all war novels must remain a mystery, for, unlike most of the novels referred to above, *Im Westen nichts Neues* contains little overt political sentiment. Nor can we draw upon circumstantial statements to help us in this matter; Remarque, perhaps in the hope of securing its popular reception, continually played down the ideological implications of his novel, emphasizing instead its imputed universal message about the horrors of war (a procedure which, as we shall see, has influenced many of his modern critics).

Once returned to its historical context, however, the critical strategy of Remarque's novel becomes much clearer. For Remarque takes all the components of the nationalist view of war – the insistence upon the Ideas of 1914 and the sense of righteous purpose felt by the nation, the suggestion that comradeship and group solidarity survived the final material onslaught, and the final essential assertion that the war left a positive spiritual legacy – and subjects them to poignant and forceful rebuttal. It is, then, the *thematic symbolism* of Remarque's novel that we must look for in our second kind of political implication.

Here is a more directly factual account from the historian Arthur J. May, taken from his comprehensive account of *The Passing of the Hapsburg Monarchy* (1966):

> The foremost literary light, Hugo von Hofmannsthal – poet, librettist, playwright – while still in his teens had won general respect for the maturity, the poise, and sweep of his writings. [As librettist he was most celebrated as collaborator in the operas of Richard Strauss: together they presented the opera *Die Frau ohne Schatten* in 1915 and a revised version of *Ariadne auf Naxos* in 1916.] Adoring the Monarchy (but despising Russia), he composed patriotic little essays for the press, compiled diverting wartime reading lists, and edited propagandist tracts for the hour. But, as the fighting dragged along, Hofmannsthal switched to a pacifist credo, and in collaboration with fellow Austrian authors and the Frenchman Romain Rolland he issued a clarion declaration of independence, calling upon European man to release himself from the claims and chains of excessive nationalism.
>
> His dear friend, Prague-born Rainer Maria Rilke, pre-eminently a European conscience with a style, spent half a year as a literary propagandist, attached to the ministry of war, a frightfully irksome assignment for a sensitive, thoroughly unmilitary person, however much his superiors endeavoured to make his environment congenial. Rilke in *Five Songs* lauded the spirit of combat and the grim gods of war, tried to persuade readers that he was all athirst for victory, but his cosmopolitan past soon gained the upper hand, and he turned to acrid denunciations of the loathsome facets of human nature brought to the surface by the war – by the 'rhythmic convulsion of the universe' (in his own phrase) – profiteering, exploitation, and a holiday for truth.

Finally, I quote from the much acclaimed book, *The Great War and Modern Memory* (1975) by Paul Fussell, the distinguished American professor of English (who had first-hand experience of war with the American army in World War II). Fussell's theme here is the 'irony' of war – war is not straightforward, war is a massive cruel deception on mankind, war explodes the myth of progress (the 'Meliorist myth').

THE WAR AS IRONIC ACTION

Every war is ironic because every war is worse than expected. Every war constitutes an irony of situation because its means are so melodramatically disproportionate to its presumed ends. In the Great War eight million people were destroyed because two persons, the Archduke Francis Ferdinand and his Consort, had been shot. The Second World War offers even more preposterous ironies. Ostensibly begun to guarantee the sovereignty of Poland, that war managed to bring about Poland's bondage and humiliation. Air bombardment, which was supposed to shorten the war, prolonged it by inviting those who were its target to cast themselves in the role of victim-heroes and thus stiffen their resolve.

But the Great War was more ironic than any before or since. It was a hideous embarrassment to the prevailing Meliorist myth which had dominated the public consciousness for a century. It reversed the Idea of Progress. The day after the British entered the war Henry James wrote a friend:

> 'The plunge of civilization into this abyss of blood and darkness . . . is a thing that so gives away the whole long age during which we have supposed the world to be, with whatever abatement, gradually bettering, that to have to take it all now for what the treacherous years were all the while really making for and meaning is too tragic for any words.'

James's essential point was rendered in rowdier terms by a much smaller writer, Philip Gibbs, as he remembered the popularity during the war of what today would be called Black Humor. 'The more revolting it was,' he says, 'the more [people] shouted with laughter':

> 'It was . . . the laughter of mortals at the trick which had been played on them by an ironical fate. They had been taught to believe that the whole object of life was to reach out to beauty and love, and that mankind, in its progress to perfection, had killed the beast instinct, cruelty, blood-lust, the primitive, savage law of survival by tooth and claw and club and ax. All poetry, all art, all religion had preached this gospel and this promise. Now that ideal was broken like a china vase to the ground. The contrast between That and This was devastating . . . The war-time humor of the soul roared with mirth at the sight of all that dignity and elegance despoiled.'

The British fought the war for four years and three months. Its potential of ironic meaning, considered not now in relation to the complacencies of the past but in itself alone, emerges when we consider its events chronologically. The five last months of 1914, starting August 4, when the British declared war on the Central Powers, began with free maneuver in Belgium and Northern France and ended with both sides locked into the infamous trench system. Before this stalemate, the British engaged in one major retreat and fought two large battles, although *battles* is perhaps not the best word, having been visited upon these events by subsequent historiography in the interest of neatness and the assumption of something like a rational causality. To call these things *battles* is to imply an understandable continuity with earlier British history and to imply that the war makes sense in a traditional way. As Esmé Wingfield-Stratford points out, 'A vast literature has been produced in the attempt to bring [the Great War] into line with other wars by highlighting its so-called battles by such

impressive names as Loos, Verdun, the Somme, and Passchendaele . . .'
This is to try to suggest that these events parallel Blenheim and Waterloo
not only in glory but in structure and meaning.

IRONY AND MEMORY

The innocent army fully attained the knowledge of good and evil at the
Somme on July 1, 1916. That moment, one of the most interesting in the
whole long history of human disillusion, can stand as the type of all the
ironic actions of the war. What could remain of confidence in Divine
assistance once it was known what Haig wrote his wife just before the
attack: 'I feel that every step in my plan has been taken with the Divine
help'? 'The wire has never been so well cut,' he confided to his diary, 'nor
the artillery preparation so thorough.' His hopes were those of every man.
Private E. C. Stanley recalls: 'I was very pleased when I heard that my
battalion would be in the attack. I thought this would be the last battle of
the war and I didn't want to miss it. I remember writing to my mother,
telling her I would be home for August Bank Holiday.' Even the weather
cooperated to intensify the irony, just as during the summer of 1914. 'On
the first of July,' Sassoon says, 'the weather, after an early morning mist,
was of the kind commonly called heavenly.' Thirteen years after that day
Henry Williamson recalled it vividly:

> 'I see men arising and walking forward; and I go forward with them, in a
> glassy delirium wherein some seem to pause, with bowed heads, and
> sink carefully to their knees, and roll slowly over, and lie still. Others
> roll and roll, and scream and grip my legs in uttermost fear, and I have
> to struggle to break away, while the dust and earth on my tunic changes
> from grey to red. And I go on with aching feet, up and down across
> ground like a huge ruined honeycomb, and my wave melts away, and
> the second wave comes up, and also melts away, and then the third
> wave merges into the ruins of the first and second, and after a while the
> fourth blunders into the remnants of the others, and we begin to run
> forward to catch up with the barrage, gasping and sweating, in bunches,
> anyhow, every bit of the months of drill and rehearsal forgotten, for
> who could have imagined that the 'Big Push' was going to be this?'

What assists Williamson's recall is precisely the ironic pattern which
subsequent vision had laid over the events. In reading memoirs of the war,
one notices the same phenomenon over and over. By applying to the past a
paradigm of ironic action, a rememberer is enabled to locate, draw forth,
and finally shape into significance an event or a moment which otherwise
would merge without meaning into the general undifferentiated stream.
I am saying that there seems to be one dominating form of modern
understanding: that it is essentially ironic; and that it originates largely in
the application of mind and memory to the events of the Great War. (Paul
Fussell, *The Great War and Modern Memory*, 1975; footnotes excluded).

Discussion   My quotations, I think, give you in lucid and self-explanatory form the main
points that distinguished authorities have made about the war's effects on
literature. □

The evidence (not all of it, as we need to study writers' letters, diaries, and other
contextual matter) is in the works of literature themselves. Again the question
arises: should we be studying works *during* the war, or works written *after*?

Presumably, while we might think a Social Insurance Act passed in 1929 would perhaps only be tenuously linked to the war, a novel published in 1929, but totally preoccupied with the war, would on the contrary be a tribute to the long-lasting, if not permanent, effects of the war. Anyway, I want you now to read three texts: one from an English poem written during the war, one from a French novel written during the war, and one from a German novel written in the late 1920s.

Exercise Now turn to *Documents 1* and carefully read the three documents listed below; then in each case note down answers to the following questions:

1   What distinctive formal and stylistic elements do you think can be related to the war and/or modernism?

2   In what way is the content related to the experience of war?

3   Is the document supportive or critical of the waging of the war?

4   With respect to Extract (c), does anything indicate that, unlike *Under Fire*, this novel is the product of reflections ten years later? ∎

Extract (a): document II.13, 'Strange meeting' by Wilfred Owen.

Extract (b): document II.14, the final pages of the novel *Under Fire* (1915) by Henri Barbusse. Published quite early in the war, this novel was immensely successful, yet also highly controversial. Though an older man, Barbusse himself served in the trenches before being invalided home.

Extract (c): document II.15, the final pages of Erich Maria Remarque's novel *All Quiet on the Western Front*. Not published till 1929, this novel was also an immense success, though hated by right-wing German patriots. Remarque was of normal enlistment age, had direct front-line experience, but was also invalided home.

Specimen answers and discussion

Extract (a) 1   The most striking formal element in the poem is that it is organized in couplets, but rather strange ones: in each case the 'rhyme' is only a 'half-rhyme' – 'groined/groaned', 'tigress/progress', 'mystery/mastery', etc. This was a mode pioneered by Owen and not widely to be found, I believe, before the war. One could interpret it as a relaxation in formality induced by the upheavals of the war and developed also, perhaps, as the only possible mode for grappling with the appalling horrors and irony of war ('pretty' rhymes certainly would not do). Furthermore, Owen coins rather strange words of his own ('groined', 'richlier'). The whole, also, is in a slightly informal, narrative style. Summing this up, one might say that the quite new and awful experiences of war called forth new modes of poetic expression. These modes, of course, are very much in keeping with the innovations of modernism.

2   The poem is 'about' death on the battlefield of, it transpires, both the British narrator and his German enemy. It is about the terrible loss of war ('undone years', 'the hopelessness'), particularly for young men on the verge, the poem suggests, of great discoveries which might have been of benefit to others. The poem, of course, is 'about' – 'The pity of war, the pity war distilled', the best-remembered line in the whole poem. It is 'about', in effect, the deeper comradeship, the appalling shared experience, of men technically classed as

enemies. It is utterly and completely 'about' the experience of war, and not in any way 'about' anything else.

3   This is not an overt, violent denunciation of war. Yet in its almost understated, but profoundly moving, reflection on the pity and the tragic loss of war, it is, for all that, perhaps a profoundly effective criticism of the waging of the war. Poetry, though it is of fundamental importance to understand exactly what the poet is saying, is open to personal and subjective interpretation, so these responses of mine are offered simply as guidance on the sorts of things one might get from this poem.

Extract (b)   1   Evidently this is not a conventional ending to a conventional, 'story-telling' novel. There is a declamatory style which is both polemical and poetical. The narrator is making direct statements, rather than letting these emerge, as in the traditional novel, from the events narrated, or from the views expressed by the characters. The passage is 'non-traditional' and therefore 'modern'. Again, it is a matter for your own judgement how far you accept the argument that this 'modern' style was required to cope with the immense issues thrown up by the war.

2   This is absolutely and exclusively a scene set in the French front line. Every point made is a point about the nature and experience of war.

3   Almost the whole of the passage seems to be so vigorously critical of the waging of the war, and the governments responsible, that it is surprising to find that the novel was published while the war was still being fought. The sufferings of the soldiers are sympathetically exposed, yet at the same time, in most unheroic mode, they are recognized to be 'murderers'. There is vigorous condemnation of financiers, 'feeble-minded' jingoes, and parsons. The religion of militarism is 'bad and stupid and malignant'. Yet the ultimate conclusion is, to say the least, ambiguous. The chapter itself is entitled 'The Dawn', and it appears that Barbusse is suggesting that from all the horrific slaughter 'a tranquil gloom' will emerge, so that then all the miseries and slaughter will have resulted in at least one step of progress. There is nothing at all reprehensible in this kind of ambiguity. Barbusse, in common with Wilfred Owen, had believed that Germany was a menace to civilization. What they are both saying, perhaps, is that the war, and the way it was fought, was out of all proportion to its objectives, with Barbusse leaving a sufficiently open ending (I am not for a moment saying that this was his reason) for the French government to see it as *not being a direct and comprehensive attack on the French war effort*. But it is an utter mistake to look at these literary artefacts from the point of view of whether they are 'anti-war' or not. It is, as Fussell so brilliantly points out, the horrific irony of the war that they expose.

Extract (c)   1   If you have any familiarity at all with German literature, you will be struck by the brief, staccato, almost journalistic sentences (the translation, I should say, is absolutely faithful to the original). The contrast in sentence length compared with that of the pre-war (and post-war) novels of Thomas Mann, for example, is quite stunning. This style is very effective for conveying the direct experience of war, and it is indeed a style which characterizes a particular type of twentieth-century novel.

2   The entire short chapter is a reflection on the war which is known to be nearly over, and how life has been utterly changed by the war.

3   Again there is no violent denunciation of war. The tone is of resignation and melancholy. Because the tone was not heroic, the novel was read by German nationalists (quite correctly, in fact) as not being an endorsement of the German war effort, of Germany military valour and virtue.

4   The points about the war generation becoming a forgotten generation are, I think, very much a product of the experience which former soldiers like Remarque actually had in the 1920s. It was possible for Barbusse, perfectly genuinely I think, to perceive a glimmer of hope, to believe in some possible positive results from all the sacrifice; this was less possible for Remarque writing at the end of the 1920s. □

During the war a great deal of literature was produced, glorifying the heroism of the troops and insisting on the rightness of the national cause. It is now somewhat fashionable in historical and cultural studies to argue that since the patriotic, if rather unpretentious, novels sold far more widely than the more intellectual agonisings over, and criticisms of, the war, they are much more 'important'. (*Under Fire* and *All Quiet on the Western Front* were highly successful, but their audience, cumulatively very large over the years, was undoubtedly provided by the educated reading public, that is to say the middle class and upwards, with a leavening of politically aware, or self-improving, working-class readers).

Exercise   Do you agree with the argument that novels in general supporting the values of militarism and patriotism, which sold widely to the lower-middle class and the working class, are historically more significant than the 'élite' novels and poems I have been discussing? Give reasons for your answer. ■

Specimen answer and discussion   First of all, there *is* the very important point that, in the past, history, and particularly the history of the movement of ideas, has been written entirely on the basis of what relatively small minorities thought. It is important, especially as we go further into 'mass society' (one of the topics of Book III) to know what the mass of the people were reading and, presumably, thinking. Most people in all countries almost certainly continued to believe in the values of nationalism, and the need for military action under certain circumstances to defend the rights and interests of their own nation. There *was* much heroism in the First World War, and it was almost certainly the wish of the ordinary family to see that heroism recognized, and certainly not cynically condemned.

I started with some reasons for the significance of 'elite' novels, but arguing on lines like these, you could well say that the 'popular', 'nationalistic' novels are more important. □

Popular culture

Exercise   Turn to Roberts (the set book), p.65.

1   What reasons does he give for the expansion of popular culture *before* 1914?

2   What does he identify as a major artefact in modern popular culture?

3   What effect do you think World War I had on the history of this artefact?

4   What general reason might there be for a general expansion in popular culture related to the war? ■

Specimen answers and discussion　1　(a) Rising real wages; (b) cheaper consumer goods, big stores and central markets, and cheaper transport; (c) increased leisure activities; (d) greater well-being; (e) new pleasures; (f) popular education and increased literacy.

2　'Monster newspapers'. Of course, earlier centuries had had their own artefacts of popular culture, but modern historians often place great emphasis on the founding of *Le Journal*, the *Daily Mail*, *Le Petit Parisien*, and (in Russia) *Novoe Vremya*. Note, however, that these are papers aimed more at the lower-middle class than at the working class.

3　(a) There was a general hunger for war news. Familiarity with the notion of the newspaper expanded (particularly in the Balkans, as we saw). (b) At the same time governments everywhere exercised censorship (though note that often newspapers exercised voluntary censorship – they wanted to 'win the war' too). I think the first development had the greater long-term effect. □

Exercise　If censorship makes newspapers an unreliable source for what soldiers really felt about the war, where might we look for more reliable information? ■

Specimen answer and discussion　This is not an easy one: 'soldiers' letters (also subject to censorship) and diaries' would be a good answer. But strictly within the sphere of popular culture the really interesting area, which historians are only now beginning to explore fully, is 'the popular culture of the trenches' – 'trench newspapers', the revues, sketches, song-and-dance shows, etc., which soldiers organized for themselves (recall the page from the *Wipers Times* which was reproduced in Unit 7).

Popular war reviews, stage shows on the civilian front, etc., do give us a sense of the widespread (and genuine) feelings of patriotism on the home fronts. But if I wanted to make a really clinching argument in favour of the value to the historian of popular culture (in comparison, say, with high culture) I'd give a high place to this 'popular culture of the trenches'. Conclusions must be tentative, but on the whole this culture does seem to reflect the established patterns of pre-war years, showing that soldiers tended to accept their lot in society, treated the awful conditions of war with both resignation and great wit, had little respect for their 'betters' at home, but felt that they had no alternative to fighting on. It could be argued that forms of popular culture already developed before the war (music hall songs, certain stereotyped characters and jokes) and now taken over and adapted to trench life, helped to sustain the fighting men in their horrific tasks. (There is a brief treatment in Marc Ferro, *The Great War*, 1973, pp.155–7; a major work on the British side is being written in 1989 by John Fuller, a research student at Cambridge.) □

Exercise　In section 2.7 on customs and behaviour, I identified some new developments in popular culture. What were these, and how, if at all, do they relate to the war? ■

Specimen answer and discussion　(a)　Film.

(b)　Gramophone and records.

(c)　Public dance halls.

(d)　Radio.

I have suggested that radio depended upon technological developments fostered, though not originated, by the demands of war. The demands of war, also, I have suggested, gave middle- and upper-class respectability to film. The special experiences of war legitimized public dancing, and encouraged the import of American rhythms. The growth and extent of American influences on popular culture is one of the great issues of twentieth-century historical study. Logistically, and geopolitically, World War I brought America into Europe. The connections between the developing modes of popular culture and the war are not direct, but that they exist is beyond question. This book (and indeed much of A318 as a whole) is about teasing out with as much precision as possible just exactly what these relationships are. Some historians have seen World War I as the great divide marking the beginning of mass society and technology-based popular culture. It depends partly on which developments you emphasize, partly on what you see as the main sources of modern popular culture. Roberts obviously places the origins much further back. Some commentators stress the advent of film, some the arrival of radio in every home (often associated with World War II). □

Exercise There is one form of high cultural practice which perhaps more than any other impinges directly on the majority of the people (particularly in urban areas). What is this art form? How might it have been affected by the war? ■

Specimen answer and discussion Architecture. Wartime destruction meant a requirement for rebuilding. More important, the end of the war (with the revolutions associated with it) was seen as a time for starting anew, a time for wholeheartedly applying the tenets of modernism to architecture.

Indeed, the 1920s are seen in the realm of architecture as the 'Heroic period of the new architecture' (see Charles Jencks, *Modern Movements in Architecture*, 1982, p.32). Beginning in October 1922, the Swiss architect Le Corbusier began writing a series of articles which were influential throughout Europe. He wrote:

> A great effort has begun . . . There is a new spirit: it is a spirit of construction and of synthesis guided by a clear conception.
> (quoted by Jencks, *Modern Movements*)

In the new Russia there was the movement known as 'constructivism'. In the new Weimar Germany there was the celebrated architectural school of the Bauhaus, led by two of the most famous of all twentieth-century architects, Mies van der Rohe and Walter Gropius. □

2.10 Political institutions and values

By this point you will have picked up several hints as to what has changed within this sphere. Again, it will help your understanding if you try first of all to work out what sort of changes had taken place between the pre-war and the post-war years. To give you a basis and, as it were, a stimulus, I want you to turn to the exercise chart which I completed for you in Book I, Unit 5.

Exercise Look at the exercise chart in Book I, Unit 5. As you can see, this chart is divided up by countries. I want you to take each country in turn, going each time direct to the final section, 'political institutions and values'. In the case of each country, make notes on the main changes that have taken place, as compared with pre-war days. Try to indicate the significance of the war in bringing about these changes. ■

United Kingdom

All men now have the vote, together with women over thirty (provided they fulfil a small property qualification). Votes for all women came, without much fuss, in 1928. It could be argued that participation in the war effort was the key factor in the gaining of votes by both men and women. Events have moved decisively towards independence for the bulk of Ireland, the Irish Free State being declared in 1921. It might be argued that the war tested Britain's artificial grip on the major part of Ireland. Ideas of collectivism and state enterprise were greatly strengthened during the war, though there was a determined effort to return to the principles of *laissez faire*. Because of the rise of the Labour Party (perhaps attributable to working-class participation in the war effort) there was now a three-party system rather than the stable two-party one.

France

Adult males continued, of course, to have the vote, but, despite a significant swing of opinion, women did not get the vote at the end of the war. French socialism split (you may well not know this) between socialists and communists, but this can be more directly related to the Bolshevik revolution than to the war as such. French labour had gained something in prestige, but was still not a very strong influence on the policies of the state. France's immense sufferings and losses, despite its being on the winning side, helped to encourage right-wing nationalistic movements.

Italy

Liberal values and democratic principles were not firmly established in pre-war Italy. The exigencies of war undoubtedly had a deeply destabilizing effect, and although there were, as elsewhere, moves towards further liberal democratic reforms, an immense stimulus was also given to extreme right-wing nationalism, helping, it may be argued, to pave the way for the fascist takeover of power (these matters will be discussed much more fully in Book III).

Germany

Here the major changes were the German Revolution and the establishment of democracy; the gaining of prestige by organized labour; the split in the socialist movement; and the great stimulus, from the bitterness of defeat, to right-wing nationalism. These matters will be taken up in Units 11–13.

Russia

Obviously, the most overwhelming changes in political values and institutions took place here, and these too will be the subject matter of Units 11–13.

Austria

Here too we have immense changes, with the Habsburg monarchy disappearing. In appearance, at least, democratic values were established in Austria itself, with democratic socialism a powerful force. This again is a subject area examined in Units 11–13.

Neutral countries

The big question is whether overall there was a broad movement towards the values and institutions of 'mass society', including votes and welfare for 'everyone'. It is appropriate now to consider the question of the neutral countries and how they affect arguments about war and social change. Below is the response I made some years ago. All I will add here is that this is an issue well worth pondering over as you come to the end of these complex (but, Bill Purdue and I certainly hope, interesting) units.

At first sight it might seem that my theories are shattered by the history of those countries which, although remaining neutral, none the less underwent the same broad social changes as belligerent countries; on closer inspection the problem simply dissolves. In some degree or another, war did impinge on the several neutral countries of the First World War . . . Even in spheres where the direct impact of war was slight, or non-existent, these countries found that, after the war was over, they were inescapably part of the new social, intellectual, economic and political structures created elsewhere by war. (Broadly, this applies to Switzerland, though revealingly, women still did not have the vote there in 1972.) Spain [in 1972] has remained a backwater. Sweden in the First World War enjoyed a boom in the production of her high grade steel, and endured a blockade more complete than that of any other country save Germany. Norway in the same war suffered destruction of her shipping greater, in proportion to her shipping resources, than any other country, and in absolute terms second only to the United Kingdom. In 1921 Sweden *followed* most of the major belligerent countries in granting universal manhood suffrage and votes for women; even although there had been no participation effect, Sweden was now *joining* a new political and social order created elsewhere by the experience of war . . .

Of special interest is the range of psychological reactions to be found in the various countries which succeeded in, or desired to, remain neutral when everywhere the tides of patriotism were flowing high. This is not a subject which can be explored here; it is however worth comparing this calm Royal Message which King Christian of Denmark addressed to the nation on the outbreak of the 1914–18 war, with the jingoistic effulgences so prevalent in other countries:

'At no time more than the present has there ever been demanded a greater sense of responsibility, both in the individual and in the whole nation. Our country stands in friendly relations to all nations. We feel confident that the strict and equal neutrality which has always been maintained as the foreign policy of our country, and which now also will be unhesitatingly maintained, will be respected by all. This is the common view of the Government and of all responsible and sensible people, and we trust that no one by an untimely display of feelings, by rash demonstrations, or in any manner will violate the dignity and peace which it is of vital importance to maintain in order to create confidence in the attitude of our country. Everyone now has his responsibility and his duty. We feel convinced that the seriousness of the moment will be reflected in the actions of all Danish men and women.
God save our country
CHRISTIAN .'

(Arthur Marwick, *War and Social Change in the Twentieth Century*, 1974, pp.214–15)

REFERENCES

Aldcroft, D. H. (1977) *From Versailles to Wall Street, 1919–1929*, Harmondsworth, Penguin.

Becker, J-J. (1985) *The Great War and the French People*, trans. A. Pomerans, Leamington Spa, Berg.

Beckett, J. V. (1988) *The Aristocracy in England 1660–1914*, Oxford, Blackwell.

Cadwallader, B. (1981) *Crisis of the European Mind: A Study of André Malraux and Drieu La Rochelle*, Cardiff, University of Wales Press.

Cruickshank, J. (1982) *Variations on Catastrophe: Some French Responses to the Great War*, London, Oxford University Press.

Danaïllow, G. T. (1932) *Les effets de la guerre en Bulgarie*, Carnegie Endowment for International Peace, Yale University Press.

Feldman, G. (1966) *Army, Industry and Labor in Germany 1914–1918*, Princeton, Princeton University Press (extract reprinted in Course Reader).

Fermor, P. Leigh (1977) *A Time of Gifts*, London, John Murray.

Ferro, M. (1973) *The Great War 1914–18*, trans. Nicole Stone, London, Routledge and Kegan Paul.

Fisher, H. A. L. (1935) *A History of Europe*, vol. III, Boston, Houghton Mifflin.

Fussell, P. (1975) *The Great War and Modern Memory*, New York, Oxford University Press.

Gagnon, P. (1972) *France since 1789* (revised edn), New York, Harper and Row.

Geyer, M. (1981) 'Professionals and Junkers: German re-armament and politics in the Weimar Republic', in Bessel, R. and Feuchtwanger, E. J. (eds) *Social Change and Political Development in Weimar Germany*, London, Croom Helm.

Golovin, N. (1931) *The Russian Army in the World War*, Carnegie Endowment for International Peace, Yale University Press.

Hajnal, J. (1965) 'European marriage patterns in perspective', in D. V. C. Glass and D. E. C. Eversley (eds) *Population in History: Essays in Historical Demography*, London, Edward Arnold.

Higonnet, M. *et al.* (1987) *Behind the Lines: Gender and the Two World Wars*, New Haven, Conn., Yale University Press.

Jencks, C. (1982) *Modern Movements in Architecture*, Harmondsworth, Penguin (first pubd 1973).

Kirk D. (1946) *Europe's Population in the Interwar Years*, Geneva, League of Nations.

Lentin, A. (1985) *Lloyd George, Woodrow Wilson and the Guilt of Germany*, Leicester, Leicester University Press.

Leslie, R. F. (ed.) (1987) *The History of Poland since 1863*, Cambridge, Cambridge University Press.

Macartney, C. A. and Palmer, A. W. (1962) *Independent Eastern Europe*, London, Macmillan.

McMillan, J. (1981) *Housewife or Harlot*, Brighton, Harvester Press.

Maier, C. S. (1975) *Recasting Bourgeois Europe: Stabilization in the Decade after World War I*, Princeton, Princeton University Press.

Marwick, A. (1965) *The Deluge: British Society and the First World War*, London, Macmillan.

Marwick, A. (1968) *Britain in the Century of Total War*, London, Bodley Head.

Marwick, A. (1974) *War and Social Change in the Twentieth Century*, London, Macmillan.

May, A. J. (1966) *The Passing of the Hapsburg Monarchy 1914–1918*, Philadelphia, University of Pennsylvania Press.

Mayer, A. J. (1981) *The Persistence of the Old Regime: Europe to the Great War*, New York, Pantheon.

Medlicott, W. N. (1940) *British Foreign Policy since Versailles*, London, Methuen.

Middlemas, K. (1979) *Politics in Industrial Society: The Experience of the British System since 1911*, London, Deutsch.

Mitchell, B. R. (1975) *European Historical Statistics 1750–1970*, New York, Columbia University Press.

Mitrany, D. (1936) *The Effect of the War in South-Eastern Europe*, London, Oxford University Press.

Mommsen, W. (1988) 'The social consequences of World War I: the case of Germany', in A. Marwick (ed.) *Total War and Social Change*, London, Macmillan.

Mosse, G. L. (1988) *The Culture of Western Europe*, Boulder, Colorado, Westview Press.

Nicolson, H. (1952) *King George V*, London, Constable.

Nicolson, H. (1933) *Peacemaking 1919*, London, Constable.

Polonsky, A. (1983) in R. F. Leslie (ed.) *The History of Poland since 1863*, Cambridge University Press.

Reid, A. (1988) 'World War I and the working class in Britain', in A. Marwick (ed.) *Total War and Social Change*, London, Macmillan.

Reinhard, M. R. *et al.* (1968) *Histoire générale de la population mondiale*, Mont-chrestien.

Riasanovsky, N. V. (1984) *History of Russia*, New York, Oxford University Press.

Rogger, H. (1983) *Russia in the Age of Modernisation and Revolution 1881–1917*, London, Longman.

Rose, K. (1983) *King George V*, London, Macmillan.

Stone, N. (1983) *Europe Transformed 1878–1919*, London, Fontana.

Taylor, A. J. P. (1961) *The Origins of the Second World War*, London, Hamish Hamilton.

Thompson, F. M. L. (1963) *English Landed Society in the Nineteenth Century*, London, Routledge and Kegan Paul.

Travers, M. (1982) *German Novels on the First World War and Their Ideological Implications, 1918–1933*, Stuttgart.

Urlanis, B. C. (1970) in L. A. Kosinsky (ed.) *The Population of Europe: A Geographical Perspective*, London, Longman.

Waites, B. (1976) 'The effect of the First World War on class and status in England 1910–20', *Journal of Contemporary History*, vol. II, no. 1.

Waites, B. (1988) *A Class Society at War: England 1914–18*, Leamington Spa, Berg.

Wall, R. and Winter, J. (1989) *The Upheaval of War: Family, Work and Welfare in Europe, 1914–1918*, Cambridge University Press.

Wandycz, P. (1986) in G. Martel (ed.) *'Origins of the Second World War' Reconsidered*, London, Allen and Unwin.

Wilson, T. (1986) *The Myriad Faces of War: Britain and the Great War 1914–18*, Cambridge, Polity Press.

Winter, J. M. (1986) *The Great War and the British People*, London, Macmillan.

Woytinsky, W. S. and E. S. (1953) *World Population and Production: Trends and Outlook*, New York, Twentieth Century Fund.

Yovanovitch, D. (1929) *Les effets économiques et sociaux de la guerre en Serbie*, New York, Carnegie Endowment.

UNITS 11–13 THE RUSSIAN AND GERMAN REVOLUTIONS AND THE COLLAPSE OF THE HABSBURG EMPIRE: A COMPARATIVE STUDY

(Introduction and sections 1–5 and 9–10 by Clive Emsley; sections 6–8 by David Englander)

Open University students will need to refer to:

Set book: J. M. Roberts, *Europe 1880–1945*, Longman, 1989

Documents 1: 1900–1929, eds Arthur Marwick and Wendy Simpson, Open University Press, 1990

INTRODUCTION

In Britain our perception of World War I is dominated by images drawn from the trench warfare of the western front. The war in Central and Eastern Europe was much less static, and consequently, in addition to the enormous loss of life, the destruction and devastation wrought by modern war affected much larger expanses of territory than in the West. Also unlike the West, the war in Central and Eastern Europe concluded with dramatic political changes. In 1914 there were four empires in Central and Eastern Europe: the Austro-Hungarian, German, Russian and Turkish. Eight years later each of these had been defeated and had ceased to exist; furthermore, all have been said to have experienced 'revolution'. The small Balkan states that existed between these empires in 1914 experienced similar political and social upheaval, though their problems have not always been graced with the term 'revolution'. In the following three units we want you to think about the events of war and revolution in Central and Eastern Europe between c.1914 and c.1921.

When you have completed these three units you should:

1   appreciate some of the semantic problems that arise with the word 'revolution';

2   have a general understanding of the events of war and revolution during the period c.1914 to c.1921 in Central and Eastern Europe;

3   be able to make your own informed assessment of the interrelationship between war and revolution in these parts of Europe.

As with Units 8–10, Units 11–13 are not separated into three discrete units; nevertheless they represent three weeks' work. For the purposes of your study time, therefore, Unit 11 covers sections 1–5, Unit 12 covers sections 6–8, and Unit 13 covers sections 9 and 10.

You should note that sections 1–5 are written by Clive Emsley.

1 CONCEPTUALIZATION: REVOLUTION AND WORLD WAR I

'Revolution' is a word much used (perhaps overused) by academics as well as journalists and politicians. Thus we have references to revolutions in government, to industrial revolutions, intellectual revolutions, managerial revolutions, scientific revolutions, student revolutions, in addition to the kind of political revolutions which engulfed France during the 1790s and Russia in 1917. Generally speaking, however, all of these uses are in some way referring to change, and change which is both fundamental and sudden.

Our concern in this unit is essentially political revolution. This is defined in the *Oxford English Dictionary* as 'a complete overthrow of the established government in any country by those who were previously subject to it; a forcible substitution of a new ruler or form of government.' This definition seems to me to ignore one crucial element, mass participation, without which there is very little difference between a *coup d'état* (a 'palace revolution' if you like) and the kind of upheaval which we are discussing. Yet even the notion of the forcible and sudden overthrow of one system of government by a violent upheaval involving mass participation does not take us much further forward in explaining the process of political revolution. A consensus appears to be emerging among historians and political scientists that the process of political revolution involves:

1   A total breakdown of government and particularly of the state's monopoly of armed force, leading to

2   A struggle between different armed power blocs for control of the state. These power blocs might be organized paramilitary formations, improvised groups like the soldiers' and workers' councils in Russia, or spontaneous peasant *jacqueries*.

3   The revolution is brought to an end when one of these blocs emerges as dominant and is able to reconstitute the sovereign power of the state. Often the most violent stage of the revolution occurs when a power bloc (or an amalgam of such blocs) has made itself master in the centre and then sets out to impose its authority on the provinces.

This definition portrays revolution as a specifically political process; it is not concerned to cover the macro-conceptualization of Marxist historiography, which sees revolutions as key events in the process whereby one socio-economic system is replaced by another. In this definition it is not important whether the English Revolution of the 1640s and the French Revolution of the 1790s were crucial moments in the shift from feudalism to capitalism. Nor is it important whether the Russian Revolution, which is central to these units, was a crucial moment in the overthrow of capitalism. However, many of the individual revolutionary activists who participated in the events which we will be discussing did conceive of their action and their revolutions in these Marxist terms.

Exercise   From your basic historical and general knowledge make a list of what might be considered as the general causes of revolution. Note down both those causes which you consider valid and any which you consider invalid. ■

Specimen answer   Your list may have looked something like the following:

1   Conflict between classes, with a new and powerful class in society seeking political power commensurate with its economic and/or social prominence.

2   Conspiracy and subversion.

3   A revolutionary ideology.

4   Economic disruption or upheaval causing discontent.

5   A repressive regime causing anger and discontent.

6   Serious divisions and a crisis of confidence within the old regime which renders it powerless to suppress the initial disorders.

7   The collapse of a regime in the face of a serious external threat, e.g. war, which enables other groups to seize power. □

Discussion   This list is in no particular or significant order, and you probably noted down other different causes. I hope that I will cover them now as I look at the list in some detail, suggesting where these 'causes' may be useful, and where they may not.

1   'Class', as you will recall from Book I, Units 1 and 4, is a word which is fraught with problems of definition. For some scholars, notably Marxists, 'class' necessarily entails 'consciousness' and 'conflict'; other scholars, though they recognize

that specific tensions or specific grievances at specific times can cause conflict between certain identifiable social groups or classes, attempt to use class in a more neutral way. In phrasing my answer above I was careful not to use the term 'class conflict', though the answer did go on to suggest something of a broad Marxist interpretation. Yet it is, of course, insufficient to say that 'class conflict' or 'conflict between classes' is the cause of revolutions, since what has to be explained is why, at a particular moment, that conflict became revolution; even if 'class conflict' is perennial, revolutions are not. Furthermore, as you will recall from Unit 4, the word 'class' is fraught with semantic problems. Most of the revolutions that we will be looking at in these units involved clashes between social groups – workers against employers, peasants against wealthy landowners. They also involved clashes between ethnic groups; on some occasions ethnic divisions might be said to have corresponded with social divisions, but this was by no means always the case.

2   The notion of an 'enemy within' ever active in fermenting disorder and conspiring to overthrow a particular government continues to be popular among some politicians, government officials and journalists, even in the late twentieth century; few (if any) serious historians would see revolutionaries as important in *causing* a revolution. What is never satisfactorily explained by those who take such conspiracy theory seriously, is precisely how revolutionary activists manage first to dupe the masses and bring them on to the streets and, second, to undermine totally the police and soldiers who could normally be expected to suppress the initial disorder. However, this is not to deny that in Central and Eastern Europe at the beginning of the twentieth century there were groups of revolutionaries, and that they did agitate through deeds and through the printed and spoken word. Moreover, when revolutionary action had begun they sought to take it over and to control it.

But actions, speeches and pamphlets which criticized and perhaps, in consequence, helped to undermine the autocratic empires of 1914, were not just the work of dedicated revolutionaries. Moderate reformers, some of whom had close links with the ruling elite and/or who were willing to work within the existing system, also called for change and the correction of what they perceived as abuses.

3   The question of a revolutionary ideology as a cause of revolution is linked to my previous comments. Ideological orthodoxy became all-important for many early twentieth-century socialists; it shaped their perceptions and dictated their course of action. Arguments about orthodoxy became internecine: should socialists work within the existing order, or should they stand out against any amelioration of the working class's lot so as to hasten revolution? The war brought another debate: Lenin, most notably, savaged socialists

> who are helping 'their own' bourgeoisie to rob other countries and enslave other nations. That is the very substance of chauvinism – to defend one's 'own' Fatherland even when its acts are aimed at enslaving other peoples' Fatherlands. (V. I. Lenin, 'Opportunism and the collapse of the Second International' (1915) in *Collected Works*, vol. 22, 1964, pp.109–10)

However, these theoretical debates had little impact when it came to bringing people on to the streets in the initial disorders of the revolutions. The root causes here were generally more immediate bread-and-butter issues (often quite literally, since bread shortages could bring crowds on to the streets). The task of the revolutionary activist was then to persuade the crowds of the relevance of his (or her) party's orthodoxy to the people's needs, and to do this an ideology might need dilution or a rather different focus.

4   Economic disruption and distress brought people on to the streets, yet that in itself did not automatically create a revolution. Food riots were widespread during times of dearth throughout the eighteenth and nineteenth centuries. Leon Trotsky noted that 'the mere existence of privations is not enough to cause an insurrection; if it were the masses would always be in revolt.' Equally, C. Dobrogeanu-Gherea, a leader of the Romanian Social Democrats who made a detailed analysis of the agrarian question in his native country, concluded, with reference to the peasantry, that extreme misery 'dulls the mind, numbs the soul, destroys energy and the spirit of revolt, and leads to resignation and blind submission – a state of mind diametrically opposed to that which leads to revolt' (quoted in Henry L. Roberts, *Rumania: Political Problems of an Agrarian State*, 1951, p.5). But historians still tend to point to a link between the economic situation of a country and revolution. Much of the most recent debate has tended to suggest that revolutions have followed a period of rising economic expectations and success which has been rudely interrupted by a recession or some kind of acute economic crisis.

5   Of course, repression often can create anger and discontent among those who are being, or have been, repressed. But repression can also be effective. There are two significant things to bear in mind about the impact of repression on the beginning of a revolution: first, some repression possibly can create sufficient discontent among a large enough section of the population to prompt it into vigorous and violent action when the opportunity arises; but secondly, and perhaps more importantly, in the first act of serious revolutionary disorder the forces of repression often fail either because they are given no clear direction, or because they are reluctant to take action.

6   The idea of there being serious divisions and a crisis of confidence within the old regime is, perhaps, the element which you were least likely to have noted in my initial exercise. Most analysts of revolution, however, now seem agreed that such a crisis of confidence is a significant cause of the phenomenon both at the occasion of the outbreak of disorder (it can contribute to the failure of repression noted above) and over the longer term. I have already touched on this in point 2 above with reference to individuals linked to the elite seeking change. In his classic comparative analysis, *The Anatomy of Revolution*, Crane Brinton suggested that 'the ruling classes in our [old regime] societies seem, and not simply *a posteriori* because they were overthrown, to have been unsuccessful in fulfilling their functions.'

> The Russians here provide us with a *locus classicus*. To judge from what appears of them in print, Russian aristocrats for decades before 1917 had been in the habit of bemoaning the futility of life, the backwardness of Russia, the Slavic sorrows of their condition. No doubt this is an exaggeration. But clearly many of the Russian ruling classes had an uneasy feeling that their privileges would not last. Many of them, like Tolstoy, went over to the other side. Others turned liberal and began that process of granting concessions here and withdrawing them there . . . Even in court circles, it was quite the fashion by 1916 to ridicule the Czar and his intimates. (Crane Brinton, *The Anatomy of Revolution*, 1965, p.52)

7   The external threat bringing about the collapse of a regime draws together many of the other 'causes', but first let me reiterate that these 'causes' should not be taken either singly or together as 'fundamental laws' governing the causes of revolutions. There remains considerable debate and controversy. The list is simply to provide you with some questions to think about as you explore the upheavals in Central and Eastern Europe which followed World War I. This brings us to the key question here: what was the interrelationship between war and revolution? □

Exercise   How do you suppose the pressures of war might influence most, if not all, of the causes noted above? ∎

Specimen answer   The pressure of war, especially if it was going badly, could exacerbate, or even create, some of these causes. Low morale, for example, might worsen a crisis of confidence among a country's rulers, and might also make the police and the army unreliable when it came to internal repression. The economic disruption of war might prompt people to take to the streets and make certain revolutionary calls and slogans more attractive.

It is also worth considering here the notion that participation in war can have a radicalizing effect on men. In Book I, Unit 2 it was suggested that conscription widened some men's horizons; while it provided some with the opportunity for social mobility, it might have made others discontented with their lot in civilian life. Conscription into a wartime army might have given such discontent a rather different and a sharper focus as men asked, first, what they were fighting for, and, second, what were they going to get for their effort and sacrifice. Furthermore, if the high command and the government seemed incompetent, and either lost the war or seemed likely to lose it, the loyalty of such soldiers and sailors could become questionable. □

Exercise   Do you suppose that the demand for 'unconditional surrender' which has been common in the total wars of the twentieth century might have any impact on the government of a defeated country? ∎

Specimen answer   Having suffered defeat and been required to surrender 'unconditionally' is likely to undermine the legitimacy of any government in the eyes of its people, thus making it very difficult for such a government to continue, even supposing that the victorious power, or powers, were prepared to permit this.

In her book *On Revolution* (1963), Hannah Arendt draws attention to 'the little noticed but quite noteworthy fact that since the end of the First World War we almost automatically expect that no government, and no state or form of government, will be strong enough to survive a defeat in war' (p.15). She goes on to suggest that 'among the most certain consequences' of defeat in modern war is 'a revolutionary change in government' brought about either by the people of the defeated state or enforced by the victorious powers. □

As with the 'causes' of revolution, it is not intended that you should take these suggestions about the interrelationship between war and revolution as unproblematic. They are rather in the nature of hypotheses with which we can explore the historical evidence relating to the changes in Central and Eastern Europe in the aftermath of World War I.

2 RUSSIA: THE REVOLUTION OF 1917

Exercise   Read Roberts (set book) pp.422–6 and answer the following questions:

1   How many 'revolutions' does Roberts identify in Russia during 1917?

2   What are the differences between these 'revolutions'? ■

Specimen answers   1   Roberts identifies two Russian 'revolutions' in 1917: the first in February (March according to the Western, Gregorian calendar), and the second in October (November).

2   The essential difference is that the February Revolution was 'an extemporization', whereas that of October was a planned coup conducted by the Bolsheviks. □

Discussion   Like Roberts, many historians have written of two 'revolutions' in 1917, recognizing that the two events they are describing are very different. Thinking back to the definitions which I suggested at the beginning of the previous section and which described a revolution as a lengthy political process, it is equally possible, and equally common among historians, to regard the whole of 1917, and even the years immediately following, as the Russian Revolution.

Exercise   Documents II.16–II.19 in *Documents 1* are drawn from the proceedings of the state *Duma* between 1915 and 1916. The first of these is the programme of the Progressives, and there follow extracts from three parliamentary speeches.

Read them now, and then answer the following questions. What do they suggest to you about:

1   how the war is going at the time the documents were drafted and the speeches were made;

2   what different members of the *Duma* considered to be the necessary remedies for Russia's problems;

3   attitudes in the *Duma* towards the Tzar and his governments? ■

Specimen answers   1   The implication in the documents from both 1915 and 1916 is that the war is going badly, though no one here ever advocates anything other than pursuing the war to a successful conclusion.

2   The majority Progressive Bloc was keen to have some kind of coalition government which pursued liberal and reformist policies and behaved in a strictly legal manner and kept the military out of civilian affairs. On the political Right, Markov expressed concern that the Progressive Bloc's language could provoke the masses into revolution, while Purishkevich, a member of the same right-wing party, was critical of the hypocrisy and paralysis of government, the Germanophile tendencies in the organs of government, and the influence of Rasputin.

3   There is much criticism of the Tzar's government in all of these documents, but no direct criticisms of the Tzar himself and no calls for an end to the regime. However, the criticism of the government and of Rasputin's influence, together with the Progressive Bloc's urging of an authority 'supported by the confidence of the people', imply an increasing division between the political groups in the *Duma* and their monarch.

While Miliukov's speech suggests unity in the Progressive Bloc, there was, in fact, a growing split between the Kadets and the Octobrists, who advocated change through legal and parliamentary means, and those to the left who talked about 'action' without specifying clearly what they meant. During the winter of 1916–17 several plots were contemplated by politicians and even people close to the throne; generally the plans centred on the removal of the Tzar and/or the Tzarina and a regency under the Tzar's brother on behalf of the heir, the Tzarevitch Alexis. Sir George Buchanan, the British ambassador, found himself approached by a grand duchess proposing that the Tzarina be 'annihilated'. In the event the only plot to come to fruition was the murder of Rasputin by a group of right-wingers including Purishkevich. ☐

Exercise   Turning back to Roberts, pp.422–4, note down what he considers to be the general causes of the February Revolution. ■

Specimen answer 1   War-weariness brought about by military defeat and starvation, which fostered strikes in the factories and desertion from, and mutiny in, the army.

2   Cracking morale in the army.

3   Scandals involving the autocracy.

4   A collapse of the old order as much as an insurrection by a new order.

Roberts also warns that given the needs of Marxist orthodoxy, it has become easy to exaggerate the contribution of those with the theoretical programmes and the logic of Marxist conceptualization of revolutions as central to the working out of the process of history. ☐

I want now to expand upon, and in some instances qualify, these causes. I have little to add on the subject of (3) above, however – the principal scandal was that of Rasputin; there were also rumours and suggestions that the Tzarina, who was German by birth, was in league with the enemy.

On the home front, life in general, and the economy in particular, had been seriously disrupted by mobilization. By the end of 1916 over 14 million men had been mobilized in the empire. The heaviest burden fell on the peasantry: almost half of the male rural labour force had been called up by the end of 1916, and the census of 1917 revealed that in most of the Russian provinces anything from one-third to two-thirds of the peasant households had lost their male workers. The demands of war drastically reduced the number of draft animals on the land; most plants responsible for producing agricultural machinery were turned over to war production, while those that were left were last in line for fuel and metal supplies. Urban workers were hit by mobilization to a much lesser extent; those working directly for the war effort were generally exempt from military service, and in trades where skills and demands for their product were at a premium, workers used the strike weapon to push up wages. Wartime inflation, however, tended increasingly to cancel out wage increases. In October 1916 the Petrograd Security Police reported that 'While the wages of the masses have risen 50 per cent, and only in certain categories 100 to 200 per cent (metal workers, machinists, electricians), the prices on all products have increased 100 to 500 per cent.' The report went on to give data based on one plant to demonstrate how wages were affected by wartime inflation (see Table 11–13.1). Table 11–13.2 gives some idea of the impact of wartime inflation on the increasing wages of one group of skilled Moscow workers. Table 11–13.3 shows the impact of inflation on an average worker's daily food basket.

Table 11–13.1   *Cost of different items in Petrograd*

Item	Cost (pre-war)	Cost (October 1916)
Rent for a corner	2 to 3 rubles monthly	8 to 12 rubles
Dinner (in a tearoom)	15 to 20 kopeks	1 ruble to 1 ruble 20 kopeks (at the same place)
Tea (in a tearoom)	7 kopeks	35 kopeks
Boots	5 to 6 rubles	20 to 30 rubles
Skirt	75 to 90 kopeks	2 rubles 50 kopeks to 3 rubles

Source: George Vernadsky *et al.* (eds) *A Source Book for Russian History from Early Times to 1917*, 1972, vol. 3, p. 868.

Table 11–13.2   *Moscow machine-worker's annual wages, 1913–17*

Year	Annual wage (in rubles)	Annual wage (at 1913 money rate)
1913	469	469
1916	1062	516
1917	2382	308

Source: based on Diane Koenker, 'Moscow workers in 1917', 1976, pp.123–4.

Table 11–13.3   *Cost of a Moscow worker's daily food basket[1]*

Year	Daily cost (kopeks)	Change (1913 = 100)
1913	24.23	100
1914	26.53	109
1915	31.70	131
1916	49.47	204
1917 (January)	87.51	361

[1] This is based on the experience of textile workers; it does not take account of the change of eating habits brought about by shortages and the increasing prices of meat and potatoes.

Source: Koenker, 'Moscow workers in 1917', p.125.

Wartime production demands led to an overall increase in the number of factory workers in the big cities: there were 242,600 workers in Petrograd in 1914 and 391,800 in 1917; in Moscow, during the same period, the factory labour force increased from 153,223 to 205,919. The Tzarist government took extensive powers against organized labour and strike activity, yet after a brief respite during the first five months of the war the number of strikes began to rise inexorably (see Table 11–13.4). The authorities were inclined to see political agitators at the back of every strike; in fact it is difficult to assess the role of union activists and political agitators. The giant Putilov Works in Petrograd had 20,000 workers, but only 150 of them were Bolsheviks in February 1917. Agitators and activists did begin receiving German financial support in March 1915, though it is unlikely that many knew where the money was actually coming from, least of all the strikers in Petrograd and in the Nikolayev naval yard, whose strike pay in January 1916 came from this source.

Russian military losses were enormous. While the statistics are unreliable because of the haphazard way in which they were collected, it seems generally accepted that by the end of October 1916 the Russian army had lost between 1.6

Table 11–13.4   *Strikes, 1905–17[1]*

Year	Strikes	Strikers (in 000s)	Political strikers
1905	13,995	2,863	6,024
1906	6,114	1,108	2,950
1907	3,573	740	2,558
1908	892	176	464
1909	340	64	50
1910	222	47	8
1911	466	105	24
1912	2,032	725	1,300
1913	2,404	887	1,034
1914 (total)	3,535	1,337	2,401
1914 (Aug.–Dec.)	68	35	—
1915	928	540	213
1916	1,284	952	243
1917 (Jan.–Feb.)	1,330	676	—

[1] Based on the reports of the Factory Inspectorate, which by 1917 supervised 12,392 institutions employing two million workers, respectively 40 per cent of factories and 70 per cent of factory workers.

and 1.8 million killed, with another two million as prisoners of war and over one million more 'missing'. Early in 1916 there had been reports of troops fraternizing with the enemy. General Brusilov briefly improved discipline and morale, and his summer offensive met with early success, but some troops disappeared from the front and there were occasional mutinies. The military postal censors reported that letters from the home front were increasingly expressing the desire for peace and that they were having a depressive effect on the troops; the soldiers' letters home were full of complaints. Yet while senior officers at the front expressed alarm about morale and about replacements (some of whom were political exiles or exiled strikers) they also spoke of 'excellent' discipline. In part this may have been bravado and a reluctance to admit discipline problems; nevertheless it must be remembered that the crucial breakdown of military discipline occurred not at the front but in Petrograd.

The precise number of troops in the Petrograd garrison early in 1917 is unclear; there appear to have been between 322,000 and 466,800 men in the city and its vicinity. After the police (3,500 men) and the Cossacks (3,200 cavalry) they constituted the third line of defence in case of disorder. The morale of the troops in Petrograd was particularly low. They were bored with barrack life and highly resentful of their officers – at least at the front, junior officers shared the privations of their men. A large number of the soldiers in Petrograd were in their forties; younger men were the first choice for the front. There were also men recuperating from wounds or sickness, as well as strikers mobilized as a punishment. When the strikes and food riots began, some troops obeyed orders and acted against the crowds; others, even the usually loyal Cossacks, began to fraternize. Then, on 11 March (26 February 'old style') fraternization turned into a full-scale mutiny as one unit and then another killed their officers and began exchanging fire with those troops who remained loyal.

In addition to soldiers there were large numbers of sailors in the immediate vicinity of Petrograd. The city itself is at the eastern end of the Gulf of Finland, which juts off the Baltic Sea. Some fifteen miles west of Petrograd, in the Gulf, lies Kottin Island with the town of Kronstadt at its eastern tip. Kronstadt was the headquarters of the Russian Baltic Fleet (see Map 4 in the *Maps Booklet*). There had been spasmodic fighting between warships in the Baltic, but much of the time the Russian sailors were idle, cooped up below decks on their ships or else idle in barracks. Naval officers enforced a harsh and brutal discipline on their men. The sailors, while conscripts, were generally from a different social background to the largely peasant soldiers. One of their number recalled:

> The Kronstadt sailors were a politically advanced element. The point is that the very conditions of service in the Navy call for persons who possess special technical training, that is they require skilled workers. Every sailor is, in the first place, a specialist: a minelayer, an electrician, a gunner, an engineer, and so on. Every special trade presupposes a certain body of knowledge and a certain technical training obtained through practice. Consequently, those accepted into the Navy were in the main workers who had passed through a trade school and had by practical experience mastered some special skill. The Navy was particularly keen to take in fitters, electricians, engineers, mechanics, blacksmiths, and so on.
> (Quoted in F. F. Raskolnikov, *Kronstadt and Petrograd in 1917*, 1982, p.36)

The sailors of Kronstadt were not important in the initial trouble in Petrograd, but they seized the opportunity offered by the army mutinies in the city to execute unpopular officers (including the two principal admirals) and to imprison many more. Later on they were to play a significant role in the revolutionary events.

Against the advice of many advisers who feared that military disaster which could be attributed to the Tzar would compromise the monarchy, Nicholas II had taken personal command of the army in 1915. In March 1917, while at his military headquarters, he received regular reports on the situation in Petrograd from police and garrison commanders. He ordered them to suppress the disorder. On 11 March the chairman of the *Duma*, Mikhail V. Rodzianko, telegraphed the Tzar urging him of the necessity 'that some person enjoying the confidence of the country be entrusted immediately with the formation of a new government.' Nicholas suspended the *Duma*. This, together with the trouble on the streets, prompted the *Duma* into action. It refused to disperse and, following a popular invasion of the Tauride Palace where the *Duma* met, the party leaders decided to establish themselves as a provisional committee. On 14 March (1 March 'old style') the committee nominated a Provisional Government; the following day the Tzar abdicated.

Exercise   Document II.20 in *Documents 1* is the proclamation issued by a committee of the *Duma* announcing the formation of the Provisional Government. Read it now and answer the following questions:

1   Is the opening paragraph a fair reflection of events?

2   What kinds of reforms are promised in the document?

3   What promises are made about the war and the economic difficulties? ∎

Specimen answers   1   The implication here is that the *Duma* was the prime mover in the events which brought down the old regime – hardly a fair representation of what had happened.

2   Essentially the document promises liberal constitutional reforms.

3   There is no mention of either the war or the economic difficulties of the country. ☐

Exercise   Document II.21 in *Documents 1* is 'Order No 1' issued by the Petrograd Soviet of Workers' and Soldiers' Deputies on the same day that the *Duma* announced the Provisional Government. Read it now and answer the following questions:

1   What is created by this document?

2   Does the document suggest any potential for friction between the Petrograd Soviet and the *Duma*? ■

Specimen answers   1   Committees of elected representatives of the lower military ranks who, in turn, are to send representatives to the Soviet.

2   In some instances Order No 1 appears to be authorizing some of the same things as the Proclamation of the Provisional Government (see in particular principle 8 of the latter and resolutions 6 and 7 of the former). But, obviously, two organizations, even if in agreement on some things, have the potential for friction; and resolution 4 of Order No 1 states clearly that the Soviet will not adhere to orders with which it disagrees. □

The existence of the Petrograd Soviet and the Provisional Government responsible to the *Duma* created the problem of what was subsequently referred to as 'dual power'. Initially the Soviet was not as suspicious of, or hostile towards, the *Duma* and the Provisional Government as these latter were of the Soviet. The Soviet was predominantly Menshevik with a sprinkling of Socialist Revolutionaries (if you are unsure of, or have forgotten, the different political groupings on the Russian Left see Roberts pp.194–5). The Mensheviks wanted to use their influence in the Soviet to keep the Provisional Government from veering off on the path of old regime reaction; under Lenin the Bolsheviks were later to use their growing influence in the Soviet to undermine the Provisional Government. Other towns and cities followed up the example of Petrograd and established soviets of their own; seventy-seven were in communication with Petrograd within a month of the March uprising; in addition there were other elected committees in factories and in the army. Order No 1 was significant in inspiring those in the army. Most of these other soviets had, initially, Menshevik majorities; generally speaking, however, they sought to establish local coalition governments drawn from all parties and clauses.

The weeks following the Tzar's abdication were a period of tremendous hope and excitement. Peasants, workers and soldiers meeting in different committees and soviets passed resolutions outlining their aspirations under the new order. These broad aspirations are shown in Tables 11–13.5 to 11–13.7.

Exercise   Study the demands outlined in Tables 11–13.5, 11–13.6 and 11–13.7.

1   Are the most common demands of workers and peasants economic or political?

2   What do these demands suggest in general about attitudes towards:
(a)   the old order;
(b)   the war?

3   While there are no percentages given for the soldiers' demands, what seem to be the similarities, and what seem to be the differences between them and the workers and peasants? ■

Table 11–13.5   *The aspirations of the working class: table of statistics (based on 100 motions voted in March 1917)*[1]

General policy		Percentage of motions in support of policy
A	Measures against the Tzar	2
B	Measures against the old administration	3
C	Formation of a democratic republic	14
D	Universal suffrage	5
E	Confidence in government	3
F	Distrust of government	11
G	Decentralization	0
H	Hasten meeting of Constituent Assembly	12
I	Free education	3
J	Graduated tax	0
K	Defence proclamations	3
L	In favour of peace without annexations or revolutionary contributions	3
M	Elimination of professional army	1
Problems pertaining to the workers		
N	Eight-hour day	51
O	No overtime (7 times formally, 7 times with the addition 'unless better paid')	14
P	Guaranteed wages and social security	11
Q	Pay rise	18
R	Hiring question	7
S	Foreman and choice of foremen	2
T	Sanitary conditions	15
U	Factory committee role	12
V	Worker administration	4
W	International slogans	7
X	Land for the peasants	9
Y	To learn to wait for pay rises and various advantages, to be patient	1

[1] These first hundred motions are valid for the period March 3 to March 28. They concern factory workers. The regional breakdown is as follows: Petrograd 40 per cent, Moscow 25 per cent, other cities 35 per cent.

Source: Marc Ferro, *The Russian Revolution of February 1917*, 1972, p.115.

Table 11–13.6 *The aspirations of the peasantry: table of statistics*[1]

General policies		Percentage of motions in support of policy
A	Measures against the Tzar	4
B	Measures against the old administration	16
C	Formation of a democratic republic	24
D	Universal suffrage	9
E	Confidence in government	10 (7 in March)
F	Distrust of government	10 (in April)
G	Decentralization	12
H	Hasten meeting of the Constituent [Assembly]	17
I	Free public education	10
J	Graduated income tax and no other	6
K	Defence proclamation	4
L	In favour of a quick, just peace	23
M	Abolition of professional army	3
N	Measures of safeguards against large landowners	11

Agricultural questions		
O	Lowering of land rents	17
P	Forbidding of sale of land until [discussion in] Constituent	13
Q	No squatting	4
R	The Constituent will settle the questions of lands and agrarian questions	15
S	Seizure of state lands, crown lands (fiefs)	20
T	Seizure of state lands, crown lands, and large estates	31
U	Seizure of land without compensation	15
V	Abolition of private property	7
W	Socialization of land, nationalization	12
X	Give land back to the *obschchina*	2
Y	The land to those who work it, in accordance with their strength (no pay)	18
Z	Egalitarian status (norm)	8
AA	Administration and distribution of the lands by the municipalities, soviets, etc.	15

[1] This table has been compiled from the first one hundred resolutions found among the three hundred documents assembled by the Soviet historians on the agrarian question for the months of March and April. This sample is as good as any other, since there is a correlation between the selection made here and the breakdown of the agrarian troubles between February and October. It should be noted that in the gathering of documents there is an overrepresentation of the Moscow and Valdimir regions (near Moscow) which is due to the greater development of historical research in the capital. Aside from this distortion, the governments of Tula (9 resolutions), Ryazan (6 resolutions), Kaluga, Pskov and Smolensk are represented in this table by five or more resolutions. These are the regions where the agrarian troubles were the most numerous. Half of these hundred resolutions bear on the regions which saw the most intense agrarian troubles. The rest bear on the most diversified provinces – thirty-three governments are represented out of about fifty for European Russia. It can be estimated that this sample gives an indication of the aspirations of the Russian peasantry.

Source: Ferro, *The Russian Revolution of February 1917*, pp.124–5.

Table 11–13.7   *The aspirations of the soldiers*

1   A soldiers' organization to fight attempts to restore the old régime.

2   The organization of the army in such a way that Socialists will be elected to the Constituent.

3   While maintaining an active defence, we demand that steps be taken for peace negotiations between all belligerents.

4   That soldiers' committees control the operations decided on by the general staff.

5   An immediate meeting of the Constituent Assembly, which by equal and secret vote, will immediately decide on the form of government. We will give our full support to the formation of a democratic republic.

6   Recognition of the freedom of assembly, press, and speech, of the right to form unions and to strike; the extension of political rights to the armed forces.

7   The end of discrimination on account of religion or nationality.

8   Formation of militia, with elected commanders, for the maintenance of local governments.

9   Election of local authorities.

10 Graduated income tax.

11 Separation of Church and State.

12 Confiscation of lands from owners, the State, the Church, etc.; the land to belong to those who work it.

13 The eight-hour day.

14 Social security for workers, providing for old age, disability, sickness, pregnancy.

15 Pension for disabled war veterans.

16 Compulsory education to sixteen years of age.

17 Formation of a League of Nations for Disarmament.

18 The Petrograd Soviet, Defender of the People, will be defended with all our might.

Source: Ferro, *The Russian Revolution of February 1917*, p.134.

Specimen answers   1   The most common demands are economic rather than political: 51 per cent of the workers' motions included demands for the eight-hour day; 50 per cent of the peasants' motions included demands for the seizure of land.

2   (a) There were few demands for action against the Tzar and the old administration; the peasants were much keener on the latter than the workers. (b) The war, too, was not central to the aspirations of the workers but, possibly because of the impact of the war in rural areas, between one-fifth and one-quarter of the peasant resolutions called for a speedy but just peace.

3   As might be expected, the soldiers' demands reflect those of the workers and peasants – the confiscation of land, the eight-hour day, a Constituent Assembly. There are demands for peace negotiation between all belligerents, but not the demands for an immediate peace. Some of the soldiers' resolutions were much broader than those on the home front – a League of Nations for Disarmament, compulsory education to the age of 16; others, like war pensions and soldiers' committees, related directly to their current experience. □

Discussion   It is worth emphasizing here that immediately after the February Revolution the troops were not calling for peace at any price. It seems that the troops at the front believed they should continue fighting for the honour of Russia and their revolution; if fighting the Germans was to be considered as a mark of patriotism, they did not want their officers to have a monopoly on patriotism. Bolshevik militants who urged a stand for peace in front-line soldiers' meetings found the troops reluctant to embrace the idea. When they were engaged in combat in the spring and summer of 1917, most Russian troops continued to fight in a courageous and disciplined manner. The troops who did participate in calls for peace appear, most commonly, to have been those in reserve regiments and especially those billeted in large cities.

Exercise   Remembering the ethnic diversity of the Russian Empire discussed in Book I, Unit 3, what other aspirations do you suppose could have been encouraged by the fall of the old order? ■

Specimen answer   National aspirations among the minority peoples. The fall of the Tzar fostered the hopes of the Finns for a restoration of their autonomy. Poles demanded autonomy, as well as a separate Polish army serving within the Russian army. (Similar demands for their own national army were later taken up by other ethnic groups.) The situation with regard to Poland was complicated by the fact that Russian Poland was occupied by German and Austro-Hungarian troops, which had recognized Polish independence in November 1916. Demands for autonomy were also heard from other Baltic peoples in the provinces of Estonia, Latvia and Lithuania. In Kiev, Ukrainian nationalists formed a Central Ukrainian Council, the *Rada*, and called for autonomy. The Cossacks had special privileges in return for the obligation of all men to serve in the army for twenty years from the age of 18. The Cossack village held its land in common and the villages were run by elected assemblies. Cossack landholdings were larger than those of ordinary peasants in the empire; during the summer of 1917 many Cossacks were concerned that the peasants would seize their land while they were away serving in the army – Cossack units were less prone to the general disintegration, being more cohesive and having fewer grievances. In September 1917 a Cossack *Rada* was formed. Russian Jews tended to act rather differently from other ethnic groups. The end of the old order promised an end to discrimination and periodic pogroms. While extreme Zionists campaigned eagerly for a Jewish homeland in Palestine, many more Russian Jews discarded their separate identity and sought to merge with the mass of new Russian citizens. □

The Provisional Government was worried by the demands of minority peoples, but it made some concessions: Finnish autonomy was restored; Polish independence was recognized in principle; the use of national languages was permitted, and some of the restrictions imposed by the Tzarist regime were lifted. A series of other reforms was introduced, many of which were promised in the Provisional Government's manifesto – freedom of the press, of worship and of association; local militias to replace Tzarist police; the abolition of the death penalty; the disestablishment of the Church; and the independence of the judiciary. But problems mounted. The overthrow of the old regime did not suddenly change the unfavourable war situation. The Provisional Government was determined to continue the war, partly to win international recognition (Britain and France had recognized the government providing Russia remained their ally), and partly in the hope that the war would unify people behind the new regime (Miliukov, now foreign minister, was a historian, and both he and others looked back to the way in which the French people appeared to have been united during the French revolutionary wars). Perhaps most important to the Provisional Government, however, was the way they perceived Russia as a liberal democracy, in league with other liberal democracies against reactionary monarchies.

If the fall of the old order did not immediately change the situation on the battle fronts, nor did it immediately achieve the aspirations of workers and peasants. Both groups began taking action on their own behalf. In 47 out of 73 Moscow factories for which we have information, the workers implemented the eight-hour day themselves; only afterwards did the city's soviet order all Moscow enterprises to institute the eight-hour day with no reduction in salary and overtime for extra hours, and pass a resolution calling on the Provisional Government to legislate nationally. In the countryside the peasants began seizing land, sometimes clashing with the new militia as they did so. As the internal disorder increased, so the army began to melt away. Initially it seems to have been the troops furthest from the front who deserted, but as troops at the front became infected with radical propaganda, as they heard of land seizures (and they wanted their 'share'), as negotiations for peace failed to materialize, and as fears increased that many officers wanted to reimpose the old system of discipline, so the front-line soldiers also began to go home. In February there were reported to be about 1,700 desertions a week; this rose to 8,600 in May and 12,000 in July. Deserters, soldiers on leave, and delegates from soldiers' committees were alleged to be radicalizing the peasantry and were commonly identified as being involved in peasant action; but it was also known for peasants to turn on deserters whom they did not know and send them back to the front or kill them. Separate localities began following policies which most appealed to those running them; they had little idea of what was going on in Petrograd, while the Provisional Government had little idea of, and virtually no control over, events in the provinces.

It was in this increasing anarchy that Lenin, returning from exile in April 1917, introduced his slogan 'All power to the soviets'. As noted above, the Bolsheviks were not a majority in the soviets, but Lenin saw these bodies as instruments with which to undermine the Provisional Government and within which he could develop a power base. He was the only political leader to oppose the new regime, and this brought him and his party increasing popularity as the Provisional Government was regarded with mounting frustration and suspicion for its inability to alleviate continuing shortages and inflation. Furthermore, the government repeatedly postponed the election which would have given the new regime some semblance of legitimacy. These postponements were partly due to the difficulty of compiling the necessary electoral registers and organizing elections in wartime; but it is also probable that the ministers, aware of their diminishing standing in the country, feared defeat. Twice the Provisional Government reconstituted itself, the first time in May, the second time in August. On each occasion there was a shift to the left, but insufficient to satisfy the militants like the Kronstadt sailors, who took to the streets of Petrograd in July; yet such shifts were too far for others, like General Kornilov, the new supreme commander, who attempted an abortive coup in August.

The 'revolution' of October/November was not the end of violence and upheaval in Russia; nor, arguably, was it the end of the process of political revolution. But before moving on to post-1917 events I want you to think again about the interrelationship of war and revolution. Some soviet historians maintain that the revolution would have occurred even without the war, since the conflict of classes made it inevitable. Indeed, they have argued that the war actually retarded the revolution by bringing about an initial degree of false national solidarity. The strike figures in Table 11–13.4 might be said to support their argument, though a Bolshevik call for a general strike in the summer of 1914 (and before the war) met with very little support outside Petrograd. In other quarters it has been argued that the revolution was the result of structural problems within the old regime (particularly the repressive, reactionary nature of the autocracy) which were exacerbated by the war; this view was popular among both Soviet and Western historians during the inter-war years. However, since World War II some Western historians, including Alexander Gerschenkron (whose theories concerning economic backwardness were discussed in Book I, Unit 3), have asserted that the reforms following the revolution of 1905 promised, albeit gradually and haltingly, to put Russia on the road to political and social stability. Stolypin's economic reforms, moreover, seem to have started the process of modernizing the economy. In the opinion of these historians it was the war which brought about revolution by imposing intolerable strain on government and people.

3 RUSSIA: PEACE, CIVIL WAR AND INTERVENTION

(You will probably find it helpful to refer to Map 4 in your *Maps Booklet* while studying this section.)

Exercise   Read Roberts, pp.305–8 and 426–8; then study Map 5 on p.602 of Roberts and answer the following questions:

1   Why did the Russians agree to the Treaty of Brest-Litovsk?

2   What were the results of the treaty? ■

Specimen answers   1   While opinion, even among the Bolsheviks, was divided over signing the treaty when it was initially drafted, once the Germans resumed their offensive the Russians had very little choice but to agree.

2   Russia lost vast tracts of territory by the treaty, principally lands in which there were ethnic groups calling for independence. By accentuating some of the divisions between the Bolsheviks and others, the treaty also accelerated civil war. □

Hopes that the peace treaty would offer the chance of some internal stability were quickly dashed. During the four years following Brest-Litovsk, foreign powers intervened in Russia's affairs, while civil war aggravated economic problems which, in turn, provoked still more unrest.

The initial intervention was made by German and Austro-Hungarian troops. After forcing the issue of the peace treaty the Germans occupied the Ukraine briefly, and a small Austrian force established itself in Odessa. The Germans were also active in the Baltic, notably driving Red troops from Helsinki and thus assisting in the creation of a liberal, democratic Finnish state. Article 12 of the armistice signed between Germany and the Allies towards the end of 1918 revealed the latter's fears of Bolshevism and insisted that German troops maintain their presence in the Baltic. In fact the German army entrusted with this task melted away much as Russian troops had melted away from the fronts in 1917, but this was not the end of German involvement. Early in 1919 the largest of the *Freikorps* units – the Baltic *Landeswehr* and the Iron Division – marched into the Baltic lands to 'defend the Fatherland from Russian Bolshevism'. They also had plans for German *Lebensraum* (living space), with the promise of land and Latvian citizenship being held out to the *Freikorps* volunteers. Eventually, their supply lines were cut by a Franco-British naval squadron and they were defeated by combined Latvian and Estonian armies.

British, French, United States and Japanese troops were also deployed at different extremities of Russia during 1918 and 1919. Fearful of a German and Turkish push on the oilfields around Baku as the Russian armies dissolved, small British units were ordered into Transcaspia. The first of these, 'Dunsterforce', was dispatched in January 1918, with a larger contingent stationed in the region from August 1918 to April 1919. A few British troops were landed at Murmansk in March 1918; these were not unwelcome to the Bolsheviks, who were then concerned about a German advance. In August many more troops from Britain and other Allied powers began disembarking at Archangel and Vladivostok. Most of the Allied intervention in Russian affairs, however, was in sending military equipment and supplies; initially, it was maintained that the supplies were for those troops continuing the war against the Germans, although, as time went on, the supplies were clearly meant for those fighting the Bolsheviks. Only towards the end of their stay were the Allied troops themselves fully committed to action against the Bolsheviks. Most of the intervention forces were withdrawn in September and October 1919; only the Japanese continued to keep troops in Siberia until 1922.

The White armies did not call for a return of the Tzar. They claimed to want a restoration of military discipline but, above all, an end to both the Bolshevik regime and the anarchy which was sweeping through Russia. As something of an afterthought their leaders also spoke of reconvening the Constituent Assembly so that the people could decide on their form of government. A large White army was originally established in the Don region towards the end of 1917; it later named itself the Armed Forces of South Russia. The Don was a Cossack region: some Cossacks joined the army; others were wary, not wishing to bring Bolshevik troops into their lands to fight the Whites; other Cossacks, accepting a Bolshevik promise that their lands were now safe in their own hands, were Red. A second, large White army was organized in central Russia; towards the end of 1918 it was put under the command of Admiral Kolchak with its headquarters in Omsk. The civil war ebbed and flowed, but 1919 was the high point for the Whites: Kolchak's forces moved west in the spring, meeting with early successes; later in the year General Deniken, in command of the southern army, advanced on Moscow, while a third White army, under General Yudenich, pushed along the Baltic coast into the outskirts of Petrograd. But the Whites were weakened by their failure to win peasant support. The peasants seem to have seen little difference between the Reds and the Whites: both factions wanted the peasants' young men for their armies; both requisitioned their produce – and Deniken's army developed an appalling reputation for its corruption and anti-semitism. If anything, the peasants seem marginally to have preferred the Bolsheviks, who were, after all, clearly opposed to the old order, and had sanctioned land seizure by the peasants. Nor were the Whites prepared to make any promises to insurgent nationalities about the future; this was one reason why Estonians and Finns did not help

Yudenich in his drive on Petrograd. Although all of the White advances were driven back in 1919, it was not until the defeat of General Wrangel (who replaced Deniken in the south) in the Caucasus and the Crimea towards the end of 1920 that the civil war was effectively over.

If Estonians and Finns felt that it was against their interests to embroil themselves in conflict with the Bolsheviks, this was not the case with every national army. The Czech Legion was the inspiration of Thomas Masaryk, a former philosophy professor at the University of Prague who had become a leading spokesman for the Bohemian people before the war. Masaryk believed that an army recruited from Czechs and Slovaks and fighting beside the Allies was a means of securing Czech nationhood. The first legionnaires were recruited from Czechs and Slovaks living outside the Austro-Hungarian Empire, or from deserters (especially on the Italian front) who had no desire to fight for a German victory. In the summer of 1917 the Russian Provisional Government agreed to the formation of a legion from among Czech and Slovak prisoners of war. Following the events of November and the opening of peace talks with the Germans, it became clear that the Russian Czech Legion was not going to be able to fight on the eastern front. In February 1918 agreement was reached with the Bolsheviks for the Legion to travel by train to Vladivostok, where it would embark for Europe and the western front; by now the Legion was technically a part of the French army. Clashes with local Bolsheviks as the Czechs travelled east resulted in the Legion, some 30,000 strong, seizing all but one of the principal towns and cities along 2,500 miles of the Trans-Siberian Railway; as an additional means of ensuring their passage to France, the Czechs linked with the White armies of Kolchak. In the end the legionnaires finished their war service in Russia, continuing technically as part of the French intervention force.

A few months after the last Czechs left Vladivostok bound for their new nation state, the armies of another nation state created (or rather, in this instance, recreated) by the Treaty of Versailles marched across Russia's western border. Josef Pilsudski, leader of the new Poland, dreamed of restoring the vast Greater Poland of the eighteenth century. In June 1919 Pilsudski's army occupied Kiev, the capital of the Ukraine. A Red army counter-attack pushed the Poles to within fifteen miles of Warsaw. For Bolshevik leaders the speed and success of their advance seemed to presage the success of a world-wide communist advance; similar thoughts crossed the minds of the British and French governments. Inspired and guided by the French General Weygand, the Poles counter-attacked in their turn and drove the Russians back across their frontiers, seizing a chunk of Lithuania while they were about it. The ensuing peace also secured the Polish frontier much further to the east than originally planned.

Baltic peoples, Czechs and Poles all ended World War I with their own nation states. But not all of the ethnic minorities who became involved against the Bolsheviks were as successful. The army of the Ukrainian *Rada* is an obvious example; it was fairly rapidly overwhelmed by the forces of the Bolsheviks, yet this did not prevent the Ukraine from becoming a battleground throughout the period 1918 to 1920. Deniken and Wrangel fought the Bolsheviks there, as did the Poles of Pilsudski; and the partisan army of Nestor Ivanovich Makhno fought them all. Makhno was a peasant born in the Ukraine; imprisoned for his anarchist associations by the Tzarist regime in 1908, he was released by the revolutionary crowds in Moscow in March 1917. The Makhnovschchina were, generally speaking, peasants of the southern Ukraine whose main influence lay in a semi-circle with a 150-mile radius drawn from the northern shore of the Sea of Azov. They had seized the land when the opportunity presented itself in 1917. They were opposed to the idea of the state, and suspicious of towns and cities. They envisaged a society of self-governing, largely self-sufficient communes. 'Every commune', recalled Makhno,

> comprised ten families of peasants and workers, i.e. a total of 100, 200 or 300 members. By decision of the regional Congress of agrarian communes every commune received a normal amount of land, i.e. as much as its members could cultivate, situated in the immediate vicinity of the commune and composed of land formerly belonging to the *pomeschiki* [aristocrats and landowning gentry]. They also received cattle and farm-equipment from these former estates. (quoted in E. J. Hobsbawm, *Primitive Rebels*, 1971, p.184)

Makhno was an extremely capable guerilla commander who first led his men against the forces of the Ukrainian *Rada*, then against German and Austro-Hungarian occupation units. The Makhnovschchina were prepared to ally with the Bolsheviks against the Whites, but there was little common ground between them. The Bolsheviks labelled the Makhnovschchina as 'bandits', a charge in which there was probably an element of truth. Makhnovist theorists (and these were very few in number) condemned the Bolsheviks for subordinating everything to the state:

> The State is everything, the individual worker – nothing. This is the main precept of Bolshevism. For the State is personified by functionaries, and in fact it is they who are everything; the working class is nothing. (Peter Arshinov, *History of the Makhnovist Movement (1918–1921)*, 1974, p.70)

The Makhnovschchina were finally beaten by the Reds in 1921, and Makhno himself was forced into exile.

Other peasants also rose against the Bolsheviks. In the central province of Tambov, some 50,000 insurgents led by A. S. Antonov were active during 1920 and 1921. Like Makhno, Antonov proved to be a very capable partisan leader. He was a former SR, a member of the Social Revolutionary party which had developed a large following among the peasantry. But it was less political ideology, and more hostility to the excesses of war communism, that prompted the insurrection in Tambov.

The Bolsheviks' ultimate military success in the civil war was achieved by the new Red Army. During 1917 the Bolsheviks had relied on their cadres within the old army and navy and on Red Guards for their military shock troops. The Red Guards were not affiliated to the Bolsheviks; they were militias generally organized at individual factories. As might be expected, the Guards were overwhelmingly young working-class men and, like most of Russia's urban workers, a high proportion of them (perhaps just over half) had been born in rural districts. Along with much of the urban working class, the Red Guards were Bolshevized between March and November, but the Bolsheviks still preferred to rely on cadres within the existing armed forces, and notably on the Kronstadt sailors, in the crucial events of November. When the Germans renewed their offensive in January 1918, some hoped to see the Red Guard extended and transformed into a new proletarian army; the general staff of the Petrograd Red Guard, for example, had a plan which would have authorized the committees in each factory to mobilize 20 per cent of their workforce, thus producing 80,000 fighting men.

> Of this, 12.5 per cent or 10,000 men must be on active service for a whole week, after which they will return to the factory as a reserve. In this way, in two months, the 80,000 men will have carried out their service.
>
> The 10,000 Red Guards on active service will be split into two parts: one half (5,000) for defence of the town, which will pay the Guards; the other will be the factory reserve, the Red Guards receiving their pay from factory managements or the government. (Quoted in Marc Ferro, *October 1917*, 1980, p.283)

The Bolsheviks did not follow up such proposals and sought to halt the German advance with volunteers. But volunteers proved to be insufficient to stop the Germans; then, as the civil war developed, there was an even greater need for men. In the early summer of 1918, universal, compulsory military service was introduced and social groups and professions such as former lawyers (the Bolsheviks had abolished the bar), priests, monks and bourgeois (i.e. non-Communist) journalists, were no longer exempt. At the same time strict military discipline was re-introduced and the election of officers, which had begun in March 1917 and had been legally sanctioned the following December, was abolished. More than two-thirds of the officers in this new army were former Tzarist officers. Trotsky, the People's Commissar for War, reasoned thus to Lenin:

> Many of them commit acts of treachery. But on the railways, too, instances of sabotage are in evidence in the routing of troop trains. Yet nobody suggests replacing railway engineers by Communists . . . It is essential to make the entire military hierarchy more compact and get rid of the ballast by extracting those general staff officers that are efficient and loyal to use and not on any account by replacing them by party ignoramuses. (Quoted in John Ellis, *Armies in Revolution*, 1973, p.192)

These military 'experts' from the old army were supervised, however, by political commissars in the individual armies on the different fronts. Also, military party members were shifted when and where possible to weak areas, since it appeared that the presence of committed Communists in a unit considerably improved effectiveness in combat (though the best troops were not always card-carrying Bolsheviks – the 40,000 sailors who provided Trotsky with some of his finest shock troops were unquestionably revolutionary militants, but not necessarily Bolsheviks). At the beginning of 1919 the Red Army numbered just under 400,000; by the close of the following year it had reached more than three million and it was still growing.

An army of such size needed feeding, and so too did the urban workers. A blockade imposed by the capitalist powers, together with their military intervention, shut off the possibility of purchasing food abroad. These problems coalesced with Bolshevik ideology to produce the system known as 'war communism'. The centralized Bolshevik state nationalized major industry and sought to control both production and distribution. The intention was that the peasants would supply the towns and cities in return for industrial products. However, the shortage of raw materials and fuel meant that very little was produced in the factories; furthermore there were major problems of organizing distribution in a country as vast as Russia when the men responsible had little experience and when war and civil war had disrupted, and continued to disrupt and destroy, the transport system (see Table 11–13.8). The peasants understandably had little desire to part with produce for nothing. They began sowing fewer crops and reverting to subsistence agriculture; in 1920 the sown acreage of Russia was three-fifths of what it had been in 1913. The Red Army began requisitioning to feed itself; the *Cheka* began requisitioning to feed the towns and cities. This, together with conscription, provoked many of the peasant risings. The Tambov insurgents sang:

> Oh, sorrow, oh, sorrow, the soldier tortures the peasant and still takes, oh, sorrow, three poods [a pood is thirty-six pounds] for each eater.

They also sang:

> Deserter I was born, deserter I shall die. Shoot me on the spot; I don't go into the Red Army. To us came a commissar and two Red Army soldiers. All the same we won't go. Don't hope for us. (Both quotations from W. H. Chamberlain, *The Russian Revolution*, 1965, vol. 2, p. 438)

Table 11–13.8 *Russian railways, 1917–19*

Date	No. of locomotives	Percent fit for use	No. of freight wagons	Percent fit for use
Jan. 1917	20,394	83.5	537,328	95.8
Dec. 1918	8,955	52.2		
Dec. 1919			244,443	83.4

Source: based on Chamberlain, *The Russian Revolution*, vol. 2, p.108.

Table 11–13.9 *Paper rubles in circulation, 1914–21*

Date	No. of paper rubles
1 July 1914	1,630,400,000
1 March 1917	10,044,000,000
1 Nov. 1917	19,477,900,000
1 Jan. 1918	27,650,000,000
1 Jan. 1919	61,326,000,000
1 Jan. 1920	225,015,000,000
1 Jan. 1921	1,168,596,000,000

Source: based on Chamberlain, *The Russian Revolution*, vol. 2, p. 103.

The economic problems of 1918 to 1921 aggravated the inflation created during the war; both the Tzarist and the Provisional Government had sought, in part, to finance the war by printing money (see Table 11–13.9). Moreover, as the number of paper rubles grew, there was a decline in the value of gold rubles; the gold ruble of January 1921 was worth just over 5 per cent of that of January 1918. Urban workers were paid in food, clothing and shoes; but peasant recalcitrance, distribution problems and rationing reduced thousands to the brink of starvation. The population of the large cities of northern Russia declined by over a half between 1916 and 1920. People returned to the villages where they were born either for good or to get and take back food for their starving families in the cities. In the latter case they ran the risk of being branded as 'speculators' and losing their goods to the armed road-block detachments; these squads were regularly con-demned for arbitrariness, brutality, and for keeping the goods which they confiscated for their own use. Workers who stayed in the cities periodically absented themselves from their factories to steal or to make small household articles which could then be exchanged on the black market for food. The decline in standards of nutrition and the lack of fuel to heat homes in the bitter winters weakened people's resistance to disease; between January 1918 and January 1920 an estimated seven million died from malnutrition and epidemic.

The question might be asked: why did the urban industrial workers who had contributed so significantly to the downfall of the Tzar not rise up against the rigours of war communism? Several reasons might be advanced by way of explanation. The few benefits which workers had secured may have blunted the militancy of a few: some workers moved from their poor quarters into the homes of the well-to-do which had either been abandoned or confiscated; also, Bolshevik labour and welfare legislation, while often violated, did promise, and sometimes deliver, new benefits. Possibly the day-to-day struggle against starvation sapped the energies of many. The number of active young workers in the cities declined with mobilization for the Red Army and with the exodus into the countryside. The activity of the *Cheka* probably reduced the potential anti-Bolshevik shop-floor leadership; certainly many Mensheviks and SRs were arrested. However, it would be wrong to assume that the urban workers remained quiescent. While evidence is fragmentary, there were strikes in 1918, rather fewer in 1919 and 1920, but an upsurge in the winter of 1920 to 1921 when the civil war was over; the capitalist states' blockade ended but conditions did not improve; and the Red Army was not demobilized – flushed with the army's military success Trotsky was keen to employ it as forced labour in rebuilding the country. The most serious protest against the Bolsheviks came from a group of what might be called sympathetic workers early in 1921 with the Kronstadt Mutiny.

Exercise   Turn to *Documents 1* and read the declarations of the Kronstadt mutineers in documents II.22 and II.23; then answer the following questions:

1   What were the principal objects of the sailors' complaints?

2   What did the sailors want? ■

Specimen answers   1   The sailors condemned the Bolsheviks/Communist Party for being unrep-resentative and in some ways worse than the Tzarist regime. They objected to the imprisonment of other left-wingers, to war communism and the way in which the Communists were endeavouring to enforce their ideas on the Russian people.

2   They wanted a 'third revolution' to overthrow the Bolshevik/Communist dictatorship and to establish a system of free associations which truly represented peasants and workers. They wanted peasants to be able to work their own land and workers to be able to produce their own handicrafts if they so wished. □

In essence the Kronstadt sailors appear to have wanted a decentralized state with local elected soviets running society. Kronstadt itself had been run on similar lines since early 1917. The local soviet, with a mixture of Bolsheviks, anarchists, left-wing SRs and other radicals, had stood out against the Provisional Govern-ment and declared itself to be the sole power in the city. General meetings were held, almost daily, at the city's focal point, Anchor Square, which was capable of holding 25,000 or more people. During the period 1917 to 1920 local committees organized everything: there were committees to run houses, ships and factories. Neighbourhoods established agricultural communes of about fifty persons each which cultivated every piece of arable land on the island; these collective vegetable gardens helped the city through the worst of the food shortages during the civil war. While the sailors were not, as a body, anarchists, the spirit of anarchism (which we met earlier among the Makhnovschchina) was clearly present and was reflected in such slogans as 'All power to the soviets but not the parties'.

There was no widespread planning and organization behind the Kronstadt rising. In some respects the sailors chose a bad time; the strikes in Petrograd were collapsing, and since the civil war and the Russo-Polish war were over, the best units of the Red Army were available. Also, since the spring thaw had yet to come, the Reds could attack the city over the ice. Kronstadt held out for just over two weeks; the ferocious fighting resulted in probably 10,000 Red Army casualties, 1,600 Kronstadters killed and wounded, 2,500 of them taken prisoner and over 8,000 fleeing to Finland.

The rising was in full swing when the 10th Party Congress of the Bolsheviks assembled in Moscow. It would be wrong to say that the sailors' action led to the abolition of war communism; Lenin was already considering the end of food requisitioning in December 1920, together with the idea of introducing taxation in kind and allowing peasants to dispose of any surplus as they wished, once they had met their obligation to the state. Nevertheless, events at Kronstadt did focus the delegates' minds, and the Congress took the first steps in dismantling war communism and permitting the development of a mixed economy. The tax in kind and the peasants' right to dispose of their surplus were agreed; Trotsky's labour armies were disbanded, and trades unions were granted new freedoms, notably the election of officials and free debate on issues affecting their members.

4 GERMANY: WAR AND REVOLUTION

Exercise   Read Roberts, pp.287 and 298–305, concentrating on his discussion of the internal politics of wartime Germany; read also document II.24 in *Documents 1*, the *Reichstag* Resolution of 19 July 1917, and then answer the following questions:

1   How did the government of Germany change during the war?

2   What happened to the SPD during the war?

3   What is the essential demand voiced in document II.24?

Specimen answers and discussion   1   The military became dominant in government, pushing civilian politicans and even Wilhelm II even further into the background.

From Units 2 and 3 you will recall how, before the war, the military were able to bypass civilian ministers and communicate directly with the Kaiser, while the *Reichstag* had no say in the selection of ministers and virtually no influence in government. The war accentuated these traits. Contemporaries in First World War Germany began speaking of the development of a military 'dictatorship', an idea taken up by subsequent historians. The driving force behind the military assumption of government was Ludendorff. Under Ludendorff, in the last two years of war, the *Oberste Heeresleitung* (the Supreme Command) became involved in labour policy and the problems of food supply and raw materials; Ludendorff was also influential in the resignations of Bethmann Hollweg as Chancellor and

Richard von Kühlmann as foreign minister. However, in spite of Ludendorff's ability and efficiency in organizing armies in the field, his organization of the home front was not successful. In his influential analysis of the military role in internal politics Gerald Feldman concludes:

> Unlike the later totalitarian dictatorship of Hitler, whose mad imperialist adventure was preceded by a ruthless 'coordination' (*Gleichschaltung*) of German society, the dictatorship of Ludendorff was dependent upon the acquiescence of an independent labor movement and of a military and civilian bureaucracy whose traditional modes of operation were unsuitable for the conduct of a total war . . . [Also] like Bethmann Hollweg, Ludendorff tended to vacillate. (Gerald Feldman, *Army, Industry and Labor in Germany 1914–1918*, 1966, p.407)

2   The SPD split between those still prepared to support the government in the prosecution of the war and a new Independent Socialist Party, which demanded peace.

The war created new difficulties for the SPD and for the Imperial government in its relations with the SPD. Patriotic political and trade union leaders of the party were keen to develop a new relationship with the government, even to the extent of accepting a monarchical system. However, they recognized that such a policy would need explaining to the rank and file, which had been given pre-war instruction in a party line of revolution and republicanism. The government, eager for labour's support in the war, recognized the need at least to promise some concessions. A memorandum emanating from the Imperial Chancellory on 27 October 1914 noted:

> There is no doubt that the common danger has won the German workers for the nation. It offers perhaps the last opportunity to win them not only for the nation, but also for the state. The workers who return home as soldiers crowned with victory will not be disposed to follow a Social Democracy that is an enemy of the Fatherland and revolutionary. But they will remain workers. The state must seek to avoid treating the labor movement as an enemy. It must call upon the unions and avoid giving the anti-state dogmatists of the old Social Democracy slogans under which they can again lead the workers against the state. (Quoted in Feldman, *Army, Industry and Labor*, p.119)

But the promises were vague, and the SPD had to deliver something to convince its membership of the validity of its new policy. The length of the war helped the SPD and convinced the government that it must make some concessions; most notably, in 1916, there was a relaxation in trade union legislation which allowed the recruitment of workers under 18. The SPD's attempts to secure a reform of the Prussian suffrage, however, came to nothing. After the 'Peace Resolution' of 1917, the SPD were taken rather more into the government's confidence, and its leaders appear to have believed that the party was now recognized and accepted as a force of some significance in the state. The new party programme, announced in May 1918, made little reference to socialism, no reference to the collective ownership of the means of production, and could, in many ways, be described as liberal democratic.

As Roberts notes, the split in the socialists crossed the old divisions in the party. The bond which united the Independent Socialists (*Unabhängige Social-*

demokratische Partei Deutschlands – USPD) was the demand for a prompt end to the war. The USPD included Eduard Bernstein, the theorist of revisionism who might, in normal times, have been expected to go along with some improvement in relations with the government. It also included some of Bernstein's fiercest critics on the subject of revisionism, notably Karl Liebknecht and Rosa Luxemburg. Liebknecht and Luxemburg, both imprisoned during the second half of the war, were also recognized as leaders of the Spartacists. Though not a separate party during the war, on 30 December 1918 the Spartacists became the core of the new *Kommunistische Partei Deutschlands* (KPD).

3   The wording of the document is imprecise. In the resolution the *Reichstag* essentially expresses a desire for peace without forced acquisitions and without economic, financial or political oppression.

This, in spite of its woolly phrasing, is the document known as the 'Peace Resolution'. It marked the end of the *Burgfrieden* (fortress truce) which had existed since August 1914 and which had united all parties in the *Reichstag* behind the government in the prosecution of the war. While the military still spoke confidently in terms of total victory over the enemy, more and more deputies began voicing doubts about the conduct of the war, the dominance of the military, and the need for negotiated peace. □

Exercise   Read Roberts, pp.317–18 and 460–1, and then answer the following questions:

1   What events constitute the German Revolution in Roberts's account?

2   What were the causes of this revolution? ■

Specimen answers   1   Roberts's account is not really very clear about what constituted the revolution, but a succession of events in October and November 1918 brought about the collapse of the old order: the army's call for an armistice; naval mutiny; the abdication of Wilhelm II; the socialists in government; uprising in Bavaria spreading to Berlin. Then, early in 1919, there was a 'minor civil war' with a Spartacist uprising in Berlin and the destruction of the Soviet Republic in Bavaria.

2   The collapse of Germany's allies and the army announcing the need for an armistice; the beginning of cracks in morale. □

Exercise   Read document II.25 in *Documents 1*, the extract from Hans Peter Hanssen's diary. What elements does this extract suggest contributed to the Revolution? ■

Specimen answer   Starvation; dissatisfaction even in the army; hostility to the Kaiser; the inability of the police to act against at least some critics. □

The traditional view is that the German Revolution of November 1918 was brought about largely by war-weariness. During the war the German people had suffered severely from food shortages and inflation. General rationing was introduced in 1916, but the allowance of food was below subsistence level in some instances, and it was considerably below that which even some of the most unfortunate had experienced in peacetime (see Tables 11–13.10 and 11–13.11). The problems were aggravated by the fact that the stipulated ration allowances were not always available; imports from overseas were shut off by the Allied blockade, and little could be expected from Germany's own allies. The winter of 1916–17 became known as 'the turnip winter', as that root vegetable became a staple food; the cereal harvest had been poor and there were extreme difficulties of supply transport. A black market flourished and substitute (*ersatz*) foods were developed. Some of the latter were worthless in terms of nutritional value. In March 1918 a system of compulsory regulation and licensing was introduced when there were more than 11,000 such products on the market.

Table 11–13.10 Wartime rations and peacetime consumption for Germany as a whole (peacetime consumption = 100)

	July 1916 to June 1917	July 1917 to June 1918	July 1918 to December 1918
Meat	31	20	12
Fish	51	—	5
Eggs	18	13	13
Lard	14	11	7
Butter	22	21	28
Cheese	3	4	15
Rice	4	—	—
Pulses	14	1	7
Sugar	49	56–67	80
Vegetable fats	39	41	17
Potatoes	71	94	94
Flour	53	47	48

Source: Gerd Hardach, *The First World War 1914–1918*, 1977, p.119.

Table 11–13.11 Weekly diets for one adult

Hamburg poorhouse, 1900	Düsseldorf rations, January 1917	Düsseldorf rations, April 1918
potatoes 8.3lb	potatoes 3lb	potatoes 7lb
rye bread 9.6lb	'war bread'[1] 3.5lb	'war bread' 4lb
meat 600g	meat, sausage 200g	meat, sausage 200g
sausage 60g	—	—
whole milk 1,400g	whole milk 100g	whole milk 90g
skim milk 1,000g	—	canned milk 126g
flour 185g	milling product 120g	milling product 170g
		soup flour 50g
sugar 90g	sugar 200g	sugar 200g
butter 260g	butter, fats 62.5g	butter, fats 62.5g
pork lard 110g	—	—
eggs 1	—	eggs 1
cheese 60g	—	cheese 12.5g
Quark [like cream cheese] 100g	spread 60g	spread 200g
herring 350g	—	bouillon cube 1
dried fruit 280g	—	pudding powder 57g
honey 350g	—	—
rice 160g	—	—
lentils 460g	—	—
barley 80g	—	—
beer 350g	—	—
syrup 55g	—	—
cabbage 750g	vegetables?	vegetables?
Nutritional value of above		
calories 26,500	7,900	11,200
protein (g) 1,000	260	350

Source: Elizabeth H. Tobin, 'War and the working class: the case of Düsseldorf 1914–1918', 1985, pp.282 and 284.

[1] 'K-brot', K for *Krieg* (war), or *Kartoffel* (potato). The variety manufactured in Düsseldorf was 85 per cent rye flour and 15 per cent potato flour.

Before the war the peasantry had been inclined to find a variety of scapegoats for their problems – American farmers, commercial capitalists, middlemen. Management of the economy by the government during wartime, however, provided a different scapegoat. The government's management of the agricultural sector was often ill-conceived and clumsy. In October 1914, for example, it set maximum prices for bread grain but not for feed grain; when the latter rose rapidly, peasants fed their livestock on potatoes and, in consequence, potatoes virtually disappeared from the market in early 1915. Wartime controls became tougher, more rational and rather better enforced in the second half of the war, but no more popular with the peasants; searches for hidden farm produce early in 1918 embittered the peasantry still more. The peasants resisted and circumvented the regulations where possible; they also profited from the black market as both sellers and, in the case of chemical fertilizers which were in short supply because of the war, as buyers. In spite of the interrelationship which developed between the peasantry and the urban dwellers through the black market, a profound hostility began to emerge in the way that rural producer and urban consumer regarded each other. The peasants, especially the farmers and smallholders of the west and south, saw the war economy as working solely for the benefit of the urban consumer; the latter, discontented by rationing and shortages, believed that there was always plenty of food available in the countryside.

The experience of urban dwellers varied greatly during the war. The shortage of male workers encouraged the use of new flow production techniques, especially in the important war industries of optics and metallurgy. These changes, in turn, levelled some traditional wage differentials. But the war economy also fostered the growth of differentials between pay in war industries and civilian industries. In the former, between 1914 and 1918 the daily earnings of male workers increased by 152 per cent and those of female workers by 186 per cent; in the latter the increases were 81 per cent and 102 per cent respectively. (It is important to note that, on average, women continued to earn about half the wages of men.) Those in the war industries were also better off because they received most of the food premiums given to 'hard working' and 'hardest working' members of the workforce. With pay increases, some working-class families managed to approach the living standards of some of the middle class. This was due equally to an overall decline in the position of many members of the middle class, especially those on fixed incomes who suffered acutely from the wartime inflation. Nor were white-collar workers and independent artisans entitled to the extra food rations given to munitions workers, or able to benefit from the illegal bonuses provided by some industrial employers. The decline in their living standards fuelled discontent among sections of the middle class and made them rather more sympathetic to demands for reform and even socialist ideas. The corresponding rise in the living standards of sections of the working class, however, did not end discontent in that quarter. The problems of inflation, rationing and shortages appeared large in working-class family budgets, prompting disorder and increasing participation in strikes (see Table 11–13.12).

Most of these strikes were organized at shop-floor level, not by the trades unions' leadership, and they were indicative of a growing split between the rank and file and the leadership. Like the political chiefs of the majority SPD, trades union leaders increasingly allied with the military authorities to support the war effort; this was particularly the case with the announcement of the Hindenburg programme for war production and the Patriotic Auxiliary Service Law (*Vater-*

Table 11–13.12   *Average number of people participating in strikes per month, August 1914–18*

1914 (August)	0
1915	1,000
1916	10,000
1917	50,000
1918	100,000

Source: Hardach, *The First World War*, pp. 183–4.

ländischer Hilfsdienst) of December 1916. This law effectively militarized both the economy and the workforce: all males between 17 and 60 who were not in the army were henceforth regarded as members of the auxiliary services under the authority of the Minister for War; compulsory arbitration was established for labour disputes; local workers' committees were to be elected in factories employing fifty or more workers. The trades union leaders were generally satisfied with this system in as much as it gave them the recognition they had long sought from both employers and the state; at the same time they were alarmed by the way in which the elected factory committees tended to go their own ways against the national leadership. The declining authority of the leadership at shop-floor level was exposed by the massive strike in Berlin in January 1918, which eventually involved perhaps as many as half a million workers whose elected council demanded:

1   a prompt peace without annexations or reparations;

2   workers' participation in the negotiations for peace;

3   the democratization of the Prussian franchise;

4   the democratization of the *Reich*;

5   the abolition of the Patriotic Auxiliary Service Law and of the *Belagerungszustand* (siege law) which had been in operation since 1914 and which gave the army wide powers to curtail civil liberties and political activity;

6   an amnesty for all political prisoners;

7   improvements in the supply and quality of food.

The leaders of the socialist trades unions refused to give any backing to the strike; the majority SPD hierarchy dared not condemn it and sought to negotiate; the military authorities used force. While the actual figures are unreliable, it is possible that as many as 50,000 strikers were subsequently conscripted.

The conscription of strikers brought men into the army who were as likely to undermine morale and discipline as to yield to the latter. The German military was not falling apart in 1918 as the Russian military had done in the previous year, but there were problems. Letters sent home by troops at the front, and comments made by troops on leave, were increasingly hostile to the war. Challenging the notion that the army had been stabbed in the back by a crumbling home front, a Bavarian officer recalled

> . . . that the mood of dissatisfaction was carried into the homeland by the troops on leave . . . at a time when the homeland did not think of opposing the war and its leaders. Many an open-hearted member of the *Landwehr* told me how he found things out there, how badly they were fed, how everything meant for the front was left in the occupied areas, how

senseless and purposeless the whole story was, how the men were
mistreated in this or that unit, etc. If there was much exaggeration and if
the individual soldier used individual instances to judge the entire
situation, there were still many people smart enough and clear minded
enough to recognize that everything was not in order. And this conviction
was carried from the front to the homeland and not vice versa. (Quoted in
Feldman, *Army, Industry and Labor*, p.507)

On 1 October Ludendorff is reported to have told his staff that the army was
'unfortunately, heavily infected with the poison of Spartacist-Socialist ideas'
(quoted in Feldman, p.515). Desertion, or at best men going absent without leave,
began to be a serious problem in the closing months of the war. Soldiers' councils
(*Soldatenräte*) appeared in the army; obviously there was some inspiration from
Russia, but there was also encouragement and guidance from those conscripted
as a punishment for strike activity. As in Russia, the navy, with its large numbers
of skilled workmen, was especially radical. The naval mutiny at Kiel in October
1918 (and there had been a similar, unsuccessful mutiny among sailors during the
previous year) sparked off much revolutionary activity. Mobile flying squads of
sailors spread revolutionary ideas throughout Germany, and the People's Naval
Division (*Volksmarine*) provided dedicated shock troops for the revolution in
Berlin.

'Soviets' were not confined to the military. The first had appeared briefly in
Leipzig in 1917, directing a strike against a reduction in the bread ration. In
November 1918 they were established in every major town and city. Concern
about an Allied invasion after the collapse of Austria-Hungary, together with a
resurgence of separatist feeling, gave the Workers' and Soldiers' Council in
Munich the opportunity to declare an independent Bavarian republic on 8
November. These councils were not Bolshevik; that in Munich was led by Kurt
Eisner, a member of the USPD, but most of the councils were prepared to go along
with the majority socialist leaders who found themselves running Germany. The
congress of the councils which met in Berlin in December co-operated with the
majority SPD leaders in setting National Assembly elections for the following
January; the USPD did not and, outmanoeuvred, its leaders resigned from the
provisional government and withdrew its co-operation with the majority party.
However, whether or not they worked with the SPD leaders, the councils were
tainted by the Russian example and were eyed with suspicion. Philipp Scheide-
mann, the SPD leader who had proclaimed the new German republic on 9
November, expressed concern that:

They come in from the street and hold placards under our noses saying: All
Power to the Workers' and Soldiers' Councils! At the same time, however,
they let you understand: If you do not do what we want, we will kick you
out . . . They can only represent a force as long as they are in the
possession of the majority of machine guns. What is Russia's present
would then become a certain future for Germany . . . We need bread,
peace and work . . . The Councils can bring us neither bread nor peace.
They will create civil war for us. (Quoted in Koppel S. Pinson, *Modern
Germany: Its History and Civilization*, 1966, pp.370–1)

Exercise   To whom could the majority SPD turn for 'machine guns' to combat any threat
from the councils or the Left? ■

Specimen answer   Those sections of the army which were not disintegrating. □

Discussion   In return for promises that the new government would support the officer corps in maintaining army discipline, endeavour to keep the army supplied, and oppose 'Bolshevism', General Wilhelm Groener, who had replaced Ludendorff, assured Ebert of the army's support.

Exercise   Given the events of the war years, do you think it surprising that the SPD leaders and the army's officer corps should have become allies in 1918? ■

Specimen answer   While the majority SPD remained Marxist in theory, in practice it had become much more like a liberal democratic party. Furthermore, during the war years its leaders and the army command had got to know each other and had, to some extent, worked together in the war effort. In 1918, since both saw a threat from the Left, it was logical that, whether they liked each other or not, they should decide to work together to stabilize the changes that had been made. □

Discussion   The army was not alone in accepting, at least temporarily, the collapse of the old order and the need to make some links with moderates so as to check Bolshevism. On 15 November 1918 the Association of Employers, representing industrialists throughout Germany, agreed to many of the demands that had been pressed by the socialist trades unions before 1914: the recognition of unions as the official representatives of the labour force and of the worker's rights to join a union; collective bargaining; and the eight-hour day. In return the industrialists received the implicit acceptance of their right to own and run their factories.

5 GERMANY: UPRISING AND PUTSCH

For most historians, as for most contemporaries who lived through the events, the collapse of the old order and the sporadic fighting of November and December 1918, as reactionary groups were mopped up and elements of the Left clashed for the first time, constitute the 'German Revolution'. However, disorder continued over a much longer period as the Weimar regime sought to establish itself as the sole recognized sovereign authority. Given the definition of the political process of revolution in section 1, there is some justification in looking at the uprisings and putsches of the period 1918–23 as the working out of the German Revolution.

The initial trouble was at the centre of political power in Berlin as, during January 1919, the SPD government confronted a Left coalition of revolutionary shop stewards, the radical Berlin USPD and the new KPD. Liebknecht and other leaders of the KPD did not consider the time opportune for an armed insurrection, but they were swept along by the enthusiasm of others, notably the shop stewards. The Spartacist uprising of January was a disaster and was brutally crushed; Liebknecht and Luxemburg were murdered after their capture. However, Spartacist and left-wing USPD activity continued: a general strike in Berlin in March led to the imposition of martial law and to more fighting, and throughout the industrial districts of Germany there were strikes and risings in the first half of 1919. The Kapp putsch of 1920 provoked insurrectionary strikes in central Germany and particularly in the Ruhr. There were abortive KPD risings in 1921 and again in 1923.

The Spartacists, the KPD and the left USPD drew support from the unemployed, of whom there were thousands in Germany during the early months of peace as demobilized soldiers and sailors looked for work and as the economy had to reorganize for peace. Throughout the Weimar period the Communists continued to recruit from the unemployed, but they also found strong support among certain trades and in certain cities. It can be argued that disillusion with the SPD leadership in wartime, coupled with that leadership's hostility to workers' militancy early in 1919, fostered support for the Left. But it is also true that some of the most militant centres during the Weimar Republic (such as Brunswick, Düsseldorf and Wuppertal) and some of the most militant trade groups (such as metalworkers and the miners of the Ruhr) were also noted for their militancy before 1914. The Ruhr miners were not to be bought off with the shorter hours and better pay granted at the end of the war; they wanted, as they had when their union was established in 1890, control of their workplace; in 1919 and 1920 they took up arms to achieve this end.

The SPD government had also to contend with the problem of Bavaria. Local elections at the beginning of 1919 had resulted in a major defeat for Kurt Eisner and the USPD. There was doubt as to how Eisner and the Workers' and Soldiers' Council would respond, but before he could make his intentions known, Eisner was shot dead by a reactionary student. Out of the developing shambles three rival governments emerged; a coalition under Johannes Hoffman of the SPD established itself eventually in Nürnberg; a soviet government led by a group of young romantic intellectuals, largely members of the USPD, was established in Munich; and a second soviet government, also in Munich, was set up by an altogether tougher and more down-to-earth Spartacist group. Hoffmann, like the SPD in Berlin, looked for assistance from the old army in Bavaria, but an early defeat sent him begging for troops from the federal government in Berlin. After a week of savage fighting at the end of April and beginning of May 1919, the soviets in Munich were destroyed; the soviets' leaders who were not killed in the fighting were either murdered after capture, or sentenced to death or to long prison terms.

Eisner's Bavarian Republic was the only one of the radical uprisings to receive peasant support, and even this was limited and short-lived. Eisner cultivated his ties with local peasant leaders and built on long-standing progressive interest groups established among the Bavarian peasantry and their antipathy towards a central government dominated by Prussians.

Exercise   In what ways do you suppose that the war may have made the peasantry disinclined to support urban uprisings? ∎

Specimen answer   The war economy, generally speaking, made the peasants suspicious of, and hostile towards, urban consumers. □

Discussion   The peasant councils that appeared at the end of the war tended to be dominated by the same people who had taken charge of agrarian interest groups before 1914, namely estate owners, often aristocrats. During the war this élite had been patriotic, often ultranationalist, but they had also condemned the injustices of the war economy. Furthermore, while they criticized the controls on agricultural production, they were not slow to point out to the peasantry that the individuals calling most vociferously for such controls were invariably those who also called for political reform. Until the publication of recent research, which has concentrated on the countryside and rural dwellers, historians tended to argue that the peasantry was largely unthinkingly conservative or that it allowed itself to be manipulated by the agrarian élite in its own conservative interest. It is now clear, however, that the criticism levelled at the economic policies of the wartime government and the immediate post-war regime reflected very much the interests of the peasants themselves. In both the east and the more advanced west of Germany, it is at least arguable that while the leadership remained largely unchanged, the radical tone of agricultural interest groups and particularly the open criticism of government policy, were in keeping with grassroots feeling.

> Claims of the unity of all agricultural producers had a firm basis in the common experience of all peasants under the war economy, a system which all peasants saw as making impossible demands and intervening at will into their economic lives. Protest against state intervention into agricultural production was not orchestrated from above but originated in the daily experience of the individual agricultural producer . . . Even where new and independent agricultural organizations, outside the traditional interest-groups framework, emerged in the months following the end of the war, they showed no sympathy to the new order, and shared the common demand for an immediate end to state intervention into the agricultural sector. (Robert G. Moeller, 'Dimensions of social conflict in the Great War: the view from the German countryside', 1981, pp.167–8)

As noted in the preceding section, in order to maintain their position and deal with threats from the Left, the SPD leadership entered into an agreement with the officer corps, as troops were needed to do the fighting. The gradual disintegration of the army before the armistice gathered pace rapidly as troops left the front lines and crossed back into Germany. A few units maintained a modicum of order, but the answer to the immediate military need was found, not in the surviving remnants of the imperial army, but in the *Freikorps*. The idea of the *Freikorps* appears to have originated with General Georg von Maercker. Early in December 1918, concerned by the military collapse all around him, Maercker requested, and received, authorization from his military superiors to form a corps of volunteer rifles. The force was to be selected from the best men who volunteered out of the old army. It was to be organized along the lines of the élite storm troops (*Sturmbataillone*) which had proved so effective in the later stages of the war. Although the corps was to be disciplined, the discipline was to be based on consent, as in the *Sturmbataillone*, rather than the rigid, unthinking discipline of much of the old army. The privates of each company were to elect *Vertrauensleute* (trusted men) who were to be the channel for any complaints and who were to be consulted by the officers on questions of food and leave. Maercker found no shortage of volunteers; some were professional soldiers with nothing to return to in civilian life, and among many of these the notion that a weak home front had stabbed the army in the back in 1918 seems already to have been present; others were motivated primarily by patriotism and/or a fear and loathing of Bolshevism. By 4 January, when Maercker paraded his men before Chancellor Ebert and the defence minister, Gustav Noske, the volunteer rifles numbered 4,000 men and were equipped with machine guns and even artillery. By the same date other *Freikorps* were being organized on similar grounds. These were the units which brutally smashed the Spartacist risings, but as the demands for them increased, there was a change in the character of the volunteers. By April, when the *Freikorps* approached 400,000 men, many of the new recruits were not drawn from the old army or from former front-line soldiers. The new volunteers were often conservative, middle-class young men who had missed the war but who were motivated by fanatical anti-socialism, sometimes also by monarchism, German 'Volk-ishness' and overt anti-semitism; it was not lost on these volunteers that many of the Left's theorists and leaders (for example Eisner, Liebknecht, Luxemburg and, of course, Marx) were Jews. Some of the later Freikorps consisted of only a few hundred men and were set up by junior officers; they were able to maintain a degree of independence by accepting finance, not from the government, but from the Anti-Bolshevik League established by a group of wealthy industrialists. The suppression of the Spartacist rising in Berlin in January had been savage; the terror unleashed on Munich by the Freikorps in May 1919 terrified even the respectable middle-class burghers who had hailed them as liberators.

When the Freikorps' tasks were completed (at least in the eyes of the government) a new and major problem developed: how to get them to disband? The Allies protested about the activities of the Iron Division in the Baltic states, but the SPD leaders had no way of making General von Goltz and his men come home; indeed, they were concerned that the Baltic Freikorps might decide to march on Berlin. The government's powerlessness was exposed in November 1919, when a new Freikorps was openly recruited in Berlin to assist Goltz in Latvia. In March 1920 some of the Baltic Freikorps joined with Ehrhardt's Freikorps when it refused to disband, and set in motion the Kapp putsch. The government fled before the disgruntled troops as they entered Berlin to be greeted, 'by chance', by Ludendorff; Wolfgang Kapp, an obscure civil servant and previously an organizer of the Vaterlandspartei, was proclaimed Chancellor. Kapp's administration lasted five days. He was ineffectual, his supporters were divided, the civil service in general (largely left over from the old regime) remained loyal to the Weimar government, but perhaps most important, Berlin was completely paralysed by a general strike called against the putsch. Significantly the Reichswehr, the small army of 100,000 men authorized by the Versailles treaty, took no action against the putsch.

Government financial support of the Freikorps finished early in 1920. Officially the units were disbanded, but some continued as units of the Black Reichswehr, a clandestine reserve army maintained in defiance of the Versailles treaty and which virtually doubled the size of the authorized Reichswehr. In October 1923 groups of the Black Reichswehr were involved in the Küstin putsch. On this occasion the regular army did act against them; generals in the regular army were responsible for organizing and equipping the Black Reichswehr and they were not prepared to have their authority and discipline challenged. Some Freikorps continued as military clubs; a few followed their leaders as a body into the paramilitary Sturmabteilung of the infant Nazi party, which, in alliance with Ludendorff, staged its own putsch in Munich in 1923. Some involved themselves in right-wing political murder gangs: members of the Ehrhardt Freikorps, for example, formed 'Organization Consul' which, in August 1921, carried out the assassination of Matthias Erzberger, the leader of the Catholic Centre Party who was hated by the extreme Right because he had led the German armistice delegation of November 1918.

Note: sections 6–8 are written by David Englander.

6 *AUSTRIA-HUNGARY AT WAR*

6.1   Introduction

If you had been around in the summer of 1914 and were asked to bet on the victor of the First World War, would you have put money on Austria-Hungary? Of course not! To the intelligent punter the ramshackle multinational empire, which sprawled across East-Central Europe, must have looked less like a winner than any of the other combatants. The Austro-Hungarian Empire in 1914 possessed neither political nor economic unity. The Dual Monarchy represented the negation of nationalism and the denial of political independence at a time when these forces were burning with unprecedented intensity. Its brittle stability rested on the skilful application of the age-old principle of divide and rule, so that loyalty to the Emperor was, for its oppressed nationalities, the best safeguard against local domination by a bigger minority. This precarious balance was not only difficult to sustain; it was also costly.

Far from proceeding towards an integrated economy, therefore, the Habsburg Empire in 1914 was in the process of recession, moving rapidly towards a set of self-sufficient units, each concerned to escape the pull of the industrially more advanced provinces of the north and west. For fear that it would bring Dalmatia into the Austrian economic sphere, Hungary opposed the construction of an inter-connecting railroad; it also obstructed the development of closer economic ties between Serbia and the Monarchy for fear that it would disadvantage its own agricultural exports. The Empire's relatively poor inland waterway facilities underscored the economic importance of railways, for the Danube, by comparison with the Rhine, is inferior both in terms of its location and navigability. The politico-economic particularism of Austria and Hungary nevertheless conspired to limit the development of an extensive and efficient railway system. Magyar nationalism prevented the centralized administration of the network, which remained under separate control from Austria, Hungary and Bosnia. The system – or more accurately the want of a system – provoked a good deal of chaos and conflict. Goods shipped by train were loaded on ships at Trieste and reloaded on a train at a Dalmatian seaport simply because Hungarian intransigence prevented the construction of a railway across Croatia. Equally, the Austrians refused to permit the Hungarians to ship goods directly to Prussian Silesia or Berlin. By comparison with Germany, the Austro-Hungarian network was stunted. Pre-war Austro-Hungarian mileage totalled 277,036 miles in a 264,204 square mile area. German railway lines, by contrast, were three times as long in a 208,830 square mile area.

The effect of these antagonistic relationships on the monarchy's war-making capacities were almost totally negative. In an old but useful study of the process of disintegration, *The Dissolution of the Habsburg Monarchy* (1929), Oscar Jaszi argued that attempts to mobilize the Austro-Hungarian economy were destined to fail because the economy remained unbalanced, being dominated by primary production and with an industrial base that was insufficient to meet the requirements of mass industrialized warfare. The imbalance between agriculture and industry was certainly striking. Industrial development was highly localized; most of it was confined to the areas around Vienna, Gras-Loeben, northern Bohemia and Silesia. Agricultural products accounted for an average 75 per cent of the Monarchy's exports before the war. Industrial employment in 1900 absorbed a mere 13.4 per cent of the active population in Hungary and only 23.3 per cent in Austria, compared with 37.5 per cent in Germany.

Though small, the industrial sector was dynamic. Growth rates in the Dual Monarchy rose sharply in the generation before 1914 and bore comparison with the more advanced European powers. Not so absolute quantities. Mineral resources, in particular, remained insufficient and underdeveloped. Austro-Hungarian raw material production reached 359 million German marks in 1913 compared to a production value of 1,845 million marks in Germany. The Monarchy wanted for everything except wood, lignite and petroleum. Although a world leader in iron production, the total output from Austro-Hungarian furnaces was easily dwarfed by that of its rivals. Indeed, by comparison with the output of the leading iron-producing states, Austria-Hungary's iron production was puny. The United States, Germany, Great Britain, France and Russia with 33, 18.8, 11, 5.4 and 4.9 million tons output respectively were all far in advance of Austria-Hungary's 2.5 million tons. Although the Empire was a producer of high-grade steel, Austria-Hungary was well behind other belligerents in terms of output. Even before the war brought unprecedented demands for consumption, pig-iron producers within the Dual Monarchy were suffering from a massive shortage of capacity and could not meet the growth in demand. Its machine industry, too, was undersized and inadequate for the requirements of modern warfare.

Additional burdens shouldered by industry included capital shortages, penal taxation and extensive cartelization. The Austro-Hungarian economy was dominated by industrial monopolies who sought, through restricted competition, low wages and high prices, to secure profits rather than production. These conditions, taken together, were sufficient to convince some that the Danube Monarchy had lost the war even before the first shot was fired. Oscar Jaszi, who was so minded, wrote that, 'in 1913, the Austro-Hungarian Monarchy was already a defeated empire from the economic point of view and as such went into the world war in 1914'. Jaszi's views, echoed by A. J. P. Taylor in a more amusing study published in 1948 (*The Habsburg Monarchy*), have not been seriously challenged by more recent scholarship. General monographs and textbook accounts are in the main dismissive of the Austro-Hungarian war economy. Roberts, for example, does not bother to mention it at all!

The Habsburg army has been equally neglected. On the eve of war the army was certainly in a parlous condition. In structure and composition it mirrored the complexities of the Empire it claimed to defend. The joint Austro-Hungarian army (the Imperial and Royal army) was supplemented by the Austrian defence army, the *Landwehr*, and its Hungarian variant, the *Honved*. Beneath them the *Landsturm*, the ultimate reserve, sought recruits from able-bodied men who were not required by the other three formations. Responsibility for these various forces was equally diffuse. The Austro-Hungarian army was administered by the War Ministry under the direction of the Austrian and Hungarian parliamentary delegations who controlled the purse strings; the *Landwehr* was controlled by the Austrian Ministry of Defence, and the *Honved* by its Hungarian analogue.

It was not an impressive force. On the eve of war the Habsburg armed forces were under-powered and under-strength. There was, in fact, a marked disparity between the growth of the population of the Empire and the size of its armed forces. Between 1870 and 1914 the former rose 40 per cent, while the increase in the military establishment was only 12 per cent. Trained manpower was insufficient because spending was insufficient. Austria-Hungary, writes A. J. P. Taylor in *The Habsburg Monarchy*, 'though ranking only after Russia and Germany in population . . . spent less than any Great Power – a quarter of Russian or German expenditure, a third of British or French, and even less than Italian'. In 1914 Austria-Hungary could mobilize a mere forty-eight infantry divisions – and that was only attained through the inclusion of the second-line units of the *Landwehr* and the *Honved* – compared with ninety-three for Russia, eighty-eight for France and eleven for Serbia.

The Habsburg army was short on equipment as well as manpower. In both weight and quality it was wanting. Its firepower was farcical: about 66 per cent of the rifles supplied to the troops in 1914/15 were antiquated 1888 models. Austro-Hungarian divisions were also woefully deficient in artillery: a German, a Russian and a Serbian division possessed eighty, fifty-nine and forty guns respectively in comparison to thirty-two in the Balkans and forty-two in the north for an Austro-Hungarian division. Habsburg artillery was, in fact, relatively weaker in 1914 than it had been in 1866, since in the move to rapid-firing guns with six rather than eight guns per battery, the Monarchy had not raised the number of batteries as other states had done.

The joint Austro-Hungarian army was more than a military formation, however. Apart from the Monarchy, it was the main focus of supranationality. Its role as a nursery of dynastic feeling was taken seriously. Measures were introduced to prevent the over-representation of the Empire's numerous nationalities, so that for every 1,000 men in the ranks of the Imperial and Royal army, there were 267 Germans, 223 Magyars, 135 Czechs, 85 Poles, 81 Ruthenes, 67 Croats and Serbs, 64 Romanians, 38 Slovaks, 26 Slovenes, and 14 Italians. Command of this multilingual and multicultural force posed problems which were formidable but not without precedent. The British had managed to weld the disparate elements of the Indian sub-continent into a cohesive and effective fighting formation; and the Habsburg generals were no less skilful. Polish, Czech, South Slav and Ruthene regiments received their orders in the limited vocabulary of the *Kommandosprache*, the sixty-odd words of German that constituted the language of command; for the rest, instruction was in the *Regimentssprache*, given in their own tongue. Officers were drawn from the middle class: one-third were Magyars and Slavs, the remainder Germans, a reflection of their numerical weight within the educated and better-off elements. Whatever their origin, officers were expected to master the language of the regiment to which they had been posted and familiarize themselves with the customs of the men under their command. Those who failed to establish such rapport were transferred or dismissed from the service.

The military value of the Habsburg army, though, was not immediately apparent. Contemporary analysts, distracted by its diversity, underestimated the stamina of its soldiery, their corporate spirit and dedication to duty. The Austro-Hungarian High Command was equally sceptical; fears of nationalist subversion prompted its demand for a pre-emptive war before the morale and fighting efficiency of the troops were fatally impaired. German commanders were contemptuous of an ally whom they regarded as inefficient, slovenly and degenerate. The experience of the eastern front confirmed these prejudices; their post-war writings are peppered with caustic comments on the third-rate fighting qualities of 'the Austrians', their incompetence and lack of moral fibre. Historians, taking their cue from the generals, have tended to present the Austro-Hungarian army as a shambles – less an example of lions led by donkeys, as with the British, and more a case of *schmucks* led by even greater *schmucks*. In recent years the clearest statement of this sort comes from the pen of Norman Stone. His book, *The Eastern Front 1914–1917* (1975), is a stylish study, which supplies an English audience with a panoramic survey of a neglected but crucial theatre of war. In his prize-winning account – it won the Wolfson Prize for the best historical work of the year – Stone identifies the lack of aggression as one of the principal defects of the military forces of the Monarchy. The problem, he tells us, was that 'the army was not ruthlessly tyrannical, in the Prussian style. The Austrians did not have the Prussian knack of making anybody and everybody fight for Prussia, by virtue of a ruthless authoritarianism.' The Austrian war effort, we are led to believe, was directed by duds and *dummkopfs*. Stone is an authority on East-Central Europe and so we must treat his views with respect. In the sections that follow we shall consider the adequacy of the Prussian perspective in relation to the military effort of the Habsburg Empire. Specifically, we shall examine the organization of the war economy, its effect upon the performance of the armed forces, and the social and political consequences arising therefrom. I shall suggest that the war effort of the Austro-Hungarian Empire, as presented by Stone and others, is in need of revision. The Empire's military effort wasn't good; but neither was it the unholy mess portrayed by the critics.

6.2   War economy

Austria-Hungary was no worse prepared for war than any other belligerent. Its statesmen and soldiers, like their compeers in Paris, Berlin and St Petersburg, anticipated a short, sharp encounter on the field of glory and had made no comprehensive plans for the mobilization of the Monarchy's human and productive resources. Partial measures, however, were better than none. The War Service Law of 1912, a piece of legislation prompted by fear of fall-out from the Balkan Wars, provided for the militarization of the economy in the event of an emergency. Baldly summarized, the Act placed the entire population of the Empire and its industrial and agricultural resources at the disposal of the military. The War Ministry was empowered to requisition and direct factories, to bypass market mechanisms and commandeer essential military supplies, and to draft labour for industry. Provision was included for the industrial conscription of all able-bodied adult males; freedom of movement was abolished and workers were placed under military discipline and law. Loss of production due to industrial unrest was to be minimal until the second half of the war.

Loss of production due to error and inefficiency in the organization of the Monarchy's resources was another matter. At the close of September 1916, von Tschirschky, the knowledgeable German ambassador in Vienna, reported on the internal situation of the Monarchy. His pessimistic prognosis identified seven major areas in which Austrian economic mobilization was deficient.

Exercise   Turn now to document II.26 in *Documents 1*. Read the report carefully and then list the principal sources of ambassadorial concern. ■

Specimen answer   Manpower shortages, a lack of co-ordination in the management of the war economy, consumer shortages, a crisis of distribution, currency depreciation, a resurgent nationalism, and internal unrest – these, Berlin was informed, raised doubts about the Monarchy's ability to prolong the struggle.

It is, of course, a biased document, full of national prejudice: the Austrians advance under German tutelage; their faults are of their own making. Nevertheless, von Tschirschky's comments are not without insight. His report emphasizes the fact that mass industrialized warfare is largely a matter of real resources – labour, raw materials and productive capacity; that fighting power is determined by the manner in which resources are allocated among the armed forces, the armament industry, producers of capital goods, and the suppliers of the civilian population. In short, defeat or victory depends upon the optimal allocation of resources.

The resource-led character of the ambassador's report might seem surprising; it shouldn't. It was the Germans under Rathenau's leadership who formulated the concept of a special 'war economy' (*Kriegswirtschaft*) characterized by the control and co-ordination of raw material supplies and the elimination of wasteful competition. His strictures upon the Monarchy's fragmented war effort, the evils of protectionism and nationalism, were unquestionably major sources of weakness. So was the collapse of the currency. But it was the imbalance between military-industrial needs and civilian consumption which ultimately proved fatal. Notwithstanding von Tschirschky's belief in German superiority, it was the same defect which proved to be the undoing of the German war economy.

In Austria-Hungary, as in Germany, the authorities were slow to realize that in total war civilians as well as soldiers must march on their stomachs. Failure to maintain a proper relationship between agriculture and industry brought famine, civil unrest and growing demands for 'bread and peace'. Had the central powers (Germany and Austria-Hungary) adopted measures to sustain civilian consumption comparable with those of the British, the outcome of the war might well have been different. In 1916, however, the emphasis was on maximizing the output of armaments and ammunition; in this sphere, as von Tschirschky readily agreed, the Austro-Hungarians had made 'surprising progress'. □

6.3   Industrial mobilization

German industrial mobilization provided a model for the organization and development of the Austrian war economy. The Austrians were persuaded to establish a whole range of trusts, boards, combines and commissions to procure and distribute raw materials and labour. As in Germany – indeed, as everywhere else – experiments in state control were accompanied by a good deal of waste and inefficiency. There were many mistakes. Indiscriminate recruitment for the armed forces meant that precious skilled labour was lost to vital war industries. Large numbers of miners and metal-workers, inducted into the army at the opening and bloodiest phase of the fighting, never returned; as one authority put it, 'the best qualified workers were left lying in the Carpathian mountains'. Conflict and chaos emerged from the competing claims of the War Ministry and the Trade Ministry to organize production. There was much muddle, unnecessary duplication of effort, and overlapping jurisdictions. Agencies proliferated: five were required to process a single ox – one for leather, one for meat, one for bone, one for fat, and one for procurement. No governmental body with control over the entire economy existed until the formation of the Commission for War and Transitional Economy in 1917.

For all that, there were a lot of positive achievements, some of which were remarkable. The military authorities, in particular, displayed energy and enterprise in organizing heavy industry and mining. In the Monarchy, as elsewhere, changes in the composition of the workforce followed as production processes were restructured to alleviate labour shortages and increase output. Replacements for men called to the colours were found from women, juveniles and prisoners of war. The feminization of the armaments and metal manufacturing industries was particularly pronounced, as Table 11–13.13 shows. In some factories women made up more than half the labour force, and until 1917, when their numbers were halved by the substitution of prisoners of war, women comprised 15 per cent of the workforce engaged in the manufacture of coke. The overall increase in the female labour force has been put at about 40 per cent; in all, about one million women entered the labour force in Austria during World War I.

Table 11–13.13   *Proportion of female workers in Viennese metal industries*

Year	Total workforce	Female workers	% female
1913	65,789	12,180	18.51
1914	69,065	15,407	22.31
1915	78,068	20,767	26.60
1916	70,124	24,401	34.80
1917	86,807	31,401	36.17

Source: R. Wall and J. M. Winter (eds) *The Upheaval of War*, 1988, p.119.

The restructuring of the labour force and the standardization of production worked wonders. So too did the battery of measures brought forward by the War Ministry to mobilize heavy industry. Through the use of direct grants and subsidies, extensive substitution, careful husbandry and close regulation of minerals and metals, output was massively increased; new factories were built, old mines re-opened and new mines sunk. Less than three weeks before the armistice, there were still fifty-seven Austro-Hungarian divisions engaged on the southern front against a formidable Entente force, while another six divisions were fighting alongside the Germans on the western front. The presence of the Austro-Hungarian army in the field in late 1918 confirms the substantial achievements of the war economy. Some measure of those achievements can be gauged from the production statistics shown in Table 11–13.14. It will be seen that, once the industrial dislocation of the opening phase of the war had been overcome, output rose spectacularly. The production of iron ore, pig iron and steel increased by 11, 5 and 25 per cent respectively in 1915 and attained new heights thereafter. In 1916 the production of ferrous metals soared above the record year of 1913: iron ore and pig iron production rose 15 per cent and steel output leapt 33 per cent over the record 1913 output; high productivity in the iron and steel industry was in fact sufficient to satisfy most of the ferrous metal requirements of the armaments industry during the first half of the fighting. It could not be sustained beyond 1917, but it was impressive while it lasted.

From the non-ferrous metals there came a similar story. Of strategic importance in the manufacture of armaments, these were even more scarce than iron and steel. Pre-war production satisfied the demand for aluminium, but was unable to supply any of the tin and nickel demand from internal sources. In 1913 domestic production accounted for only 4,052 tons of pure copper, and 36,500 tons were imported to meet industrial requirements. After 1914 imports from Germany made good some of the deficit; intensive recycling provided the rest. Industry was

Table 11–13.14   *Ferrous metal production (tons) 1913–18*

Year	Iron ore	Pig iron	Steel
1913	3,343,356	1,632,874	1,840,000
1914	2,509,365	1,487,822	1,539,000
1915	2,901,599	1,572,325	1,979,000
1916	3,900,000	1,900,000	2,750,000
1917	2,829,000	1,595,000	2,424,000
1918	n.a.	n.a.	1,461,000

Source: J. Robert Wegs, 'Austrian economic mobilization during World War I, with particular emphasis on heavy industry', 1970, p.89.

progressively stripped of its non-ferrous metals; householders, too, were compelled to contribute. Ultimately every copper-containing item was taken. Household goods and fittings were surrendered; copper was removed from roofs and lightning rods; and chandeliers, bathtubs, brass crucifixes, even church bells, were mobilized in defence of the realm.

Exercise   Examine Table 11–13.15 and briefly summarize the effect of these measures. ■

Table 11–13.15   *Copper production and acquisition (tons) during the World War I*

	1915	1916	1917	1918 (until Sept)
(a) Domestic copper				
Foundry production	6,528	7,774	5,279	3,330
Commandeered copper	2,298	5,727	1,715	641
Direct purchase by the Central Metal Authority:				
Scrap metal	1,148	1,268	2,537	1,343
Metal equipment	434	3,480	72	46
Industrial metal	4,272	4,392	2,741	756
Total	14,680	22,641	12,344	6,116
(b) Domestic copper alloy				
Commandeered:				
Church bells	—	3,703	9,771	1,119
Other	2,597	1,621	137	6
Purchased by the Central Metal Authority:				
Scrap metal	817	1,650	1,282	703
Metal equipment	625	1,969	59	91
Industrial metal	1,613	2,887	1,008	458
Total	5,652	11,830	12,257	2,377
(c) Foreign purchases				
Central Metal Authority Purchases:				
Copper	4,829	6,904	2,585	
Copper alloy	754	28	—	
Consignments from Germany:				
Copper	9,493	3,095	2,695	
Copper alloy	825	—	—	
Total	15,901	10,027	5,280	

Source: J. Robert Wegs, 'The marshalling of copper: an index of Austro-Hungarian economic mobilization during World War 1', 1976/7, p.193.

Specimen answer   It will be seen that record production increases in 1916 exceeded the 1913 production by 48 per cent. The importance of the state procurement agency, the Central Metal Authority, is clearly shown. In 1916, its interventions accounted for 45 per cent of the 34,471 tons that were available before imports; the inclusion of copper purchases from Germany brings its contribution to more than half the total supply. Its unremitting efforts also helped mitigate the effects of the fall-off in production in 1917. However, the church bells, which played so signal a part in offsetting the reduction in output in that year, could only be commandeered once. As production plummeted, ever more desperate measures were required. In 1918 the military authorities, following the example set by Germany, confiscated brass door-latches; shop windows, too, were dismantled and stripped of their copper content.

The same drive and initiative characterized the procurement and substitution of zinc, tin and lead, but to no avail. By the close of 1917 the non-ferrous metal industry had reached its limits, and much the same was true of other sectors of heavy industry. Output had attained record levels, and there might have been still greater production triumphs had the central powers been better able to co-ordinate their war effort.

6.4   The central powers: conflict and co-operation

Apart from foodstuffs, allied co-operation in the economic sphere was limited in range and effectiveness. Co-operation between the two powers took the form of bilateral trade deals whereby the Monarchy received supplies for its metal and armament industries and in exchange provided the Germans with petroleum, bauxite and other scarce commodities. Beyond that, however, there was little unity. On the exploitation of the occupied territories, for example, neither side could agree. Austrian attempts to secure a fixed share of captured material in France and the Low Countries were curtly brushed aside; German demands for dominion in Poland likewise received short shrift from a once great power that had come to fear its ally more than the enemy. These fears were justified. German ambitions, if realized, entailed the demise of the Danube Monarchy; as these ambitions unfolded, Habsburg hackles rose appreciably. *Mitteleuropa*, the organizing concept of the war aims of the central powers, was increasingly viewed as a source of coercion rather than co-ordination. The Austro-Hungarians, however, would not willingly comply; absorption into a Central European confederation under German tutelage was steadfastly resisted. To the end, the Monarchy retained its political and economic independence.

Its status as a military power, though, was compromised by the poor performance of its generals. Until the summer of 1916 the Habsburg armed forces had held their own on all fronts, being neither more nor less successful than either their allies or their opponents. The Brusilov offensive, however, dealt the Austro-Hungarian forces a shattering blow from which they never quite recovered. Thereafter the military was unable to resist pressure for the establishment of a unified command under the direction of German generals. The formation of a Supreme War Command, in September 1916, signalled the end of Austria-Hungary as an independent military power. Still, the economies which might have followed were not realized, and there was no standardization of weapons systems.

Friction, moreover, was not eliminated. As casualties spiralled and victory receded, and as shortages became ever more acute, the central powers grew peevish and recriminatory: the Germans were accused of arrogance, the Austrians of ineptitude; each blamed the other for their own failings. Habsburg soldiers were convinced that Austrian blood was shed needlessly to reduce German losses, while the Germans were aggrieved at being 'shackled to a corpse'. Faced with these contentious parties, the historian is inclined to act as a policeman called to a domestic quarrel. Wherever the fault lies, it is clear that the central powers failed to achieve a degree of co-operation and co-ordination comparable with that of their enemies (see Roberts, p.286).

6.5   Transport

By the close of 1917 industrial mobilization had passed its peak. The exhaustion of resources, human and physical, made it impossible to sustain output, let alone increase it further. In the armaments industry, for example, a critical shortage of horses for moving artillery pieces meant that field cannon lay idle when horses were required for newly created howitzer batteries. Transportation, or the want thereof, was without doubt the principal impediment to the smooth functioning of the war economy. Quite simply, the railway network did not possess sufficient carrying capacity to service the exceptional demands of the state at war. Of the 12,000 locomotives available at the beginning of the war, anything from two-fifths to one-half were constantly in repair, while enemy captures and depredations depleted the stock of railway cars – in 1914 alone the Monarchy lost 15,000 to the Russians in the retreat from Galicia. Furthermore, the loss of qualified personnel to the military reduced the productivity of labour at a time of greater need. Efficiency inevitably suffered: load limits fell, speeds were reduced, freight deteriorated in unattended cars, and locomotives became unserviceable. Some of this was avoidable. Indiscriminate military recruitment made the crisis worse than it need have been, as did the activities of those politicians who, in order to protect domestic industry from foreign competition, opposed purchases of additional locomotives and rolling stock from abroad. In consequence there was a growing discrepancy between production and consumption. Producers, inadequately supplied with railway cars, could not get food to the cities, iron to the foundries, oil to the refineries, or coal to the factories. In July 1918 vast quantities of coal were stockpiled at the pithead: the Ostrau-Karwiner coal district had 73,600 tons of coal and 35,300 tons of coke awaiting transport, while the northwest Bohemian lignite district had 37,400 tons of coal and the Carlsbad district 7,160 tons. Ironically, it was the slump in industrial activity in 1918 that created the additional capacity which enabled the defeated Habsburg armies to be returned home within one month of the conclusion of hostilities. The railways lost the Empire the war but saved the new Republic.

6.6   Currency depreciation

How was the massive increase in public expenditure to be paid for? The principles of Austrian war finance were fairly straightforward: loans were preferred to taxation on the assumption that the enemy would foot the bill on the morrow of victory; in the meantime outstanding differences between income and expenditure were settled by printing more money. War loans were obtained in the capital market and supplied a further opportunity for public participation and legitimation of the war effort; bank credits, by contrast, were secret and obtained principally by printing new paper currency of the Austro-Hungarian Bank. From July 1914 to October 1918 the amount of money in circulation rose from 2.19 milliard to 35.53 milliard kronen. No comparable increase in the quantity of goods and services available accompanied this extraordinary expansion of the money supply, and prices soared. Between 1914 and 1918 the official cost of living index in Austria registered an increase of 1,226 per cent. Against such a background, 'the amazing patience and self-abnegation of the people', to quote Redilich, the historian of Austrian war government, was truly remarkable. By the end of the war the real income of industrial workers had fallen to less than half of the pre-war level. Inflation, however, struck with even greater severity at civil servants, salaried workers, pensioners, and others on fixed incomes.

6.7   Industrial unrest

The end of the war saw professors wandering the streets of Vienna without a shirt on their back, and white-collar workers taking handouts from communal kitchens set up to sustain the starving. Shortages were such that scientists turned in vain to chestnuts, even to rats, in pursuit of substitutes for scarce fats! Although the Austro-Hungarian Monarchy before the war was more self-sufficient in food production than Germany, France or Britain, the reduction in deliveries from Hungary and the reduction in the peasant population as a result of conscription created a crisis of subsistence. Grain production fell from 9.2 million tons in 1914 to 6.2 million tons in 1917 and 5.3 million tons in 1918. Inevitably, the lack of food, fuel and clothing took its toll of civilian health. In the three years up to 1917, said Vienna's chief health officer, the incidence of tuberculosis had more than doubled. 'The physical strength of the great part of the population', he added, 'is so undermined with insufficient nourishment that they are unable to withstand sickness, and unless food conditions speedily improve the death rate from tuberculosis will run much higher.' The political repercussions were equally grave.

As early as 1915 miners had gone on strike in protest against unsatisfactory and uncertain food supplies; the same shortage of comestibles provoked further stoppages in January and March the following year. Thereafter, notwithstanding military repression, strikes grew in frequency and intensity. The halving of the flour ration in January 1918 set off a strike wave which engulfed the whole of industrial Austria and brought Budapest to a standstill. Workers' councils were elected and demonstrations for bread and peace and against the militarization of the factories were held.

But for the restraining hand of social democracy, the Habsburgs might have gone the same way as the Romanovs there and then. Convinced that a socialist seizure of power would convert the Monarchy into a battlefield on which the German and Entente forces would meet, the Social Democratic Party acted as an intermediary between government and workers, performing a critical role in the restoration of order. Its tribunal function, performed with great gusto, was sufficient to marginalize the Austrian Communist Party, which had emerged out of the crisis, and retain its leadership of a radicalized labour movement that was itself in process of transformation.

As in Britain, military participation was accompanied by increased partici-pation from unskilled elements who were previously excluded from the labour movement. In the year 1913, the Social Democratic Party had 91,000 members in the German districts of Inner Austria; in 1919, the number was 332,391. In 1913 the trades unions in the same area enrolled 253,137 members; in 1919 the number was 772,146. Two-thirds of the party and trades union membership were new recruits. These untrained and inexperienced workers were welcomed by the Social Democrats as a master receives an apprentice. The masses were to be taken in hand so that they were not seduced by the growing consciousness of their own power into dangerous and ill-considered assaults upon the polity.

6.8   The May mutinies

Until the closing stages of the war, the combat effectiveness of the Austro-Hungarian army remained unimpaired. At the beginning of 1918 it was a confident, conquering force occupying vast tracts of the Ukraine, the Balkans and Upper Italy. Support for the Monarchy held firm. The disposition of the Romanian, Ruthenian and Bosnian troops summoned to crush the January strikes in Vienna, for example, was not in question. 'There was no doubt', wrote a leader of the Social Democrats, 'that these troops were strong and reliable enough to put down any attempt among the masses to transform the strike into an act of revolution'. The armed forces, however, could not indefinitely withstand the process of decay and disintegration within the supranational empire. The red flag hoisted at Cattaro, in February 1918, signified the extent of disaffection within the navy. From the fleet to the army, sedition spread fast. Beginning in the spring, the military was convulsed by a rash of desertions, depredations, mutinies and other disturbances. Slovene troops mutinied in Judenberg; Serbian troops in Fünf-kirchen; Czech troops in Ljubljana; and Magyar troops in Budapest. In Croatia-Slavonia and Bosnia armed bands of deserters, the self-styled 'Green Cadres', plundered the countryside in defiance of both the civil and military authorities; others volunteered for service with the various 'legions' that began to proliferate among the oppressed national minorities. Military service, far from promoting supranational sentiment, was fast destroying it. Combat, it seemed, had transformed peasants into politicians; conscripts with no previous political experience had become an insurgent force that threatened the safety of the realm. Is such an interpretation accurate or are appearances deceiving? To help us form a judgement we shall examine the first of these incidents a little more closely.

For two days in May 1918 the small German town of Judenberg in Upper Styria was at the mercy of mutinous troops of the reserve battalion of the 17th Infantry Regiment. Soldiers, many the worse for drink, roamed the streets abusing civilians, pillaging shops and shouting slogans. In all, 1,181 men participated in the mutiny; almost half were convicted by courts-martial and seven were executed. The Judenberg mutiny, the first serious outbreak, exemplified the radicalizing process within the military. In the course of their peregrinations through the town the rebels shouted:

> Let us go home comrades, this is not for us but also for our friends in the fronts. The war must be ended now, whoever is a Slovene, join us. We are going home; they should give us more bread to eat and end the war; up with the Bolsheviks, long live bread, down with the war. (Quoted in Z. A. B. Zeman, *The Break-up of the Habsburg Empire 1914–1918*, 1961, p.143)

Exercise   What do these slogans tell you about the outlook of the mutineers? Re-read them carefully and then itemize the sources of unrest. Now see how your list compares with mine. ■

Specimen answer   The appeal to Slovene troops suggests elements of nationalism; support for Bolshevism would seem to indicate a political perspective – Roberts certainly thinks so (see p.311); and there are signs, too, of war-weariness, possibly pacifism, homesickness and hunger. The precise balance, though, is difficult to determine. Just how difficult will become clear as we examine each element separately. Since the last item is both easiest to deal with and the most significant, we shall take it first. □

Hunger

Exercise   Table 11–13.16 shows the state of the daily military bread ration (in grams) during the war. Does it tell you anything of significance about the timing and character of unrest in the military? ■

Table 11–13.16   *Austro-Hungarian army's daily bread rations, 1917–18*

	Up to 15 April 1917	After 15 April 1917	After 11 Aug. 1917
Field army:	500	478	480
Ersatz [reserve] and rear:	400	240	240

	September 1917	December 1917	April 1918	August 1918
Field army:	470	470	283	300
Ersatz and rear:	263	320	180	200

Source: Richard B. Spence, 'Yugoslavs, the Austro-Hungarian army and the First World War', 1981, p.249.

Specimen answer   Two aspects are outstanding. Note, first, the striking difference between the rations supplied to combatants and others. The explanation is straightforward: fighting being more arduous than training, those at the sharp end were deemed to be more deserving than reserve formations in the rear. It will also be seen that, with respect to the reduction and re-allocation of rations, those in the rear received less but lost more than soldiers at the front. It should be added that the figures shown in the table are nominal quantities; as a rule the difference between allocation and consumption was considerable.

Note, too, the course of the cuts; the drastic reduction of April 1918 – in the rear the bread ration was more than halved – directly preceded the outbreak of the major mutinies. 'I went hungry in Russia long enough, and I won't go hungry here too', exclaimed one of the Judenberg mutineers to a terrified resident. 'Why do you Germans have enough to eat and we so little?' The fact that such troops were eating less than the surrounding population also had a disastrous effect on discipline; the prospect of a square meal prompted many a deserter.

But while food was in short supply, wine was readily available and consumed in vast quantities. Hungry soldiers from *Ersatz* casernes were often drunk and disorderly, and in all the mutinies listed above, such soldiers were prominent. □

Political awareness

Protest against deprivation and the failure to satisfy material wants was one thing; unrest due to political subversion was something else. The latter was an undoubted feature of the May mutinies; pro-Bolshevik slogans were adopted by disaffected soldiers in all the units involved. The Austro-Hungarian High Command found the source of subversion easy to identify. The fault, the generals concluded, lay neither with themselves nor in their stars, but in the revolutionary agitation spread by repatriated prisoners of war who had been indoctrinated in the course of their captivity. Their numbers were considerable. By the close of 1917 there were an estimated two million Austro-Hungarian soldiers imprisoned in Russia whom the Bolsheviks sought to influence. The methods of mass psychological warfare were applied to persuade captive soldiers to take up arms in defence of socialism, peace and brotherhood. The compliant were rewarded, whereas intransigents were punished and the indifferent neglected. To the Soviet regime the potential of the prisoners of war was twofold; on the one hand they represented a trained reserve on which the Red Army might draw; on the other, properly educated, they might form politically conscious cadres to promote permanent revolution. 'The proletariat', they were reminded, 'has no homeland.' Those awaiting repatriation were enjoined to 'Inflame the country you are returning to, but inflame it not with hatred, but with true fire. Put an end to the state of the capitalists, priests and robber barons. Returning prisoners of war: REVOLT.'

Following the peace of Brest-Litovsk, hundreds of thousands of Austro-Hungarian soldiers were returned from Russian prisoner-of-war camps. The generals, though keen to restore them to active service, were concerned to exclude communist infiltrators from the army. A network of ideological decontamination units was created through which the returned prisoners were passed in order to separate suspect and unreliable elements. Those considered sound – and they constituted the vast majority – were posted to army retraining centres for reconditioning in tactics, discipline and army life. Having completed the four-week course, the ex-prisoners were given a month's leave and then required to report to their reserve units in preparation for the resumption of front-line service.

The screening process was not foolproof, however, and subversives slipped through, although their influence should not be unduly magnified. Bolshevik attempts to undermine the loyalties of prisoners of war and mobilize them in defence of world revolution met with a muted response from the captive masses; the turncoats who fought with the Reds were a tiny minority who were driven by instrumental rather than by ideological considerations. The length of service of the estimated 85,000 to 100,000 Hungarian prisoners who took arms on the Bolshevik side, for example, was limited to days and weeks; as the opportunity arose they deserted and made for home. One in three, possibly more, never arrived. Still, conditions in the camps were such that death *en route* seemed worth the gamble. Pro-Bolshevik sentiment among Austrian and Magyar prisoners was more a matter of personal protection than political commitment. By the spring of 1917, at least 600,000 prisoners of war had died in captivity. To inmates suffering and starving in disease-ridden camps the appeal of Bolshevism was like the alternative to old age; in short, Habsburg soldiers were better Red than dead.

Unrest among returned prisoners of war was not, therefore, political in provenance. The vast majority, though unaffected by Bolshevism, were reluctant to rejoin their units at the front. Having been captured and imprisoned they felt that they had 'done their bit' for 'Emperor, king and fatherland' and should be replaced by shirkers in the rear. Not only were they unprepared for the resumption of active service, the ex-prisoners of war were infuriated by the brevity of their leave and disturbed by the hunger, privations and distress encountered during their four weeks *en famille*. The Bolshevik slogans expressed by such men during the May mutinies were a vehicle for the dramatic registration of protest, not the prelude to an armed uprising and seizure of power. In this their conduct was comparable with the British soldiers at Shoreham who in 1917 broke camp shouting in similar terms in order to ventilate their grievances. Hoisting the Red flag was a signal to the authorities, not a statement of political commitment.

Homesickness, war-weariness and pacifism

Of these, the last is of least importance. There is little evidence that the mutineers were animated by a coherent body of anti-war thought. War-weariness, by contrast, was a form of non-doctrinal pacifism which was not unrelated to the enormous number of casualties sustained in the previous three years. Slovene losses were particularly heavy; by the close of 1917 there were on average 28 dead for every 1,000 of their number, a casualty rate exceeded only by the Austro-Germans. Croat casualties, too, were heavy and bore comparison with those of the Slovenes; Bosnia had a casualty rate of 19.1 and Dalmatia 18.1. All in all, something like 2,500,000 Austro-Hungarian soldiers had been killed or permanently disabled by the end of 1917. Among the warring nations, the Austro-Hungarian Empire had the highest ratio of casualties. Of the 8,300,000 men called to the colours during the war, at least 6,200,000 became casualties. 'It is no exaggeration to say', writes Istvan Deak, 'that, towards the end of the war, the Austro-Hungarian army was made up of men who had been wounded earlier, who had been seriously ill or frostbitten, or who had returned from Russian POW camps' ('Shades of 1848: war, revolution and nationality conflict in Austria-Hungary 1914–20', 1977).

Death and injury on such a scale affected the composure and cohesion of the armed forces. War losses were unevenly distributed. Among Bosnian regiments, for example, it was the higher level of casualties among Moslems and Croats which made the Serbs unmanageable. In short, the most effective troops were the most vulnerable; replacements were often less fit and invariably less committed.

The *Ersatz* Reserve, the principal source of supply, was a receptacle for troops deemed to be unsuitable for combat duties. Students, teachers and priests, who were exempted from active service, were assigned to support roles along with those conscripts who for some reason were best kept out of the front line. Exposed to agitation from the native population among whom they were stationed, these troops gave constant trouble. 'Throughout the war', writes Richard B. Spence, 'the vast majority of disciplinary problems, and outright criminal activity, would occur in the Ersatz and rear service units which became the dumping grounds for troops and officers considered unfit for service at the front.' Significantly, the May mutineers were all drawn from *Ersatz* battalions.

The increase in disaffection among Yugoslav soldiers was also related to the deterioration of political and economic conditions in the territories from which they were drawn. Professor Stone's conviction that the Austrian military were insufficiently tough and wanting in the animality of their ally, was not shared by the oppressed nationalities of the Empire, particularly the Slav and Latin elements who, in the words of Redilich, the historian of Austrian war government, were subjected to 'the unrestricted, unlimited and quite ruthless use of the power of command and punishment'. Note, too, von Tschirschky's observations (document II.26). The application of unlimited dictatorial authority to secure the submission of a suspect population was accompanied by summary executions and a good deal of brutality on the part of the military, which did nothing for the fighting spirit of loyal Slavic soldiers at the front.

Conditions at home and the high level of casualties affected the spirit as well as the structure of the army. The carnage dampened the conscript's resolve to enter or remain with his unit. This was so in all armies, but the peasant character of the Habsburg army made the problem more acute.

Peasant armies are particularly susceptible to a form of homesickness which limits the field of their operations. Although World War I provides nothing comparable with the *nostalgie* which so devastated the French revolutionary armies, the peasant character of the continental powers meant that such influences were still present, as the French army mutinies of 1907 indicate (see Book I, Unit 2). The collapse of the Russian armies ten years later pinpoints the potent effect of peasant localism. During the course of the October Revolution peasant conscripts were heard to say: 'We are from Tambov, or Penza. The enemy is far from our province. What is the point of fighting?' In the Habsburg army, too, peasant recruits, taken far from home, often arrived at the front subdued, bewildered and depressed. Desertion to the enemy was much less of a problem than desertion to go home; the Green Cadres drew much of their strength from this appeal.

Nationalism

It had long been assumed that the bitter national antagonisms between Magyars and Germans, and practically all the other peoples of the Empire, would be the undoing of the armed forces and the state they served. These fears were exaggerated: mobilization proceeded without hindrance, Slavic troops did not desert *en masse*, and the army did not fall apart. True, there were some local difficulties: anti-war riots among reserve formations in Bohemia in September 1914 were followed by the wholesale defection of the 29th Infantry from Prague in April 1915. In the main, however, loyalty to the dynasty was stronger than expected. This is not to say that within the Habsburg army nationalism was negligible. Nor was it a negative force. Whether separatist sentiment acted as a source of cohesion or disintegration depended on local circumstances. There was in fact a good deal of variation between national groups and the particular fronts on which they were engaged. Roman Catholic Croat and Slovene troops and Bosnian Moslems were generally more reliable than the Orthodox Serbs; Slavs pitted against Italians fought with great enthusiasm; Croats against Serbs were savage; Bosnian Moslems were brutal. Against Russians, however, Slavic soldiers were markedly less effective, though here, too, variations were pronounced. Serbs excepted, South Slavs were more steadfast than Czech, Ukrainian or Romanians, who were more prone to surrender or desert. But whereas their Russophile propensities made the latter more or less useless on the eastern front, the deep ethnic, religious and cultural differences that separated Catholic Croats from Orthodox Serbs encouraged excess and the barbarization of warfare in the Balkans. Italy's cultural and territorial pretensions in the Adriatic served likewise to sustain the offensive spirit of the Yugoslav troops, who until the close of 1918 remained firmly entrenched on Italian soil.

It was the lack of homogeneity which prevented the recurrence of large-scale mutinies such as those that had immobilized the French and destroyed the Russian armies in the spring and summer of 1917. The same bitter divisions frustrated attempts to recruit volunteers from among the large number of Austro-Hungarian prisoners of war in Russia. Although Slavs received preferential treatment from their fraternal captors, ethnic antagonisms and inter-communal conflict made them reluctant to renounce their allegiance to the Emperor. Mistrust of Serbian supremacy on the part of the Croats and Slovenes, for example, was sufficient to ensure that the projected Adriatic Legion was still-born. Indeed, only 10 per cent of South Slavs joined the volunteers, and these were largely Serbs. Even the Czech Legion, the largest and most famous of these volunteer formations, enrolled between one-fourth and one-fifth of the estimated 200,000 Czech and Slovak prisoners of war. Imperial troops were not, then, anxious to tear off their rosettes and eagles in support of Greater Serbia, or take up arms in the name of multinational entities like Yugoslavia and Czechoslovakia. Among the dissidents who did respond to Russian propaganda, committed nationalists, like the socialists, were a minority; more often than not the volunteers were motivated by personal rather than political considerations.

The Green Cadres, who combined nationalist and revolutionary goals with the more traditional occupation of banditry, underscore the diverse sources of unrest in the army. The Green Cadre phenomenon was first identified in July 1916. A report from the Karlovac area noted that troops from the *Ersatz* battalion of the 96th Infantry regiment, assisted by friends and relatives, were deserting their units, hiding their arms, and taking to the forests. By the spring of 1918 bands of armed deserters, ten to forty in number, roamed the hills and woods of Croatia-Slavonia, Bosnia-Herzegovina, Dalmatia and Istria; and by the autumn an estimated 50,000 were operating throughout the region. Turnover was rapid. Bosnian bands rarely stayed together for more than a few weeks; in Croatia-Slavonia, by contrast, the bands were more orderly, with elected officers and considerable quantities of guns, booty and false documents. In some districts groups of armed deserters became the magnet for disaffected elements, civilian and military. In the Srem, where formations sometimes operated at battalion strength, the deserter bands were reported to have included 'homeless people, day-labourers, and Gypsies . . . all armed to the teeth', while the village of Davidovici was said to have been pillaged by an armed group wearing Russian, Serbian and Austrian uniforms. In other parts of Bosnia the Green Cadre bands consisted of deserters and troops absent without leave, who lived by plunder during the autumn and summer, but returned to their units in winter when food was scarce and the climate inhospitable.

What are we to make of these people? Should they be characterized as brigands, freedom fighters, revolutionaries, or what? One authority concludes that in most cases they were probably something of each. 'The relative degree of criminality, nationalism or radicalism', writes Richard Spence, 'undoubtedly depended on the mixture of individuals within each group.' The Greens were in certain respects primitive rebels – peasant protesters operating out of a remote rural setting, often with local assistance, and without a general political orientation beyond resistance to oppression and poverty. To propertied and privileged sorts they were nothing more than common criminals; historians know better. The substantial criminal component of the Greens is not denied, nor is the criminality of their conduct disputed. It is the meaning and significance of their actions that remains problematic.

For remote peasant communities without understanding of the characteristic forms of modern social movements – organization and policy, programme and ideology – social banditry represented an available and acceptable response to the disruptive effects of industrialized warfare. Historically the connection between brigands and freedom fighters was strong: Balkan bandits who engaged the Turkish oppressor were cast as national heroes; those who took to the hills in defiance of authority were likewise lionized. In these parts Robin Hood spoke a Serbo-Croatian dialect. The Green Cadres were clearly an outgrowth of this tradition; insurrectionary rather than revolutionary, anti-German or anti-Magyar rather than pro-nationalist, they represented a pre-political phenomenon which perhaps anticipated the communist partisans of World War II but remained rooted in the past.

6.9   October 1918: the collapse of the Austro-Hungarian Empire

After the May mutinies the diffusion of discontent rapidly reached a critical mass. On 21 October 1918, the deputies of German Austria constituted themselves a Provisional National Assembly and proclaimed the formation of the Austrian state. A Political Council, chosen from the Provisional National Assembly and representative of all parties, assumed the role of government. Just as the Political Council was made up of all parties in the Provisional National Assembly, so the State Secretaries it appointed were drawn from all parties; and for the first time Austrian socialists obtained a share in government. Events moved quickly (for the chronology of collapse see Roberts, pp. 316–17). By the close of the month the Italian front had collapsed and Czechoslovakia and Croatia, like Poland before them, had declared independence; in Laibach, Trieste and Bosnia, power fell from Habsburg hands; the dissolution of the Austro-Hungarian Empire was complete.

7 THE AUSTRIAN REVOLUTION

7.1   Revolution? What revolution?

Poles, Czechs, Hungarians, Serbs, Slovenes, Croatians – all experienced national and political revolution at the end of World War I. Historians, while they differ in interpretation, are agreed about the far-reaching character of the changes that took place. However, about the status of post-war Austria there is no such unanimity. Was there a revolution in Austria in 1918/19 or merely a military collapse? For some the replacement of an absolute or quasi-constitutional monarchy by a democratic republic is taken as sufficient proof. From a comparative study of Central Europe at the end of World War I, F. L. Carsten concludes unequivocally that a revolution had occurred in Austria. The sudden and dramatic circumstances that brought six hundred years of Habsburg rule to a close, transformed the political structure of the country. Carsten writes:

> The German deputies of the *Reichsrat* had no authority to appoint a
> provisional government, the emperor was forced to renounce the exercise
> of his constitutional powers, and the Habsburg state disappeared for good.
> It was replaced by something entirely new: a state of the German-speaking

provinces which also claimed authority over German-speaking Bohemia and Moravia. This in itself was a revolutionary act, as these provinces had never formed a state . . . 'German Austria' was the product of a constitutional and political revolution. (Carsten, *Revolution in Central Europe 1914–18*, 1972)

Some scholars go even further. C. A. Macartney, for example, wrote a pioneering study of the infant Republic with the revealing title *The Social Revolution in Austria* (1929).

Others are adamant that no such revolution occurred: the monarchy quit but was not overthrown; the state apparatus was modified but not transformed; social inequality persisted; and private property remained fundamentally unchanged. Martin Kitchen, in his study *The Coming of Austrian Fascism* (1980), thus places the term in quotation marks. 'It is extremely doubtful', he writes, 'whether it is permissible to use the term "revolution" to describe the events in Austria at the end of the war'; he is 'certain that the collapse of the monarchy and the establishment of the republic were not the work of the Social Democrats, but rather the result of a process of internal decay'. In short, the Monarchy had disappeared by disintegration and dismemberment. If Kitchen is right and there was no revolution, how can we characterize the changes that did take place in Austria at the end of the war? Does the emergence of the Austrian Republic provide evidence of unguided social change, or does it represent a revolution that failed?

7.2   Austro-Marxism

Document II.27 is a survey and analysis of the problems and prospects of the Austrian Revolution. The author, Otto Bauer (1881–1938), was a founder member of the school of Austro-Marxism which flourished in Vienna in the years before World War I. The Austro-Marxists, whose luminaries included Karl Renner, Rudolf Hilferding and Max Adler, were concerned to restate Marxism in the light of the material, social and political changes that had occurred since Marx's death. Their preoccupations and procedures were empirical rather than philosophical; their primary interest lay in the creation of a Marxist social science that would comprehend law, psychology, cultural history and other fields of study previously neglected by Marxist theory. The output of this gifted group of scholars was remarkable. In the pages of their theoretical journal, *Marx-Studien* (founded in 1904), there appeared Adler's first thoughts on the theoretical and methodological principles of Marxist social analysis, Hilferding on the analysis of modern capitalist society, Renner's path-breaking work on the social functions of legal institutions, and Bauer on nationalism and its relation to the development of the economy and social classes.

All produced weighty tomes. Hilferding's *Finance Capital* (1910), which sought to analyse the structural change in capitalism arising out of the separation of ownership and control of production, represents a landmark in the development of Marxist social theory. Cartelization – the suppression of competition and the trend towards planned production, which Hilferding identifies as distinctive features of finance capitalism – also sets the agenda for the state and the rational reconstruction of the social order; out of the bowels of capitalism was emerging socialism. It followed, Hilferding concluded, that revolutionary politics required the control rather than the destruction of the state, a perspective which set the

Austro-Marxists apart from Russian Bolsheviks and German revisionists. The positive role of the state was of equal concern to Karl Renner, albeit from a different standpoint. His book, *The Institutions of Private Law and their Social Functions* (1904) remains *the* seminal study in the sociology of law; Bauer, too, believed that the state might be the agent rather than the enemy of the socialist revolution.

The Austro-Marxists were more than armchair revolutionaries, however. Unlike their contemporaries in the Frankfurt Institute for Social Research, the Austro-Marxists were all deeply involved in party politics. Adler was active in party conferences and educational work; Bauer, leader of the Austrian Social Democratic Party from 1918 to 1934, served as Secretary of State for Foreign Affairs at the close of World War I; Renner (1870–1950) served as Chancellor of the first Austrian Republic and President of the second; Hilferding, too, held ministerial office. 'As a result of this involvement', writes Tom Bottomore, 'there is to be found in much of their work a practical and realistic reflection upon the relation between social theory and political action' (Bottomore and Goole (eds) *Austro-Marxism*, 1978).

Exercise   Read Bauer's analysis of the condition of post-war Austria in document II.27. What in general terms are its principal themes? More specifically, (a) what are the sources of revolutionary enthusiasm; (b) why is the author opposed to the 'dictatorship of the proletariat'; (c) how is socialism to be attained; and (d) what are the achievements of the Austrian Revolution? ■

Specimen answer   Bauer is, I think, primarily concerned with the role of the state, the class structure
and discussion   of capitalist society and the situation of the proletariat, and the nature of the transition from capitalism to socialism. Let us examine these in more detail. □

The role of the state

The Austro-Marxist conception of the transition to socialism has been aptly characterized by Tom Bottomore as one of 'revolution through reform'. It was based partly upon a preference for peaceful change and a negative appraisal of the prospects for the establishment of the dictatorship of the proletariat, and partly upon a more positive appraisal of the role of the state in creating the institutions of the socialist commonwealth. Thus in the aftermath of war, when the balance of class power favoured the socialists, SPD interventions secured substantial improvements in the condition of the working class. Hours were reduced, conditions of employment enhanced, and works committees introduced; class relations were also affected by major measures on health, housing and education initiated during the period of working-class predominance. Vienna, where the socialists were in power until 1933, became the showplace of social democracy.

The situation of the proletariat

From the outset, however, Bauer and his colleagues were under no illusion as to the constraints on revolutionary action. The problems that faced the new regime were formidable. By comparison with the Austro-Hungarian Empire the young Republic was much reduced in territory, population and mineral resources. The surrounding successor states, prompted by an atavistic hatred of things German, were reluctant to supply the new democracy with markets and materials, fuel and food. The food situation was critical. Agricultural production, disrupted by war, had fallen by 53 per cent since 1913. Austria's peasant producers – less than 1 per cent of farms were above 500 acres in size – could not provide sufficient to feed the population.

Starvation exacerbated deep and growing divisions between town and country. On the eve of war Cisleithan Austria had only seven cities of 100,000 inhabitants in a country of 28 million; Hungary, with 20 million people, had only two. Vienna, like Budapest, dwarfed all rivals. The former was more than the seat of government and a centre of conspicuous consumption; for all its *Kultur* and *fin de siècle* romance, Vienna was also a great industrial district. Under Dualism its population rose from just over half a million to 1,675,000 in 1900, and to more than two million by 1914. The dismemberment of the Habsburg Empire after the war made its proletarian and 'wen-like' character seem even more pronounced; in February 1919 there were 113,905 unemployed in Vienna, 161,803 in Austria; in the following month the Viennese jobless accounted for 42 per cent of the Austrian unemployed. Likewise, Budapest was more than Hungary's cultural and economic capital; it, too, occupied a top-heavy position in relation to the provinces; for while accounting for 5.1 per cent of Hungary's total population, the city contained 28 per cent of its workforce and two-thirds of its principal industries.

In both Austria and Hungary war had intensified antagonisms between town and country and set producers and consumers at each other's throats. Moreover, the conditions which made wartime requisitioning a necessity did not disappear with the termination of hostilities. Peasants who still found themselves compelled to sell their produce below the market price were prone to withhold supplies; landowners were equally resistant, particularly in Hungary, where uncertainty as to agrarian policy led them to refuse to cultivate their fields. The downward spiral was accelerated by the collapse in industrial production, which meant that, in any case, neither Vienna nor Budapest had much to offer the countryside in exchange for the food they required.

The transition from capitalism to socialism

A socialist transformation was, in these circumstances, not to be secured without great sacrifices. Austrian social democracy was incorrigibly majoritarian in out-look, and hesitated to proceed, fearing that, without a greater measure of consent, it must face a bloody civil war and with it the prospect of Allied intervention. Bauer's class equilibrium analysis was simply a recognition that Austria, though more advanced than Hungary, also had a large agricultural sector. By contrast with Hungary, though, land reform was a less explosive issue, Austria having abolished all feudal forms of tenure as early as 1848. The Austrian peasantry, if less prone to seize land, was nevertheless determined to retain its holdings. These, though small in scale, were large in number. But for its Catholicism, the Austrian peasantry might have become a prop to a conservative democratic order in the same way as its counterpart of the Third Republic; as it was it remained traditionalist in outlook, anti-liberal in sentiment, and counter-revolutionary in politics.

Apart from food, it was the coal supply which rapidly became the most pressing of problems. The new state had acquired about 12 per cent of the population of the Empire, 30 per cent of its industrial workers, 20 per cent of the steam-boiler heating surface, but less than 1 per cent of its coal supplies. Austrian industry ground to a standstill: iron and steel production practically ceased; metal and machine manufacturers closed down; brick, lime and cement works put out their furnaces; building operations were abandoned. Transport, too, seized up; streetcar traffic in Vienna declined dramatically; the railway passenger disappeared.

In addition to its starving population and crumbling industries, the Austrian Republic was confronted with a huge deficit in the national budget, with rocketing inflation and with failing banks whose assets and dealings were located in areas of the Empire now separated from Austria. Apart from foreign loans, the authorities sought to print their way out of the crisis. The complete collapse of the currency was narrowly averted through the intervention of the League of Nations, but only four years after the end of the war. By then the average real income of workers and employees was 25 per cent below the level of 1914; the savings of the middle classes had been wiped out.

Ironically, the inflation of the currency undermined the stability it was meant to promote. Order and stability were, indeed, the watchwords of social democracy. From the outset the SPD, fearful of the blood-bath in the making, had sought to contain the revolutionary elements whose uncontrolled actions seemed certain to provoke civil war and foreign intervention.

Principal among these were demobilized soldiers and the war disabled. 'The social revolution which arose out of the war', Bauer wrote in *The Austrian Revolution*, 'proceeded from the barracks rather than from the factories.' Bauer presented the Austrian soldiery as a disorderly and dangerous force, given to violence and excess, brutalized by war, and capable of untold mischief. 'Where blind obedience had hitherto reigned, an elemental, instinctive, anarchical revolutionary movement now set in.' Of course, not all demobilized servicemen were so susceptible. The 'overwhelming majority', he readily conceded, 'were dominated by an irresistible desire to return home to wives and children'. By sheer good fortune these were helped on their way by the last great service the railways performed. The creation of a system of labour exchanges and provision of unemployment benefit, introduced with unseemly haste between 4 and 6 November, further served to reduce the number of disorderly men roaming the streets of Vienna on the look-out for trouble.

The residue supplied Communist extremism with a convenient constituency. Unemployed and disabled veterans, particularly those who had seen service on the eastern front, coupled with romantic revolutionaries from among the reserve officers, marched about the town displaying the menacing manners of a Red Guard. In April 1919 the 'more unstable among the unemployed and the demobilized and disabled soldiers' were persuaded to participate in an armed attack on the parliament buildings. Bauer's analysis leaves no doubt that the creation of the *Volkswehr*, which he describes as 'the first act of the proletarian revolution', was designed to arrest the disorder and chaos consequent upon defeat and demobilization.

Soldiers were perceived by the Social Democrats less as a positive revolutionary force in need of encouragement and more as a wild beast in need of domestication. 'In the days of the upheaval', wrote Bauer of the immediate aftermath of war, 'the revolutionary type was the homecoming soldier, filled with wild passions by his fearful experiences, who believed that, with rifle and bomb, he could overturn everything that existed.' Like the British labour movement, the Social Democratic Party acted primarily to prevent aggrieved servicemen falling into the hands of extremists. But whereas British socialists were concerned about the activities of the Right, their Austrian compeers feared the revolutionary Left; for 'with the returned soldier', wrote Bauer, 'the revolutionary opportunist [i.e. the Austrian Communist] allied himself, hoping for power, place, dignity and income from the subversion of the existing order.' The Austro-Marxists, whose horror of disorder was surpassed only by that of Ebert and Noske, worked untiringly to isolate and undermine their Communist rivals. Bauer himself saw the growing ascendancy of social democracy in almost Darwinian terms. 'Very soon', he wrote, 'the direction of the movement passed to a quite different, intellectually and morally higher type of man. Such a type were those tens of thousands of party and trade union delegates, members of workers', works' and soldiers' councils, who, in a gigantic effort marked by the highest degree of responsibility, managed to divert the popular energies released by the revolution, which threatened to destroy the revolution itself in violence and fury, into fruitful creative work.' In short, the marginalization of ex-servicemen and their subordination to the superior sorts who made up the rank and file of the social democratic labour movement was deemed to be 'the proper achievement of the revolution'.

Similarly, the workers' councils, which had enjoyed a mushroom growth since October 1918, rapidly became an instrument of order preoccupied with the distribution of food rather than the destruction of the bourgeois state. Even their role as organs of revolutionary encroachment upon economic administration was short-lived; the workers' councils were soon acting as little more than cheer-leaders for social democracy. 'Our activities in the workers' and soldiers' councils', Bauer boasted, 'kept the masses away from the Communists.'

As with the soldiers, the war brought about a fundamental change in the outlook of the proletariat. The collapse of military power in 1918 was accompanied by a collapse in the labour discipline that had been based upon it. Austrian workers were by no means immune to the revolution in the factories in Russia, Germany and Hungary, where the socialization of industry was the number one priority. On 7 April 1919, for example, the managers of the giant Donawitz Works of the Alpine *Montangesellschaft* were deposed by workers demanding the right of self-determination in industry. The Works' Committees Law, enacted the following month, was more concerned, however, with the extension of trades union power and the restoration of labour discipline than with self-government in industry. Employers, once they had recovered their composure, were by no means uniformly hostile. 'In many large undertakings', wrote a Vienna factory inspector in his annual report for 1920, 'the works' committees maintain strict discipline among the staff, and in this respect assist the management of the enterprise.' 'In many factories', he concluded, 'the works' committees have introduced a system of fines for breach of discipline.' Bauer was equally enraptured. 'The more the employers recognized that only the influence of the works' committees made the restoration of discipline possible', he wrote, 'the stronger was the influence which they were obliged to concede to the works' committees.'

These concessions, though, were small. Austrian social democracy, for all its protestations to the contrary, recoiled from any move towards the destruction of the capitalist domination of production. Iron and wood, the two most important raw materials, and coal and water, the two key sources of energy, were thus found to be unsuited to public control for fear that any attempt at forcible expropriation might offend foreign stockholders.

Considerations of foreign policy also led to the abandonment of the proposed *Anschluss* with Germany, and with it the dream of the socialist revolution which such a union had made possible. Although the Provisional National Assembly had on 12 November proclaimed Austria to be a constituent part of the German Republic, and although there was a good deal of opinion which felt that post-imperial Austria was not viable as an independent nation state, the Entente veto upon union with Germany was held to be absolute. There was, as Bauer recognized, a twofold inner contradiction in the Austrian Revolution: the contradiction between the great political power of the working class and its crushing economic poverty; and that between the freedom of the working class at home and its dependence upon capitalists abroad.

How was that contradiction to be resolved? For all their importance, the welfare measures promoted by the Austrian Social Democrats left key problems concerning the formation of a socialist society unresolved. Bauer remained confident, however, that History was on his side. War and revolution had destroyed the class state; in the new Republic, he argued, a state of equilibrium between the class forces existed. Social democracy, if not triumphant, did possess concrete achievements worth defending. As Bauer put it in *The Austrian Revolution*, 'if our revolution could not break the capitalist domination of production, it has implanted the nuclei of the socialistic system of the future within the capitalistic mode of production, which only need to be developed in order gradually to undermine the domination of capital and eventually to abolish it.'

The Austro-Marxists were certain that force alone offered no viable route towards socialism. To declare in favour of a proletarian dictatorship was, under the international conditions which then obtained, to issue an open invitation to counter-revolutionary violence. To proceed thus was in the eyes of most Social Democrats an act of insanity which must result in the destruction of the working class. The road to socialism, for them, was not paved with futile gestures and gratuitous violence, nor with good intentions; the achievements of the Austrian Revolution had to be preserved until the revolutionary tide was again on the flood; then might the advance be resumed.

8 THE HUNGARIAN REVOLUTION

If the achievements of the Austrian Revolution remain difficult to characterize, those of the Hungarian Soviet Republic are not in doubt. On 1 August 1919, the government of Bela Kun collapsed; he and his Communist coadjutors fled the country. The revolution was over; the counter-revolution had begun. There followed an orgy of blood-letting and political violence as Hungary succumbed to a 'White Terror', directed against Communists and Jews, under the semi-fascist dictatorship of Admiral Horthy. In all, the Hungarian Soviet Republic had lasted 133 days. The question naturally arises: what went wrong? Roberts, who encapsulates the rise and fall of the revolutionary regime in four sentences (p.326), offers an account which may reasonably be considered too schematic to provide a satisfactory answer. We shall, therefore, pause to examine the character and achievements of the Hungarian Revolution to see how it compares with events in Austria. This will prepare us for a closer engagement with the general issues of war and revolution in sections 9 and 10.

8.1   Economy and society in pre-war Hungary

The Hungary that went to war in 1914 was ruled by a despotic, chauvinist and intolerant landed aristocracy to whom liberalism in most of its forms was anathema. Peasant farmers, industrial workers, domestic servants and the urban lower classes – 94 per cent of the population, in fact – were all excluded from the political process; enfranchisement was confined to a propertied Magyar establishment that lived in feudal splendour on its vast estates (nearly one-third of Hungary's cultivable land was owned by 4,000 Magyar landowners). It was a cunning and coercive elite which rigged elections, corrupted the bureaucracy, fixed the judiciary, and manipulated Magyar nationalism in order to preserve its social and political predominance. It was also an extremely prosperous elite whose privileged self-image at times reached the sublime. 'Do gentlefolk die too?', asked one young Esterhazy of his tutor.

The most striking feature of the Hungarian social structure was the absence of an economically independent, politically potent or socially significant urban bourgeoisie. Beneath the great landed magnates was a large but impoverished middle-ranking nobility, known as the gentry, which, in the aftermath of peasant emancipation, turned its attentions to the state apparatus to preserve its position. Members of the 500,000-strong gentry increasingly monopolized government posts, county administration, the army, gendarmerie and police force. Economic progress depended largely upon the resource and initiative of ethnic entrepreneurs, most notably Germans and Jews, who on the whole found Magyarization more agreeable than did other oppressed national minorities.

Magyars, the dominant nationality, made up less than half of the total population; the ethnic division of the remainder of the population is shown in Table 11–13.17. With Magyar nationalism again in the ascendant in the second half of the nineteenth century, non-Magyar minorities suffered cultural deprivation and discrimination in education and employment. From the Compromise of 1867 down to the demise of the Austro-Hungarian Empire, the Magyar aristocratic regime declined to acknowledge the political existence of the non-Magyar nationalities, refused concession of any right to self-government, gave preferment to the compliant, and discriminated against dissidents. Among the former, Jews were particularly prominent. Hungarian Jewry grew rapidly during the nineteenth century, largely by immigration, and by 1910 numbered 923,000 or 4.5 per cent of the total population. Granted full and equal civic rights in 1849 and 1867, Jews occupied a dominant position in manufacturing, commerce and finance, areas neglected by the gentry with its aristocratic disdain for trade and industry. Their presence was equally pronounced in the liberal professions and in the universities. In the absence of a Magyar middle class, Jews, like Germans, provided a surrogate middle class of doctors and lawyers, businessmen and bankers. The strong urban orientation of Hungarian Jewry was equally marked. In the bigger cities Jews comprised no less than one in five of the town-dwelling population; in Budapest, the largest Jewish community, they accounted for 23 per cent of the population. Within Hungarian Jewry acculturation and assimilation were rapid; Yiddish was displaced by Hungarian (in 1910 it was the first language of more than three in four Jews), and Zionism was but a feeble force in a community that increasingly identified with the idea of a Hungarian nation state.

By the close of the century a Jewish financial oligarchy, made up of some fifty

Table 11–13.17 *National composition of Hungary (Transleithania) in 1890 and 1910*

Nationality	% in 1890	% in 1910
Magyars	42.8	48.1
Romanians	14.9	14.1
Germans	12.2	9.8
Slovaks	11.1	9.4
Croats	9.0	8.8
Serbs	6.1	5.3
Ruthenes	2.2	2.3
Others	1.7	2.2

Source: R. Pearson, *National Minorities in Eastern Europe 1848–1945*, 1983, p.62.

families, held the commanding heights of Hungary's fast-growing economy. These wealthy and well-integrated sorts had long since dispensed with the traditional garb of the ghetto; externally they were indistinguishable from the aristocracy whose life-style and values they readily appropriated. Among Jewish families of the *haute bourgeoisie*, 346 secured ennoblement, and 28 became barons and acquired substantial mansions and vast acreages, so that, prior to the outbreak of war, Jews owned one-fifth of Hungary's principal estates.

Magyarization, though meant to promote cohesion and integration among a heterogeneous population, ultimately proved to be the undoing of the aristocratic regime it was designed to protect. When war and revolution broke the fetters that bound them, not all the offers of linguistic and cultural autonomy could persuade Romanians, Slovaks and Slovenes to remain within historic Hungary, even when under the brief rule of communist internationalism in 1918/19.

Even within the well-adjusted Jewish community, there were signs of the dissidence that made Jews prominent recruits to communism, for Jewish social and economic mobility was not without a hidden price. Although no one said so, the ticket of admission into Hungarian society was purchased through conversion to one or another of the Christian denominations. Those agnostic, free-thinking and enlightened elements within the secularized Jewish intelligentsia who declined to pay the price were disadvantaged and debarred from further advancement. In socialist internationalism, these secularized sorts found not a means of assimilation but an alternative to it; and in the promise of a political community based on universalist principles they foresaw the end of Jewish particularism and all forms of ethnocentrism. The war against ethnic false consciousness was to be fought with a peculiar savagery by the Hungarian Soviet Republic; 12 per cent of those executed and 18 per cent of those imprisoned during the period of revolutionary dictatorship were Jews.

Its backwardness notwithstanding, Hungarian society did not lack dynamism. Economic progress in the period of Austro-Hungarian dualism was considerable. Between 1867 and 1914 the gross national product of the country registered an estimated six-fold increase. From the turn of the century to the outbreak of war, growth attained an unprecedented figure of 8.5 per cent per annum. Much of this was due to the process of industrialization, which took off in earnest in the generation before 1914. In the years between 1899 and 1913 the horse-power capacity of industry increased from 262,070 to 929,868; at the same time the gross value of industrial output soared from 1,366,000,000 kronen to 3,314,000,000.

More striking still is the decrease in the proportion of the population occupied in primary production. In the twenty years 1890 to 1910, the agrarian population fell from 82 to 62.4 per cent; in the major developing economies such as Japan and Russia, the population dependent upon agriculture declined respectively from 84.8 to 61.5 per cent and from 88.8 to 82 per cent; in Austria-Hungary as a whole it fell from 67.1 to 56.8 per cent. The growth of the industrial workforce was equally spectacular. In Hungary the proportion of the active population engaged in industry rose from 12.4 per cent in 1890 to 24.2 per cent by 1910. Table 11–13.18 shows that although independent craftsmen and workshop trades remained a significant feature of industrial employment, there had emerged a factory proletariat employed in large production units.

Table 11–13.18   *Structure of the active industrial labour force, 1900 and 1910*

	1900 Number	%	1910 Number	%
Independent craftsmen	301,026	33.7	330,975	29.5
Workers in small enterprises 1–20 employees	361,665	40.5	375,166	33.4
Factory workers 20+ employees	230,641	25.8	416,543	37.1
Total	893,332	100.0	1,122,684	100.0

Source: Andrew C. Janos, *The Politics of Backwardness in Hungary 1825–1945*, 1982, p.151.

Industrial requirements and the cultural imperatives of Magyarization also initiated an educational revolution which was itself an essential precondition for the entry of the masses into politics. The provision of elementary education from the mid century onwards led to a spectacular spread of literacy among the population. In 1842, 10 per cent of adults were literate; by 1900 the number so defined accounted for 61.4 per cent of adults; ten years later the figure had climbed to 68 per cent, at which point nearly 80 per cent of males were classified as literate. Popular education, however rudimentary, had created a population that was available for political mobilization to a degree that was uncommon in traditional societies.

It was among the urban population that the new political consciousness was most evident. Notwithstanding the conjoint effects of coercive labour legislation, Bismarckian-style welfare reforms and the base, bloody and brutal interventions of police and military, Hungarian social democracy gradually established itself as a potent political force capable of mobilizing the masses in defence of universal suffrage and social justice. At the turn of the century the Hungarian Social Democratic Party enrolled 72,790 members, while its affiliated trades unions registered 130,000 in the factories. Hungary had never seen anything like it. In the years before the war the socialists could muster 150,000 to 200,000 for demonstrations and political strikes. It was the formation of the Hungarian Social Democratic Party at the close of 1890 which marked the watershed; thereafter the labour movement was never without permanent organization or means of representation. Until the 1890s political demonstrations were the prerogative of university students; henceforth the streets belonged to the socialists.

It was on the streets of Budapest where violent encounters were most likely. Factory production in pre-war Hungary was highly concentrated both geographically and industrially. Large-scale industry was centred on Budapest, the population of which grew enormously from 270,000 to nearly one million in the half century preceding World War I. The new class of factory workers were confined to a small number of gigantic enterprises. In 1907 one in four of the labour force was employed by 25 enterprises; half of the machine- and metal-workers were employed in nine plants, and 97 per cent of steel-workers in three plants. From the ranks of this nascent industrial proletariat in due course arose the revolutionary challenge that destroyed the *ancien régime*. Significantly, the strike wave that so shook the central powers at the beginning of 1918 started at the factory of Manfred Weiss in Csepel, near Budapest. It was a similar movement in this, the biggest munitions factory in the country, which later brought the Hungarian Soviet dictatorship into power.

For all its material progress, however, Hungary on the eve of war was still a backward nation that had yet to make the transition from an agrarian to an industrial economy. Industrial progress notwithstanding, economy and society in dualist Hungary remained backward. Partnership with a more advanced Austria resulted in an uneven process of capitalist development in which the relations of production and the social conditions, inherited from feudalism, continued to coexist alongside a highly concentrated and technologically advanced industrial sector. Its situation in many respects was analogous to that of Russia, with a modern but diminutive industrial base overshadowed by a restless rural proletariat who scratched a living from meagre smallholdings supplemented by seasonal work and casual labour. Equally significant is the fact that the ratio of people engaged in the liberal professions and the civil service did not rise above 3.3 per cent of the total population. As in the Russia of the Romanovs, there was no mature middle class from which liberal democracy might draw sustenance.

8.2 Hungary and the war

The outbreak of war in Hungary, as in other parts of the Empire, was received with enthusiasm. Hungarian Social Democrats, like their Austrian counterparts, were well to the fore in their resistance to 'Russian barbarism' and support of the central powers. But as casualties mounted and the fighting continued, death and disruption became less and less tolerable. In Transleithania, as elsewhere, the defective war economy proved decisive. The failure to preserve a just equilibrium between military requirements and civilian consumption led to shortages of consumer goods and a sharp deterioration in the living standards of the population. The widespread development of black-market profiteering pinpointed the inadequacies of requisitioning and rationing and the attendant problems of state control. Runaway inflation, in many respects more devastating than enemy firepower, sapped morale and provoked resistance. From 1916 onwards the labour movement revived; industrial unrest grew apace. The foundation of the Independence Party under the leadership of Count Mihaly Karolyi, with its demands for peace without annexation and far-reaching internal reforms, signified a serious lack of confidence among the ruling elite in the Monarchy's generals and politicians.

The Russian Revolution changed everything. In the words of the Social Democratic Party, 'it struck a mortal blow at every despotic power of the world'. Hungarian workers were elated and encouraged to press their claims with renewed vigour. In the spring of 1917 vital war production industries were brought to a standstill as war-weary and distressed workers downed tools in defiance of military discipline; May Day once more became the occasion for mass demonstrations; class solidarity and class awareness found organized expression in the growth of trades unions, whose membership soared in excess of 200,000. The intelligentsia, too, found wartime radicalism irresistible; new socialist groups proliferated; demands for peace and progress gathered momentum.

On 25 November 1917 at the Hall of Industry in Budapest, there took place a mass demonstration in support of the socialist revolution. Several hundred thousand workers cheered demands for a general strike and the formation of workers' councils. Hungarian social democracy was unable to contain the rising groundswell. Dissatisfaction with the reformist leadership of the party and its trades unions found expression in the formation of a breakaway Revolutionary Socialist group, which pressed for the creation of a Soviet-style republic. The climax came shortly after; the three-day strike that began on 18 January 1918 spread across the country, involved more than half a million workers and led, in some places, to the formation of workers' councils. The government, recovering from an initial fright, turned to repression; arrests followed, bans were imposed, and a special security headquarters was set up for the defence of 'internal order'.

Repression was no longer sufficient to stem the tide of revolution. By the summer of 1918 the crisis on the home front was so acute that nothing short of a miracle could resolve it. Hungary, once the bread-basket of the Empire, was on the verge of starvation, without fuel and desperate for raw materials. The real wages of workers fell to 53 per cent of their pre-war level, that of day-labourers to 46 per cent, and that of employees to 33 per cent. In these circumstances, troops firing upon strikers at the MAVAG plant in Budapest provoked a nine-day general strike and mass demonstrations against the war and the government. Significantly, it was the intervention of the Social Democrats rather than the action of the army which brought the issue to a close.

8.3   The bourgeois-democratic revolution, November 1918 to March 1919

With its armies disintegrating, its peoples starving, and the enemy at the gates, a socialist seizure of power within the Austro-Hungarian Empire seemed a distinct possibility. However, Hungarian social democracy, like its Austrian counterpart, showed no inclination to lead the working class towards the socialist common-wealth. Instead it preferred to play second fiddle to the bourgeoisie as a partner in Karolyi's National Council, a broad-based grouping of middle-class democrats and radicals, which came into being in the dying stages of the conflict to maintain public order, supervise the transition from empire to republic, and preserve Hungary's territorial integrity.

The National Council was formed on 25 October 1918; within seven days the bourgeois-democratic revolution was victorious. On the morning of 31 October soldiers and workers occupied the public buildings of Budapest (including the city commandant's headquarters), bringing to a climax several days of demon-strations in favour of a Karolyi government. By now the authorities could do no more than roll with the punches. On the same day the new coalition government took office, pledged to Hungarian independence, universal suffrage, civil rights, social reform and land reform. On 16 November 1918 the formal and the real caught up with one another: Hungary became a people's republic.

It was a bloodless business. For the government and its supporters the events of 31 October marked the end of the revolution; reconstruction was to be a gradual and peaceable process conducted within a framework of law and order. Workers, soldiers and landless peasants thought otherwise. In the countryside, news of the revolution touched off a series of arbitrary seizures of food and property: expropriators were expropriated, the gendarmerie disarmed, and local bureaucrats dismissed. Elsewhere, workers' councils and soldiers' councils erupted with equal spontaneity. The labour movement grew with celerity. Trades union membership rose from 215,000 in January 1918 to 721,000 in December 1918, and above one million by February 1919.

The creation of the Hungarian Communist Party in November 1918 gave organization and direction to the elemental passions of the peasantry and the revolutionary unrest of the workers' councils. Its convenors were former Social Democrats who had been taken prisoner of war in Russia and subsequently fought with the Bolsheviks during the October Revolution. Bela Kun, their leader, had worked with Lenin, and derived great prestige from that association. The Party, which also gained the support of the left-wing opposition within the Social Democratic Party and the Revolutionary Socialists, promptly set about organizing the factories and the fields as well as the armed forces. Its programme called for the replacement of the bourgeois polity by a socialist formation run by the workers' councils and for the crushing of the counter-revolution. This last point is significant. Disaffected landowners, uprooted by war and revolution and fearful for their person, position and property, were already massing in the various semi-fascist military detachments that were to claim 5,000 lives and 70,000 prisoners during the 'White Terror' of 1919/20.

The success or failure of the bourgeois democratic revolution, however, depended less upon internal reforms undertaken by the Karolyi government and more upon the actions and policies pursued by the victorious allies. Karolyi was known for his Wilsonian sympathies and this, it was hoped, would secure more favourable treatment from the Entente powers. Indeed, one of the cornerstones of the regime was its national minorities policy. The creation of an 'Eastern Switzerland', a new form of coexistence based on autonomous rights for Hungary's oppressed peoples, would, it was hoped, enable democratic Hungary to distance itself from the foreign, domestic and national minority policies of the Dual Monarchy and in so doing preserve the lands of historic Hungary. But it was too late: the Transylvanian Romanians wished for nothing but to join with Romania; the Slovaks of Northern Hungary with the Czechoslovak Republic; and the South Slavs with the Serb-Croat-Slovene state. The victorious great powers, who had secretly agreed during the war to transfer two-thirds of Hungary's territory to Romania, Yugoslavia and Czechoslovakia, persisted in treating the Republic as a defeated country; it was their insistence upon the violation of its territorial integrity that led directly to the collapse of Hungarian democracy. On 20 March 1919 Lieutenant-Colonel Vix, the French representative at the Paris Peace Conference, presented the Karolyi government with a demand for a substantial slice of the nation's south-eastern districts. Acceptance was out of the question. Karolyi warned the Allies that if these claims were conceded, Bolshevism in Hungary would be triumphant. His protestations were ignored and he resigned.

8.4   Proclamation of the Hungarian Soviet Republic

The Hungarian Communist Party was by now a force to be reckoned with; its support was particularly strong among war invalids, demobilized soldiers and the workless who had been drawn by Kun's promises of jobs and high wages for everyone and large indemnities for returned servicemen. By March, communist agitation had made inroads into the trades unions as bread queues lengthened and problems, for which the collaborationist Social Democrats were held responsible, mounted. The Social Democrats were themselves uncertain as to whether they should crush the Communists, outbid them, or join them. The Vix note resolved their difficulties. The choice now lay between a Communist dictatorship or counter-revolution. The Socialists could not govern alone and the Communists would not govern without them; there was no alternative to a joint revolutionary government.

The new government, called the Revolutionary Governing Council, was formed on 21 March 1919. Ministerial portfolios (commissariats) were divided equally between Communists and Social Democrats. Bela Kun, who headed the Commissariat of Foreign Affairs, was acknowledged as its head; both domestic and foreign policy rested in his hands. Its programme, announced the following day, included the establishment of the dictatorship of the proletariat and the construction of a socialist society in alliance with the Soviet Union. The new Hungarian Soviet Republic renounced all annexationist claims desiring peaceful coexistence with the Western powers and their allies.

8.5   The revolutionary dictatorship

To create socialism in a backward country like Hungary posed problems of exceptional complexity; to do so in the aftermath of the bloodiest war in history and against a background of material exhaustion and military defeat suggested the impossible. Kun and his associates recognized these constraints but refused to be bound by them. The Hungarian Soviet Republic, in their eyes, represented the beginning of a revolutionary transformation, not the end. In a backward society, lacking a self-confident and dynamic middle class, and with a proletariat of uncertain judgement, democratic politics could only be vested in the hands of a dedicated few who supplied the vanguard of the proletariat. The revolutionary regime, Kun declared, was 'a dictatorship of an active minority on behalf of the by and large passive proletariat' which must of necessity 'act in a strong and merciless fashion . . . at least until such time as the revolution spread to the European countries'.

On the first day of office, the Revolutionary Governing Council declared a state of martial law and banned the sale of alcohol as a public order measure. A number of far-reaching reforms in the machinery of state were promptly instituted. The old professional army was replaced by a new and politically aware Red Army; the police and the gendarmerie, reorganized into a unified Red Guard, were likewise presented as defenders of revolutionary virtue. The system of justice, too, was reorganized: the courts were replaced by revolutionary tribunals, and justice was administered by workers advised by trained lawyers.

Industry also felt the wind of change. Production commissars and workers' councils were set up to control and supervise the management of the newly nationalized mining, transport and manufacturing industries. Banks and financial institutions were seized and housing requisitioned. Conditions of work took a quantum leap forward: wages were raised, equal pay for women was introduced, and the eight-hour day was made compulsory. Statutory protection for children and industrial apprentices was also announced. Equally popular was the introduction of food and consumer goods rationing.

On the critical issue of land reform, the Revolutionary Governing Council was equally uncompromising. Its decree provided for nationalization without compensation of all medium-sized and large estates and the introduction of collective farming on the properties taken into public ownership. Peasant aspirations were thrust aside and the redistribution of land prohibited on grounds of efficiency. The inferior productivity of small-scale farming was such, the Council argued, that the nation's food requirements could not be met except through the modern methods and mechanized farming that were only possible on the new agricultural co-operatives.

State ownership was also extended to all primary and secondary schools which, previously, had been largely church-controlled. Plans for the introduction of a uniform eight-grade school were drawn up, new textbooks commissioned and a new curriculum proposed. Priests, friars and nuns were allowed to remain in their teaching posts on condition that they quit their orders and entered the service of the state. The cultural and scientific life of the country was revitalized: Bartok joined the Directory of Music, Lukacs the Directory of Writers.

The electoral process, too, was overhauled. The old apparatus of public administration was swept away and power vested in newly elected councils, an offshoot of the workers' councils that had sprung up earlier in Hungary, as in Soviet Russia. Elections, held on 7 April 1919, on the basis of universal suffrage and a single list, suggested a good deal of popular support for the revolutionary regime. The extraordinary way in which students and industrial workers rallied to the Red Army, and the successful counter-offensive launched against the Romanian and Czech invaders in mid-May, were further indications of a popularity that might have been strengthened enormously had the revolutionary dictatorship seized the opportunity to identify the national revolution with the cause of communism. But this it failed to do, and support for the regime remained brittle.

Part of its weakness was simply structural; the state apparatus, though reorganized, had not been transformed. The non-availability of recruits from the proletariat compelled dependence upon those of uncertain loyalties. The Red Army, for example, relied on political commissars attached to army corps and individual units to work alongside commanders who were in the main professional soldiers; the Red Guard, too, was staffed with servants of the old regime. Nowhere was the shortage of cadres more apparent than in the management of collectivization. Commissars of production, appointed to head the new state-run collectives, were drawn overwhelmingly from the former owners or stewards of the large estates; there was no other source of expertise available. The rapidity with which the collectives were dismantled and the old owners restored on the appearance of the Romanian invader indicated the fair-weather character of the state apparatus. Significantly, the counter-revolutionary uprising of June 1919, though crushed by resolute action on the part of the revolutionary forces, was led by army and gendarmerie officers with the support of wealthy peasants, dismissed bureaucrats and disgruntled clergy.

The nationalization of economic life and the shortage of personnel, which led to the delegation of authority to bourgeois experts and the re-employment of the old bureaucracy, had a negative effect on the masses. The civil service, now charged with the administration of ration distribution, was detested before the war for its corruption and rude response to those with no special claim to its favours. To entrust decisions – life and death decisions – about the allocation of bread to such people was foolhardy. Complaints from desperate women about the doings of the 'bread-chit bureaucrats' undermined morale both at home and at the front. Workers worried about the state of their families drifted home from the army, and in so doing contributed to the demise of the revolutionary regime.

By the end of June the Red Army, which had repulsed the Romanians and reconquered the whole of Slovakia, was so diminished as to be well nigh useless. The regime was simply unable to sustain a war on two fronts: against the imperialist lackeys in the field and the counter-revolutionaries at home. It was this plus the promise of a Romanian withdrawal from the food-rich areas east of the Tisza which led Kun to concede Allied demands for the military evacuation of the northern regions. The decision to pull out of Slovakia without any guarantees that the Romanians would fulfil their part of the bargain led to the resignation of the army high command, desertions, and a collapse in the morale of the population, which saw its hard-won victories squandered and its nationalist aspirations trampled upon by a regime that seemed both incompetent and insensitive.

The presentation and management of the withdrawal was, in fact, symptomatic of a certain high-handedness and contempt for the masses which cost the regime dearly. Too often Kun and his associates seemed determined to thrust communist internationalism down Magyar throats in a manner calculated to give maximum offence. Kun, who condemned all 'petty bourgeois overtures . . . to social patriotism and bourgeois nationalism' and spoke frequently about his feeling 'no more akin to the Hungarian proletariat than, let us say, the American, Czech or Russian', derided all appeals to Magyar sentiment. Upon the proclamation of the Soviet Republic, there took place an officially sanctioned iconoclasm reminiscent of that of the sixteenth century: statues of national kings and heroes were dismantled, the national anthem was banned, and the display of the national colours prohibited. Suggestions that the national flag be hoisted alongside the red flag and national emblems be attached to the caps of Red Army soldiers were rejected out of hand, even though officers and men desired nothing else.

In the countryside, too, the Communist dictatorship showed scant respect for peasant sensibilities. Lenin's advice on the primacy of land redistribution and the pressing need to satisfy the requirements of the landless peasant was disregarded; instead the agrarian proletariat was harangued by urban agitators and the idiocy of rural life was held up to ridicule. All that such people held dear – family, church and community – were mocked, derided and condemned as mindless, superstitious and retrograde. Criticism from the countryside was treated with equal contempt. Provincial delegations at the National Congress of Councils, who met on 14 June 1919, were uncompromisingly hostile to the 'Soviet bureaucracy' and 'the dictatorship over the proletariat'. Kun, impatient with this 'counter-revolutionary prattle', promptly had the proceedings adjourned.

The rough handling of the countryside was more than an expression of the personal pique of the people's commissars. The resort to revolutionary violence and excess was itself symptomatic of Hungarian backwardness. The sharp deterioration in relations between town and country, aggravated by the disruption due to war and the continued Allied economic blockade, led Kun and the commissars to adopt a variant form of 'war communism' so as to feed Budapest and its proletariat. Supplies from peasants accused of hoarding were subject to confiscation and requisition; those who resisted were condemned as enemies of the revolution and punished, as were villagers who declined to accept the paper currency of the revolutionary Republic. Coercion was also required to maintain discipline and production on unpopular agricultural collectives. The Red Terror unleashed against a recalcitrant countryside claimed between 370 and 587 lives.

8.6   The fall of the Hungarian Soviet Republic

The structural constraints upon socialism in a backward country like Hungary were, as we have seen, severe. The question nevertheless arises: were these obstacles insurmountable? The victorious counter-revolutionaries evidently thought not. But for foreign intervention, they often claimed, the regime would have survived a lot longer. The sources of opposition were numerous but not united, and might in time have been subdued. We shall never know. On 30 July 1919, the Romanian army broke through the Hungarian lines of defence, crossed the Tisza and stood within one hundred kilometres of Budapest. The Revolutionary Governing Council promptly resigned; Kun and his commissars fled the country. On 1 August the Romanians entered Budapest. Private property and the old state apparatus were restored forthwith. On 2 August the revolutionary tribunals were abolished and the courts restored; the following day saw the dissolution of the Red Guard and its replacement by the police with their previous commanders. On 4 August the nationalized tenements were returned to their former owners and rent control was abolished; two days later industrial and commercial enterprises which had been taken into the public domain were restored to private ownership. The liquidation of persons began shortly afterwards.

Conclusion

Exercise This is a convenient point to pause and consider, by way of conclusion, how the post-war situation in Hungary compares with that of Austria. From what you have read so far in these units you should, in general terms, be able to identify certain similarities and differences between the revolutionary Republics. In a paragraph or two try to list their salient characteristics. ■

Specimen answer Perhaps the most obvious conclusion you might have reached is that revolutionary situations do not necessarily produce revolutionary outcomes. In neither Austria nor Hungary was there a socialist revolution. In the former it was the initiative of the three major political parties – the Social Democrats, the Christian Social Party and the German National Party – that produced the Provisional National Assembly and coalition government that supervised the transition from empire to republic. In this drama the Social Democrats performed a supporting role; both script and direction were supplied by the bourgeois parties. The Hungarian Revolution, by contrast, was little more than a war of national defence fought in the name of proletarian internationalism. Once it was clear that 'historic Hungary' could not be entrusted to the Soviet Republic, communism was done for.

National conflict, though, was not the sole constraint. In both Austria and

Hungary the balance of class forces was against socialist revolution. In a part of the world that was still agrarian in character, the attitude of the peasants was decisive; without their co-operation the revolution could be starved into submission. In both countries the urban working class supplied too narrow a social basis for socialism. The fate of the revolution depended upon the countryside. Austrian social democracy recognized as much; Hungarian communism was more adventurous. Inspired by the prospect of world revolution, it cast caution to the winds. Never knowing what Stalin knew, it plunged into collectivization without cadres. The revolution was doomed from the start. ☐

Peasants and workers, however, were not the sole source of revolutionary enthusiasm. In both countries returning soldiers performed a prominent part in the radicalizing process. Indeed, at the outset the Hungarian Communist Party was little more than an ex-servicemen's association. 'In its early stages', wrote Franz Borkeneau in 1939, 'the communist movement in Hungary was not proletarian in character. Its mainstay was the soldiers in demobilisation, of which at least a considerable part were peasants' (*World Communism*, 1971 edn). However, neither Austrian social democracy nor Hungarian communism sought to load ex-servicemen with special rewards in order to create a privileged and loyal following. The former, relying upon the combined effects of unemployment benefit and a still-functioning train service, sought to rid itself of them as fast as possible. The *Volkswehr* and the soldiers' councils were, likewise, thought of as instruments of order. The Hungarian Communists, whose need to arm the revolution was even greater, also failed to exploit the full potential inherent in an available supply of nationalist-minded land-hungry soldiers. The Communists were in fact almost as keen as the Austrian Social Democrats to marginalize the ex-service element. Kun, who for months had encouraged radical veterans to press for back-pay of 5,400 kronen, subsequently told representatives who arrived at his commissariat 'to get out . . . or otherwise you get 5,400 machine-gun bullets in your head'.

Neither the *Volkswehr* nor the Red Army could, in any case, absorb the socially uprooted and *déclassé* elements created by the victories of the Entente, who quickly found fellowship among the opponents of the Left. In both countries defeat and demobilization produced a massive dislocation in the bourgeois class and status order; inflation and insecurity, the rise of organized labour and the loss of place and position, radicalized the middle classes. In dualist Hungary, for example, where the terms 'Jew' and 'bourgeois' were readily interchangeable, there developed a vociferous anti-semitism comparable with that of pre-war Vienna, where Jews had long been perceived as competitors by businessmen as well as the professional and lower middle classes. Antagonisms of this sort narrowed further support for socialism.

The international situation was not propitious. From the outset the success of the Hungarian Revolution hinged upon support from Soviet Russia and the spread of revolution in Central Europe. It was soon clear that the hinge had stuck fast. For Austrian social democracy the Entente's embargo on Austrian–German unification closed the democratic route to socialism without making Bolshevism seem a more viable or attractive alternative. Quite simply, the precariousness of Vienna's food supply precluded any move towards a Soviet-style regime. The socialist revolution, declared the *Arbeiter Zeitung*, waited upon the rising of the industrial workers in Britain and France. Its editorial of 23 March 1919, two days after the proclamation of the Hungarian Soviet Republic, ran:

True, we could dethrone the bourgeoisie of our own country . . . a few battalions would suffice. But in regard to the Entente bourgeoisie, we are chained in a manner quite different from that of the Hungarian proletariat. Dictatorship of the proletariat here would be equivalent to a provocation and a declaration of war. The Hungarians advise us . . . to link up with Moscow; but Moscow is far away, the Soviet armies are still more than 1000km from us . . . Today we are powerless; but when the proletariat of the Entente countries rise against their bourgeoisie, then, in alliance with it, we too shall break our chains.

Meanwhile, in pressing Austrian claims for food and credit, the Social Democrats continued to remind the Allies that they alone stood between Bolshevism and disorder. It was an argument which was plausible and probably true; but it was also an argument to which Bela Kun could not lay claim. From first to the last, the Allies used their very considerable resources to strangle the Hungarian Revolution in its cradle.

As you will see in Book III, Unit 15, historians are increasingly impressed by the strength and continuity of power and the resistance of the social order in modern societies to revolutionary political change. Now, it is unquestionably the case that the Austrian Revolution failed to transform the state apparatus. For example, the *Volkswehr* and the soldiers' councils, the most significant attempt to socialize the military, were quickly undermined by the bourgeois majority in the coalition government. Indeed, this was one of the issues that precipitated the break-up of the government and the departure of the Social Democrats into permanent opposition. As to the ephemeral achievements of the Hungarian Soviet Republic, comment is superflous.

Socialism and social change are not the same thing, however. In Austria and Hungary the collapse of the Monarchy did lead to significant alterations in the character of the regime; in Austria it also led to improvements in wages and working conditions and in welfare provision, which, if they fell short of socialism, were not negligible to those concerned. Could the Social Democrats have done more? It is a question which the catastrophe of 1934 compels us to raise again and again. Alas, ours is an age in which such things still occur.

Note: sections 9 and 10 are written by Clive Emsley.

9 THE WAR IN THE BALKANS

World War I started in the Balkans with the Austro-Hungarian ultimatum to Serbia. Fascination with the western front has tended to mean that in the British historiography of World War I the Balkans are generally ignored after the initial references to their being the 'powderkeg' of Europe. Taking the Balkan countries overall you need to learn that:

1   not every Balkan country was involved for the duration of the war from 1914 to 1918;

2   even though some countries were not engaged in the war throughout its duration, they suffered enormous losses – indeed, some of them suffered proportionately much greater losses than the great powers;

3   the Balkans underwent significant boundary changes at the end of the war;

4   there were also major changes in governments and constitutions and in land ownership; sometimes these changes involved mass action, and whether we talk in terms of coups, riots, rebellions or even revolutions is, I think, open for discussion.

Exercise   You will not find a lot of detail on events in the Balkans in Roberts. However, I would like you now to read pp.294–318 of Roberts, to study the maps on pp.599, 602 and 603 of Roberts, and to note briefly what happened during, and as a result of, the war in (a) Serbia; (b) Bulgaria; (c) Romania; and (d) Greece. ■

Specimen answers   (a)   Serbia was destroyed in the winter of 1915–16. A government in exile was established on the island of Corfu and the new state of Yugoslavia was set up during 1918–19 out of Serbia, Montenegro, Bosnia-Herzegovina, Croatia and Slovenia.

(b)   Bulgaria entered the war in September 1915 on the side of Germany and Austria-Hungary. It collapsed rapidly before an Allied offensive in September 1918 and lost considerable territory, notably to Greece.

(c)   Romania entered the war in August 1916, was effectively knocked out by early 1917, and concluded the peace treaty of Bucharest on 7 May 1918. At the end of 1918 Romania re-entered the war on the side of the Entente powers to grab a share of the spoils; in the peace treaties it acquired territory from the Austrian Empire (notably Transylvania) and from Russia (Bessarabia).

(d)   In Greece there was division between King Constantine and his Prime Minister Venizelos over whether or not to participate in the war. When an Anglo-French force landed in Salonika in 1915 there were effectively two governments in Greece: that of the King and that of Venizelos in Salonika. Allied pressure led to the abdication of Constantine and the return of Venizelos as Prime Minister for the whole of Greece. □

The upheavals in the Balkan countries during and immediately after the war are not often referred to as 'revolutions', yet they have many similarities to the events and processes which we have noted took place in Russia and Germany. I want now to look at each of the countries in rather more detail.

9.1   Serbia/Yugoslavia

As it became clear that the war was not going to be over by Christmas 1914, the Serbian government began to formulate a series of positive war aims. The Serbs recognized that if they lost the war their independence was also likely to be lost, together with that of the other independent Serbian kingdom of Montenegro. However, if Serbia were to finish on the winning side, the Serbian government saw the possibility of acting in a role similar to that of the King of Piedmont in the unification of Italy; Serbia could unite the Yugoslav (which literally means 'south slavic') peoples, particularly those in the districts of Croatia, Slovenia and Dalmatia who were under Austro-Hungarian rule. The Nis Declaration of 7 December 1914, approved by a recently formed coalition government, stated Serbia's aims as the 'liberation' of all Serbs, Croats, and Slovenes. Nikola Pasic, the Serbian prime minister, began organizing propaganda in the principal Allied nations. In November he sent two Serbs to Rome to establish the 'Yugoslav Committee', which was set up to argue the case for the new state. The Committee itself, however, was drawn largely from exiles from the Austro-Hungarian Empire who, while dreaming of a Yugoslav state, were suspicious of possible attempts by Serbia to dominate them. As a consequence the relations between Pasic's government and the Yugoslav Committee became strained. It ought also to be noted here that Serbia's allies were not keen on a Serbian-dominated Yugoslavia. Britain regarded Serbia as a client state of Russia and disliked the prospect of greater Russian influence in the Balkans. Russia, on the other hand, was reluctant to see the Austro-Hungarian Empire dismembered for the example that it might set, and it also feared that the Orthodox church in Serbia would suffer because Croats and Slovenes were Catholics, and consequently a Yugoslav state could possibly come under Vatican and Italian influence. To complicate matters further, the Entente powers were keen to persuade Bulgaria and Italy to join the war on their side, and this meant promising both Bulgaria and Italy some of the territory coveted by 'Yugoslavia'.

The Serbian army performed creditably in the early months of the war, driving back invading forces on three occasions. The last invasion force, however, left typhus in its wake, and this immobilized the Serbs in the spring of 1915, causing an estimated 300,000 deaths in the country. The close of the year witnessed an even greater disaster. A combined Austrian and German invasion was launched, Bulgaria entered the war against Serbia, Greece reneged on treaty obligations to assist Serbia if attacked, and British and French troops at Salonika were far too few to be committed to any meaningful action on Serbia's behalf. Avoiding a pincer movement between the Austro-German and Bulgarian armies during the winter of 1915–16, the Serbian army, with thousands of refugees, retreated through the mountains of Macedonia and Albania. The survivors gathered around the government in exile on the island of Corfu.

Occupied Serbia was divided between Austro-Hungarian and Bulgarian rule. The actions of the former were restrained, though the Austrians were determined to reap such economic benefits as they could from the occupied lands. Bulgarian rule was ferocious. The Bulgarians declared that the Serbian state had ceased to exist. They introduced their language into schools, courts, and on inscriptions. They exiled or executed Serbian clergy. They made men of military age liable to conscription for the Bulgarian army. The response was predictable: there was a massive insurrection against the Bulgarians, which was savagely suppressed.

Defeat and exile did not produce unity among the Serbs on Corfu, nor did it resolve the division between the Serbian government and the Yugoslav Committee. The Prince Regent, Alexander, was unhappy with Pasic, and both of them were concerned about the continuance of the secret society in the army which called itself Union or Death. The latter problem was resolved with the arrest and execution of the society's leaders in 1917 for allegedly attempting to kill Alexander on a visit to the Salonika front. Before being shot by firing squad, Colonel Dimitrivec-Apis allegedly shouted, 'Long live Greater Serbia! Long live Yugoslavia!' The friction between the Serbian government and the Yugoslav Committee was highlighted by the attempt to recruit volunteer units for the Serbian army from Serbs, Croats and Slovenes who had been captured by the Russians while fighting in the Austro-Hungarian army. Serbian officers sent by the Corfu government to command the volunteers appear to have alienated non-Serbs. The February/March Revolution in Russia exacerbated the problem when some of the volunteers and their officers demanded a committee to participate in the command of the corps. Some of the volunteers also demanded that they be known as the Yugoslav Volunteer Corps, carry Yugoslav rather than Serbian flags, and that Croats and Slovenes serve in different units from the Serbs. The squabbling led to a departure from the volunteers of about 10,000 of the 30,000 who had been recruited. In spite of requests from Pasic's government, the Yugoslav Committee was not inclined to intervene and attempt to restore order. Difficulties flared again when, in June 1918, the Allied governments recognized the right to independence of the Poles and the Czechs; the Yugoslav Committee demanded similar recognition, much to Pasic's alarm and annoyance.

In the event, it was less the discussions of diplomats and politicians in exile that initiated the formation of the Yugoslav state, and more the action of the men who remained in the territory, especially those in the south Slav provinces of the Austro-Hungarian Empire. In 1917 peasants in these provinces had begun to avoid army service or to desert, taking refuge in the woods in large numbers. As the war drew to its close more deserters, returned prisoners of war, and just returning soldiers joined the *zeleni kader* (Green Cadres), described by David Englander in section 6.8 above. As far as these were concerned, the collapse of the old order meant an opportunity for land redistribution; it also meant an opportunity for retribution against rich merchants and big landowners. A very high percentage of the landowners employing Orthodox Serbs and Catholic Croats were Muslims, which gave the uprisings of the Green Cadres a religious character. Some of the Cadres also claimed affinity with the Bolsheviks, though, as David Englander points out, it is difficult to be sure exactly what this may have meant.

In the hope of establishing a new and stable kingdom out of the wreckage, a National Council was established in Zagreb in October 1918. When the imperial government asked for an armistice it handed the local authority over to the Council which, in turn, proclaimed a new state of Croats, Serbs, and Slovenes. It also organized a national guard and proclaimed martial law, neither of which could stop the activities of the Green Cadres. Indeed, the national guard itself often perpetrated crimes against the unfortunate Muslim landowners. Units of ex-prisoners of war were also hastily organized to oppose Italian troops marching into Dalmatia. In the midst of the internal chaos the National Council opened negotiations with the Serbian government and the Yugoslav Committee in Geneva. At the same time some Serbian units, fighting their way into their native country, began taking Yugoslav names. On 1 December 1918, following an invitation from the National Council in Zagreb, Prince Alexander proclaimed an Act of Union and assumed the position of Regent of the Kingdom of the Serbs, Croats and Slovenes (the title Kingdom of Yugoslavia was not finally adopted until 1929).

For the first year of its existence the new kingdom was run by a provisional government and provisional legislature based on a union of the old Serbian parliament, the National Council, and regional representatives. No party had an overall majority; indeed, there was a plethora of political groupings, most of them with strong regional ties. The first truly Yugoslav party was the Democratic Party established by the merging of several groups from Serbia and the Habsburg lands; essentially it was liberal and progressive. To the right of the Democrats was Pasic's Serbian Radical Party, which had a firm power-base in Serbia, notably among the peasants, but which also drew support from some in the old Habsburg lands. Squabbling among different groups on the Left led to the creation of the Socialist Workers' Party of Yugoslavia (Communist) in April 1919 and ultimately to the Communist Party of Yugoslavia in June the following year. Large numbers of Yugoslav Communists had experience of revolution in Russia (20,000 of the 50,000 foreign troops in the Red Army were ex-Austro-Hungarian prisoners of war of Croat, Slovene or Serbian origin) and in Hungary; these formed a notably radical element within the party. Most notable among the remaining political groups was the Croatian Peasant Party, which was suspicious of what it considered to be Serbian centralization and which hoped for a degree of dualism within the new state.

Elections for a constitutional assembly, put off until the frontiers of the new kingdom had been resolved, were held in November 1919. The Democrats and the Radicals won 92 and 91 seats respectively. The Communists and the Croatian Peasants, the next largest parties, won 58 and 50. The remaining seats, 128 of them, were divided between Serbian agrarians, clerical groups and Muslims. The problem for the new state was that the third and fourth largest parties, the Communists and the Croatian Peasants, were opposed to the way in which it was developing. The latter were determined that Croatia should maintain its identity as a separate 'peasant republic'. Fortunately for the new state, the Peasants did not form an alliance with the Communists. As far as the Communists were concerned, the peasants were petty bourgeois and the future lay with the industrial proletariat – a group which existed in very small numbers in Yugoslavia during the immediate aftermath of the war. But there was also the problem of ethnic differences. The Croatian Peasants wanted to maintain their separate identity (and they were not the only group in Yugoslavia with this in mind – the new state had to contend with a terrorist Macedonian independence movement, IMRO, based in Bulgaria and the *Komiti* guerrillas in Montenegro, both aided by the Italians). The Communists, however, believed in centralization. Communist activists, disappointed by the failure of general strikes called in 1920, and by the inability of their deputies to achieve much in parliament, turned to terrorism in the summer of 1921. The actions were counter-productive; terrorism lost the Communists sympathy, and enabled the government to crack down on the party. By 1922 the Communist Party of Yugoslavia had almost ceased to exist.

9.2   Bulgaria

Although Bulgaria did not enter the war until 1915, it was affected by the conflict from the beginning, since both groups of belligerents established open and/or clandestine organizations within the country to purchase and export supplies. The behaviour of the Germans and Austro-Hungarians was particularly irksome in this respect, as they both used the label 'war materials' to export butter, flour and meat, and to bypass the Bulgarian customs. However, in spite of the annoyance caused by these activities, Tzar Ferdinand and Vasil Radoslavov, his chief minister, had come to the conclusion by the summer of 1915 that the war was going to be won by Germany and Austria-Hungary, and that Bulgaria could both avenge its defeat in the Second Balkan War and enlarge its territory by joining with them. However, not all politicians agreed with the King and his chief minister over the declaration of war. Prominent in the opposition was the Bulgarian Agrarian National Union (BANU) and its leader Alexander Stamboliski. BANU was a party which had its power-base in the peasantry, and in the election for the National Assembly of November 1913 it had polled 21 per cent of the votes cast and won the second largest number of seats. In the summer of 1914

Stamboliski had urged strict neutrality and warned of a repetition of Bulgaria's defeat in the Balkan Wars. When Ferdinand and Radoslavov determined on war, Stamboliski was arrested; the arrests of other deputies followed. The Bulgarian socialists were already irrevocably split between the purists, fanatical 'Narrows' and the more pragmatic 'Broads'. Both had spoken out against the war until it was declared. The Broads then, with some reservation, decided to support the government, while the Narrow deputies continued opposition but, unlike BANU, were largely unmolested.

In spite of the resounding and rapid success against Serbia, senior army officers were expressing criticism of the government's administration, particularly in the occupied territories, as early as 1916. The civilian officials appointed to these territories were, the officers maintained, totally incompetent. In August 1916 the army attempted to oust them from their positions in occupied Macedonia. More serious, though, was the growing unrest in Bulgaria itself brought about by the economic disruption created by war. Bulgaria had mobilized in 1915 during the harvest, which, together with requisitioning to supply the army, meant a severe shortage of bread in 1916. Continuing conscription, which by the end of 1918 involved nearly 40 per cent of the male population, meant that farm labour had to be performed by women, children, the old and the infirm. With artificially low prices fixed for the sale of their produce, peasants simply stopped producing for the market. The land under cultivation fell by 12 per cent and the grain harvest by 47 per cent in the years 1915–18. German and Austro-Hungarian food purchasing continued. German and Austrian troops, who were stationed in Bulgaria, also seriously affected the food supply, especially after December 1915 when their currency was made legal tender in Bulgaria. The government found itself unable to finance the war and resorted to printing money; this caused major inflation, with all the inherent problems for those on fixed incomes, the less well-off, and those who could not use their industrial muscle to increase their wages. These problems were exacerbated by rumours of the wealthy making vast profits from food speculation. Anti-government demonstrations and rioting over food shortages, with women playing a significant role, began early in 1917.

The morale of the troops at the front also deteriorated markedly as the war continued. On leave they witnessed the problems at home. But the chaotic and corrupt administrative system to supply the army virtually ground to a halt in 1917; the troops received only the most meagre rations, insufficient ammunition and medical supplies, and no replacement boots or clothing. The Bulgarian soldiers resented their better paid, better fed, better equipped German allies, and a sense of kinship developed with their Russian enemies. Those parties which had opposed the war from the beginning, BANU and the Narrows, began to win converts, and mutinies led by agricultural union or socialist activists began. So also did a rumour that the alliance with Germany was for three years only and that, in consequence, Bulgarian involvement in the war would cease on 15 September 1918. That was also the day chosen by the French general Franchet D'Espérey to launch an offensive with his French-British-Greek-Serbian armies along the Salonika front. The Bulgarian front line collapsed, the retreat became first a rout, and then a rebellion.

Thousands of retreating troops streamed back from the front and converged on the small town and railroad junction of Radomir. Here the mutinous troops appeared to be making ready to attack the capital, Sofia. Desperate to redeem the situation, Tzar Ferdinand, now without Radoslavov who had been forced to resign by events earlier in the year, released Stamboliski from prison and sent him to Radomir to pacify the troops. Stamboliski was subsequently to claim a central role for himself in proclaiming the 'Radomir Republic'. In fact the running appears to have been made by one of his lieutenants, Raiko Daskalov, who announced to the troops the deposition of Ferdinand and the creation of a provisional government. Stamboliski returned to Sofia where he endeavoured to establish an alliance with Dimitur Blagoev, leader of the Narrows. Blagoev refused; he assumed that Bulgaria was about to follow the same pattern as Russia and intended to await his opportunity in a Bulgarian 'October'. Moreover, ideologically he could not accept that a peasant party could be in the vanguard of revolution – peasants to Blagoev were petty bourgeois and in no sense progressive. While Stamboliski attempted to negotiate, Daskalov led the army of Radomir against Sofia, only to be beaten at the gates by a few troops still loyal, heavily reinforced by well equipped German units. But even as these events unfolded, the Bulgarian regime was in the process of dramatic change. On 26 September, the day before Daskalov proclaimed the republic, the government had requested an armistice, and on 29 September, the day of Daskalov's first assault on Sofia, the armistice was signed. Ferdinand abdicated in favour of his son Boris, and left the country. Within a short time the wartime coalition government was expanded to include BANU and the Broads. The Narrows were determined to maintain their ideological purity and await the 'inevitable' revolution.

Peace, as in other countries at the close of the First World war, brought almost as many problems as it solved. Rapid demobilization poured thousands of men back into the shattered economy, and while the peasantry were fairly quick to restore their pre-war living standards, the situation in the towns was appalling, with many people literally starving. The victors' demands for reparations impeded economic reorganization. The demands for Bulgarian territory, for example, meant some 400,000 refugees from lost lands entering a state much reduced in size. Among these refugees were members of the IMRO (Internal Macedonian Revolutionary Organization) who, financed partly by the Italians and partly by 'taxes' which they levied from the local population in the areas where they were based, carried out brutal raids in the Yugoslav province of Macedonia.

The appalling economic situation boosted the membership of the Narrows. In 1915 the Party had only 3,400 adherents; by December 1918 this number had risen to 6,000, by the end of January 1919 to 10,000, and at the end of 1919 there were over 30,000. The interesting point about the membership of the party was that only 10 per cent was made up of industrial workers; there were far more people drawn from professional groups, notably civil servants and teachers who, during the war years, had probably suffered a more dramatic decline in living standards than any other groups. In May 1919 the Narrows transformed themselves into the Bulgarian Communist Party with a programme for revolutionary action to overthrow the 'bourgeois' government. However, the Bulgarian population was still overwhelmingly agrarian, and the party which did best in the elections of August 1919 was Stamboliski's BANU.

Though initially without a majority in the assembly, Stamboliski and BANU dominated Bulgarian politics until the summer of 1923. Bulgaria had long been a country of small landowners, relatively prosperous in comparison with many peasants in the Balkans, but BANU still believed there was room for improvement and had an ideal based on small, profitable farms run by their owners but assisted by credit, consumer, and producer co-operatives which would provide the small farmer with the technological and economic advantages of large-scale capitalist farming. To achieve this end land was to be expropriated for the landless or for those with dwarf holdings, and Stamboliski's government encouraged the formation of co-operatives. To inculcate ideas of duty, as opposed to what BANU regarded as the militaristic nationalism taught to conscripts before the war, to break down divisions between town and country, and to enable the achievement of large-scale national development projects, compulsory labour service was introduced for all men aged 20 (for one year) and for all women aged 16 (for six months). The compulsory labour for women was never fully implemented, primarily because of the traditional view of women's role left from the Turkish occupation. Muslim women, most notably, were exempted from labour service. BANU also proposed major educational reforms and changes in the system of justice.

These reforms and changes were not universally popular. Urban workers, encouraged by the Communists as well as by the Broads (the latter now becoming more militant in the attempt to win back those supporters who had switched to the Communists) saw nothing for them in reforms which were concentrated on peasants, and they disliked the compulsory labour service. Because of the restrictions imposed on the size of the Bulgarian army by the victors, and because of his suspicions of the officer corps, Stamboliski recruited the paramilitary Orange Guard from among the peasantry to help maintain his authority against communist and socialist labour. In the strike wave which hit the country in the winter of 1919 and 1920, the Orange Guard fought alongside the army and the police in brutally repressing labour demonstrations and strikes. But the urban workers proved far less formidable than other opponents of BANU. Large landowners, who were still strong in the traditional political parties in the Assembly, condemned land reform as an attack on the sacred rights of private property; and the well-to-do disliked having to perform labour service alongside, and on an equal footing with, peasants. Many army officers hated Stamboliski for opposing the war, for the Radomir rebellion, and for signing the peace treaty. A secret military league was formed to preserve military values and to stand 'above politics'. As well as most of the serving army officers, the league's ranks included thousands of officers retired because of the reduction imposed by the victors in the war. Finally, IMRO was enraged by Stamboliski's attempts at *rapprochement* with Yugoslavia and his criticism of the Macedonian terrorists and their aspirations. In June 1923 a coup organized by the military league and IMRO toppled Stamboliski's government. Stamboliski and several others were brutally tortured and murdered. BANU, without the dominant presence of Stamboliski, dissolved into several factions, and while some of the reforms were continued by the new government, it was with little enthusiasm for idealism.

9.3   Romania

Romanian politicians were divided in 1914. A secret treaty had been negotiated with the triple alliance. King Charles, a German prince himself, together with much of the Conservative Party, was keen to honour the treaty, but the Liberal Party, which was then in office, reneged on it. The King, distraught by this action, contemplated abdication. His death, in October 1914, brought his heir Ferdinand to the throne; possibly more important, however, was the strong personality of Ferdinand's wife, Marie of Edinburgh, the grand-daughter of Queen Victoria and of the Russian Tzar Alexander II, whose sympathies were strongly pro-Entente.

For two years Romania maintained a position of armed neutrality, with both sides eager to purchase its grain and oil as well as its military allegiance: the central powers offered the Russian province of Bessarabia should Romania enter the war on their side; the Entente offered Austro-Hungarian territories. All of these territorial bribes contained large numbers of ethnic Romanians. It was alarm at the scale of the central powers' success that eventually brought Romania into the war in August 1916. The war was not popular with the Romanian Social Democratic Party. Even before Romania entered the conflict, the war was beginning to have an adverse affect on urban workers through economic disruption and rising food prices. However, strikes and demonstrations to maintain neutrality in 1916 were dealt with ferociously. Of course, the urban working class was only a tiny percentage of Romania's population, and by no means all were adherents of the Social Democrats. Romania was overwhelmingly a peasant society. Peasant concerns were different: the war and the Russian Revolution provided a new impetus for the kinds of changes which the peasants wanted.

While Romanian agriculture produced good yields, few Romanian peasants owned their land, and profits tended to go to absentee landlords. Discontent among the peasantry over land tenure and over high and rising rents had provoked a massive uprising in 1907. In the aftermath of the uprising legislation had been passed to help the peasant, but it was little enforced at the local level where it mattered. During the Balkan Wars the largely conscript peasant army was promised more land reforms; furthermore the Romanian soldiers invading Bulgaria saw an agricultural system which they envied – peasants with their own holdings, no enormous estates with absentee landlords, better built villages. On the restoration of peace the Liberal Party promised action, but with the outbreak of war in the summer of 1914, even though Romania was not directly involved, land reform was once again shelved until 'after the war'. Romania's entry into the war in 1916 soon met with disaster; troops of the central powers entered Bucharest on 6 December 1917, and the Romanian government and its army retreated, under the protection of Russian troops, into the province of Moldavia.

Exercise   What, as far as the Romanian government was concerned, were the disadvantages of being shielded by Russian troops in the winter of 1916–17 and the following spring? ■

Specimen answer   Russia was shortly to be plunged into a revolution and Russian soldiers were to start establishing soviets. □

Discussion   There was the further problem of the peasant disorders in Russia. The Romanians coveted Bessarabia, which bordered Moldavia and contained a large number of ethnic Romanians. Bessarabian peasants acted like others in the Russian Empire and, in the aftermath of the fall of the Tzar, they began seizing land. Thus in the spring of 1917 the Romanian government found itself with a demoralized and beaten army, closely allied with an army involved in revolutionary agitation (soviets were established in the Romanian army at an earlier stage), and Romanian soldiers could watch their ethnic brothers in Bessarabia appropriating land.

Exercise   What could the Romanian authorities do to prevent disorder and a breakdown of discipline in their army? ■

Specimen answer   They could promise land reform and/or crack down on all agitation. □

Discussion   In the event, the Romanian government followed both of these policies. King Ferdinand travelled to the front and spoke to the troops, promising them land reform:

> Sons of peasants, who, with your own hands, have defended the soil on which you were born, on which your lives have been passed, I, your King, tell you that besides the great recompense of victory which will assure for every one of you the nation's gratitude, you have earned the right of being masters, in a large measure, of that soil upon which you fought.
>   Land will be given you. I, your King, am the first to set the example; and you will also take a large part in public affairs. (Quoted in David Mitrany, *The Land and the Peasant in Romania*, 1930, p.101)

This promise appears to have restored morale, and Romanian troops fought courageously in the Kerensky offensive of July 1917. But, at the same time, the authorities dealt severely with any continuing agitation in the army. A Constituent Assembly meeting in the summer of 1917 amended the constitution and outlined the principles for a law of land appropriation which was to be passed six months after the liberation of national territory.

The disintegration of the Russian armies as the revolution progressed left the Romanians totally isolated. Out of necessity a preliminary treaty was negotiated in March 1918, with the Peace of Bucharest being signed in May. The terms imposed by the central powers were harsh. They were to have virtual control of Romania's oil production and railways; factories were to be dismantled, timber felled and livestock forcibly exported. This was all in addition to the destruction that had followed the central powers' invasion. The oil wells had been largely, if temporarily, destroyed by a British agent, while the troops of the German general Mackensen behaved like many other invading armies. Mackensen criticized the behaviour of his troops in an order of the day:

> They take away from the population, in a foolish way and much in excess of the needs of the troops, teams and supplies which are needed for the cultivation of the soil; refugees returning to their homes, instead of receiving help, find their poor belongings pillaged. Much wealth is being destroyed of set purpose; animals are wasted without purpose, so that meat is getting scarce, notwithstanding the former riches of the country in animals . . . The numerous stragglers who roam behind the front are causing disorders which have become a pest to the land . . . This order of the day must be expressly communicated also to the troops of the allied countries. (Quoted in David Mitrany, *The Effect of the War in South-Eastern Europe*, 1936, pp.164–5)

This particular problem continued even after the end of the fighting. In the towns, expropriation by the central powers, together with their insistence that the Romanian government print money to finance itself, made for continuing shortages and inflation, with consequent disorders and strikes.

The collapse of the central powers towards the end of 1918 gave the Romanians opportunity for prompt revenge. In the countryside there was much settling of scores with those who had informed on peasants hiding food from central powers' requisitions, and with those who had collaborated and/or profited from occupation: 508 communal councils were dissolved and 202 village mayors and local officials were dismissed for these reasons.

Joining in on the winning side in 1918 also gave the Romanian government the opportunity of securing the territories promised by both sets of combatants three years earlier. The central powers, while occupying much of Romania and negotiating the Treaty of Bucharest, had been sympathetic to the Romanian confrontation with Bolshevik forces in Bessarabia and had no objection when, in April 1918, the national council of Bessarabia voted in favour of union with Romania. Given the Entente's antipathy to Bolshevik Russia there was no suggestion that Romania should give up this territory when World War I ended. Re-entering the war on the side of the Entente gave the Romanians the opportunity to seize and incorporate the Austro-Hungarian territories of Transylvania, Bukovina and the Banat. In August 1919 the Romanian army also occupied Budapest, driving out the short-lived Hungarian Communist government of Bela Kun. The victorious Entente powers protested vigorously, but the Romanians did not withdraw until November, and during that time the Romanian army was able to pay back in kind for the destruction wrought by Mackensen's troops. Hungary, Bulgaria and Russia all had reasons to resent the new, bloated, Greater Romania which was doubled in size and population in 1919 (in 1915 Romania constituted 137,900 square kilometres with a population of 7,625,000; in 1919 it covered 294,000 square kilometres with a population of 15,500,000). The Romanians themselves, now with a greater variety of ethnic minorities than any other country in Eastern Europe, had no intention of pandering to the 30 per cent or so of the population that made up these minorities. The Romanian solution to any problems from national minorities was integration, if necessary by force, and emigration, again if necessary by force.

If peace brought extended territories and problems of national minorities, it did not mean that other internal problems were automatically solved. Land reform took much longer than the six months allowed by the constitution of the Constituent Assembly in 1917. Opposition from large landowners who, in spite of electoral reform and the granting of universal manhood suffrage, still had considerable clout in the Assembly, checked various proposals, and it was not until July 1921 that successful legislation for land reform was promulgated. The reform was not wholly satisfactory to the peasantry but it appeased them, and the new Peasant Party which was established in the aftermath of the war gave them a voice within the legislature. The Peasant Party, like most of its fellows, became violently hostile to Bolshevism.

Some communist writers have asserted that as the central powers collapsed and retreated, and before the Romanian army re-entered Bucharest and the rest of the occupied zone in November 1918, a revolutionary situation existed which the Social Democratic leadership and the proletariat failed to exploit. Admittedly a few workers' soviets were established, as were some workers' militias, but such groups were only a tiny minority of the population and never succeeded in making links with, let alone mobilizing, the peasantry. The Social Democrats made little attempt to profit from peasant exasperation over the time that land reform took; nor did they profit from unrest in the Romanian Army in 1919, when many peasant conscripts decided that, as far as they were concerned, the war was over, and deserted. The Social Democrats had little interest in intervening against

Communists in Hungary or Russia. Where the party, and especially the extreme Left, was able to win recruits was in the urban areas where workers, for some three years following the end of the war, continued to suffer from the effects of wartime inflation and from shortages of food, fuel and housing. In October 1920 the socialists determined to confront the government, demanding a series of concessions in the tough anti-labour legislation which had just been introduced, and threatening a general strike if their demands were not met. The ultimatum proved to be a disaster for the socialists. The government proclaimed martial law, arrested Social Democratic Party and labour leaders, suspended party news-papers, and gave tacit approval to the wrecking of party offices. The strike collapsed. Large numbers of strikers and socialists were given long prison sentences. Even though their economic problems continued, workers left the trades unions in droves, and since the unions provided the Social Democrats with the core of their membership, the party suffered severely. Equally serious, the Social Democrats split irrevocably between moderates and the Left, which became a separate Romanian Communist Party (to be outlawed in 1924). Throughout the interwar period Romanian governments proclaimed themselves a bastion against Soviet communism. In internal political debate 'Bolshevik' became the ultimate term of abuse.

9.4   Greece

During World War I there was very little fighting on Greek soil, and Greek troops were not seriously involved in the conflict until mid-1918. Nevertheless the war provoked serious divisions within the Greek government which led to coup and counter-coup and which left a legacy of royalist and republican divisions. The peace settlement led to an enlarged Greece and a greedy Greece. Desire for more Turkish territory led to a new war, to military disaster, to enormous shifts in population, and to further constitutional change.

   Division was apparent in Greek governing circles from the summer of 1914. The Prime Minister, Eleutherios Venizelos, had already had discussions with the British about the possibility of acquiring new territory in the event of war. He believed that Turkish involvement with the central powers would provide the opportunity for Greece to expand at the expense of the Ottoman Empire and, in particular, to redeem those Christian Greeks still living under Ottoman rule. King Constantine and his advisers, notable among whom was Colonel Iannis Metaxas, the Deputy Chief of Staff, were less sanguine; they wondered whether Greece had the strength to hold on to any new territory acquired as the result of an Entente victory. More important, they had their doubts about the likelihood of such a victory and they feared that Greece would fare very badly if it participated on the losing side. These divisions over foreign policy exacerbated the existing friction between Venizelos, a liberal who had led a Cretan secession movement in 1905, and Constantine, who had attended a German military academy, held the rank of Field Marshal in the German army, was married to the Kaiser's sister, and had a general preference for the autocratic Prussian style of government.

   The dispute between King and Prime Minister reached a climax in March 1915, and Venizelos resigned. In the general election which followed, Venizelos's majority in the assembly was reduced, but it remained workable and Constantine reluctantly invited him to serve again as Prime Minister in August. The following month, with Bulgaria's declaration of war on Serbia, the conflict between Constantine and Venizelos came to a head once again. A mutual defence treaty signed between Greece and Serbia required the former to assist Serbia with 150,000 troops in the event of an attack by Bulgaria. The King and his advisers argued that the treaty only applied in the case of war with one opponent, not in the case of a European war; besides, they pointed out, because of its commitments against Germany and Austria-Hungary, Serbia could not provide its own quota of 150,000 men to assist Greek troops against the Bulgarians. Venizelos suggested that the Serbian quota could be made up with French and British troops; the Entente powers jumped at his invitation and began to land troops at Salonika. However, Constantine and his advisers remained reluctant to enter the war and Venizelos was forced to resign. When the King called a general election in December 1915 the Liberals refused to take part, insisting that Venizelos had been dismissed unconstitutionally and that, in consequence, the election should not take place. The argument about the undermining of the Greek constitution gave France and Britain the pretext for intervening in the internal politics of Greece, since, under the nineteenth-century treaties which had established the Greek state, they were protectors of that state and its constitution. They began to violate Greek neutrality and made propaganda value, much of it unfounded, from Constantine's sympathy with the Germans.

In August 1916 a group of pro-Venizelos army officers, under the protection of the French military commander in Salonika, proclaimed a National Defence Movement and forced royalist officers to leave the region. Towards the end of the following month the French secret service organized Venizelos's departure from Athens, first to his native Crete, and from there to Salonika, where he took over the leadership of the National Defence Movement and proclaimed a provisional government. The provisional government began raising an army to fight with the Entente, and called on the Greek people to save their nation's honour by driving Bulgarian troops from their country. (The royalist government had withdrawn before Bulgarian troops entering East Macedonia, arguing that the Bulgarians' presence there was just like that of the Franco-British force in Salonika.) The Greek people in the area of the provisional government did not show themselves particularly enthusiastic about 'national honour'. Most of them were peasants with more pressing day-to-day concerns, and they had developed an intense dislike of the high-handed and sometimes brutal behaviour of the Franco-British expeditionary force. Their reluctance was increased by violence and brutality committed by Venizelos's recruiting officers, who burned the houses of men who would not enlist in their army. France and Britain, meanwhile, exerted further pressure on Constantine's government in Athens, notably with a blockade, and they compelled the King to abdicate in favour of his second son, Alexander. In June 1917 Greece was reunited under a single government headed by Venizelos, and it declared war on the central powers.

Greece did well out of the peace settlement, and together with France, Britain and Italy, established occupation forces in Turkey in 1919. Backed by Lloyd George, Venizelos hoped to incorporate more former Ottoman territory into Greece, and during the second half of 1919 Greek troops cleared Turkish forces out of Thrace (on the western side of the Dardanelles) and began advancing east through Anatolia. Both Venizelos and Lloyd George had reckoned without the new Turkish nationalism being fostered by Mustafa Kemal (Ataturk), but the main problems for Venizelos developed out of a tragic farce in Greece. In October 1920 King Alexander was bitten by a pet monkey; he contracted blood poisoning and died. Venizelos invited Alexander's elder brother, Paul, to take the crown, but, mindful of his father's forced abdication, Paul refused the crown unless his father was first rejected by the Greek people. A general election was called and, much to his surprise, as well as that of his Entente allies, Venizelos was overwhelmingly defeated, even to the extent of losing his own seat. The unpopularity of the Entente army and the brutal recruitment in Salonika was at least one reason for his loss of popularity. As a consequence of the election, Constantine was restored to the throne.

Constantine had been unsure about the Greek army's ability to secure greatly expanded national territory in 1914, but in 1921 he had lost such inhibitions and determined to press on with the war against Turkey. It was a serious error. Not only did the Turks regroup and reorganize under the growing authority of Mustafa Kemal, but the Greeks lost the support of the victorious Entente powers: the Italians did not look kindly on Greek expansion in Asia Minor, while Britain and France had no love for the restored Constantine. The war began to go badly for Greece. The climax came in September 1922, when the Turks reoccupied Smyrna and, a few days later, the city was burned to the ground: each side blamed the other for the destruction. Military disaster led to military mutiny as Colonel Nikolaos Plastiras, who had rallied the remnants of the defeated Greek army, proclaimed a new government. Plastiras's troops forced Constantine to abdicate once again; six of Constantine's principal ministers and generals were court martialled and shot.

Peace with Turkey led to a massive exchange of minority populations (see the *Maps Booklet*); Turkish massacres of Christian Armenians, if not the destruction of Smyrna, showed the dangers faced by minorities in the disputed regions. It is estimated that more than a million Greeks and about half a million Turks were uprooted as a result of the exchange. Such an exchange, of course, meant economic dislocation in both countries. Many of the Greeks from Anatolia were skilled artisans, notably carpet weavers, whose crafts simply disappeared from that part of the new Turkey. But there were also advantages: the Greek refugees colonized hitherto waste areas of Macedonia and Western Thrace, while Greek land reform legislation in 1924 broke up large estates especially for the refugees. Politically, peace with Turkey resolved little. Though Constantine abdicated in favour of his third son, George, real power lay in the hands of the army officers around Plastiras. A rising in October 1923, allegedly the work of Metaxas and royalist officers, led to George's being forced to leave the country. A republic was proclaimed in March 1924.

9.5   Turkey: empire to republic

(You will probably find it useful to study this section with your *Maps Booklet* open beside you at Map 5.)

The Turkish Empire, the other great multinational combatant, did not long survive World War I. In Book I, Unit 2, I described very briefly the rise of the Young Turks in the decade before the outbreak of the war. The Young Turks, increasingly dominated by a triumvirate of army officers, were seeking to create a modern, secular state. The Empire had received a battering during the century before 1914 as many of its Christian subject peoples had fought for, and won, their independence. The Balkan Wars had seen further defeats and further territorial losses. Consequently when war broke out in 1914, many of the imperial elite were keen to remain neutral. The military triumvirate, led by Enver Pasha, had other ideas.

Initially the Young Turks had been lionized in liberal circles in Western Europe, where they were seen as fellow liberals. They had, after all, compelled the autocratic Sultan to accept a constitution in 1908 and reconvene the Chamber of Deputies (dissolved thirty years before). However, attitudes in the West had begun to change when, once in power, the Young Turks had shown themselves to be aggressively nationalist, espousing a racial philosophy which stressed the Turkish and Islamic elements in the Empire, centred primarily in the imperial heartland of Anatolia, and alienating the minority races and religions. Enver Pasha himself had served as a military attaché in Berlin and, with the aid of German military advisers, he had sought to recreate the imperial army in the Prussian mould. He hoped that participation in the war which broke out in 1914 would enable the Empire to settle the score with the traditional enemy, Russia, who had aided and abetted the Slav Christians in their struggles for independence. He hoped also that victory would enable the Empire to reimpose control over Egypt (now under British protection), acquire the Suez Canal, dominate Persia and Transcaucasia, and threaten British India with a drive through Afghanistan.

Enver's enthusiasm for the war and his faith in the Prussianization of the Turkish army blinded him to the Empire's problems. The loyalty of the non-Turkish peoples in the Empire was already faltering before the nationalism of the Young Turks weakened it further. Army morale was low following the defeats in the Balkan Wars, and the German military advisers were often resented. Although a few railways had been built and some externally financed industry established, communications within the Empire were poor and the economy remained centred on subsistence agriculture. The war exacerbated all of these problems.

The Turks began the war with a drive against the Russians in Transcaucasia. They met with some initial success, but in the winter of 1914–15 the campaign turned into a disaster, with the Turkish army losing some 75,000 of the 95,000 men which it had committed. Enver and his generals looked for scapegoats and found them in the last sizeable Christian racial group remaining within the Empire, the Armenians. There is some controversy over the causes of, and the scale of, the Armenian genocide. In their *History of the Ottoman Empire and Modern Turkey* (1977) Standford J. Shaw and Ezel Kural Shaw argue that the Armenians seriously disrupted the Turkish campaign in Transcaucasia by cutting the army's supply lines – there were, after all, Christian Armenians on the other side of the Turkish-Russian frontier in Transcaucasia, and the Russian army was a Christian army. This view has been strongly criticized as an apology for the behaviour of Enver's government, most recently by the contributors to Richard G. Hovanissian's collection of essays, *The Armenian Genocide in Perspective* (1986), who draw parallels between the Turks' treatment of the Armenians and the Nazis' 'Final Solution'. It would seem that at least 1.5 million of the 2.3 million Armenians in the Empire died as a result of the massacres and deportations. A few of the German consular officials resident in Turkey complained to the imperial government, but were fobbed off with excuses or told to mind their own business; some of the German troops in the Empire have even been accused of participating in the massacres. As the massacres and deportations commenced, Armenian troops in the Russian army moved into north eastern Anatolia in the wake of the retreating

Turks and, calling themselves the Christian Army of Revenge, conducted their own massacres, though on a much smaller and less organized scale.

The Armenians were a particularly vulnerable group, since most of them lived in Anatolia, the centre of the Turkish racial group. The Arabs were a different problem, inhabiting those territories which they claimed as their own. The Arab Revolt began in 1916, and while it was rather more of a side-show than the heroic images surrounding Lawrence of Arabia might suggest, it became a steady drain on the Turkish war effort and a useful appendage to British imperial forces as they pushed into Palestine and Mesopotamia.

After the disaster in Transcaucasia the Turkish army settled down to fight a largely defensive war. It met with some successes: although the Turks lost more men than the attackers, the British and French forces landed at Gallipoli in April 1915 were withdrawn the following January; in April 1916 a British and Indian army of some 13,000 men surrendered to the Turks at Kut; the Russian collapse enabled the Turks to advance, once again, into Transcaucasia. Yet the Empire found itself increasingly in difficulty: desertion increased – in December 1916 there were an estimated 30,000 deserters; a drought combined with the shortage of male labour on the land to produce a famine; and the distribution of such food as there was became a lottery as the feeble communications system of the Empire grew more and more chaotic.

On 30 October 1918 the Mudros armistice was signed. This authorized warships of the Entente powers to enter the Bosphorus and enabled their troops to occupy any strategic area which they considered necessary. Enver Pasha fled to Russia, but the Sultan still reigned. The army began to demobilize. Skilled Turkish workers and students, who had been sent to Germany during the war, began to come home, as did thousands of Turkish soldiers who had been made prisoners of war.

Exercise Can you think of any ideas or experiences which these returning soldiers, students and workers might have brought with them and which would create problems for the Sultan's regime? ■

Specimen answer Men returning from both Russia and Germany at the end of 1918 and early in 1919 would have seen revolutionary behaviour and heard revolutionary ideas. □

Discussion It was only a tiny minority of the men who returned from Russia and Germany who came back as committed socialists, yet they did inject new, radical ideas into Turkish politics and nationalism. The Turkish Spartacists, some of whom had participated in the German Revolution, organized the Turkish Worker and Peasant Socialist Party in 1919; they conflated Marxist and nationalist ideology in as much as they tended to equate the Turks with the proletariat, and the victorious Entente powers then became agents of the bourgeoisie. In general the Turkish intelligentsia was sympathetic to the Russian Revolution, and both they and the nationalists believed that it contained lessons for a modernizing Turkey. On the popular level, possibly fostered by the Turkish peasants and workers who, as soldiers, had been captured by the Russians, there was a common belief that communism was a restatement of Islam, notably because it advocated that goods be shared with the poor. However, it was not socialism or Islam that inspired the events leading, eventually, to the creation of the republic.

Turkey was in total disarray at the beginning of 1919. The Sultan's government had little authority outside of the capital, Istanbul, and even here it appeared to function only because the Allied occupying forces permitted it. The Allied occupation provoked resentment; in eastern Anatolia nationalist groups began organizing, regardless of the Sultan and Allied occupation forces, to oppose the creation of an Armenian Republic; similar groups began organizing for national defence following the Greek invasion and accompanying massacres in May 1919. The leadership of these nationalist groups was increasingly assumed by Mustafa Kemal, who had become a popular hero during the war, first as a successful divisional commander at Gallipoli, and later for refusing to comply with orders given by German officers. Kemal had been sent by the Sultan to bring the nationalist groups in eastern Anatolia to heel in the spring of 1919, but he opted to join and lead them. By mid 1920 there were two governments in Turkey: that of the Sultan in Istanbul and that of Kemal and the nationalists in Ankara. The Sultan had the nationalist leaders declared outlaws and he sought to raise an army against them around Ankara. The Sultan's forces were quickly defeated and Kemal, anxious not to offend anyone who had a lingering sympathy for the Sultan, excused the Sultan's actions on the grounds that he was a virtual prisoner of the Allies. Indeed, Kemal was prepared to work with anyone who, he believed, would help him create a modern nation state. He sought, and received, aid from the Soviet Union, and socialists and communists were welcome under the nationalist banner, though Kemal clamped down on them if their propaganda appeared to provoke discord. In 1921, for example, the communist paper *Emek* (Labour) was closed down, and various party leaders were arrested, after it declared:

> Kemal is the absolute ruler of Anatolia. Say he wins victory. Will the position of the peasantry be better for this? Whatever victory Kemal wins it will not benefit the people of Anatolia. One man alone . . . can never deliver the country from need . . . Only a social revolution can free the people of Anatolia from the yoke of capital. Thus as soon as the war with the Greek imperialists is over, a civil war will begin in Anatolia. (Quoted in George S. Harris, *The Origins of Communism in Turkey*, 1967, p.92)

The original nationalist groups that had sprung up to oppose the Armenian Republic and the Greek invasion were drawn predominantly from the old imperial elite of army officers, bureaucrats and the intelligentsia. Kemal succeeded in fusing these with the illiterate Anatolian peasants and creating a common idea of the Turkish nation. War against the Armenian and the neighbouring Georgian republics, and above all against the Greeks, helped. So too did the continuing presence of Allied troops in Istanbul and elsewhere. Kemal was prepared to indulge in brinkmanship with these troops, as, most notably, in September 1922 when the Turkish forces came close to joining battle with British troops at Chanak.

The Entente powers had signed the peace treaty of Sèvres with the Sultan's government in August 1920. Kemal's destruction of the Greek invaders and his confrontation with the British at Chanak led to a new peace conference. The Allies invited both Kemal's nationalist government and the Sultan's government to attend the new conference, and this brought to a head the question of who was the ruler of Turkey. Kemal and the nationalists – the men with a strong, victorious army – were not prepared to let the Sultan take credit for their achievements and they engineered a resolution in the Grand National Assembly which abolished the sultanate. The resolution demonstrated, once again, Kemal's political acumen. He was conscious of the continuing power of Islam in Turkey and of lingering sympathy for the Sultan Mohammed VI and the ruling house of Osman; consequently, while the Assembly abolished the sultanate, it maintained the caliphate by which Mohammed VI was a religious leader and 'defender of the faith'. The caliphate was to remain in the house of Osman. However, as his government departments were moved from Istanbul to Ankara, Mohammed VI played into Kemal's hands by taking refuge on a British warship; he, and his dynasty, could now be branded traitors. When the peace conference met at Lausanne on 20 November 1922, only Kemal's government was present to represent Turkey, and it succeeded in negotiating a treaty (that of Lausanne, 24 July 1923) which, for a defeated state, was the most favourable of any of those which concluded World War I.

On 29 October 1923 Turkey became a republic and Kemal became its first President. While the new constitution accepted that the republic was to be an Islamic state, a succession of laws passed in March 1924 expelled the Osman dynasty, abolished the caliphate, broke the power of Islam within the state, and thus allowed Kemal's policies of secularization and modernization on a Western model to proceed unimpeded.

Exercise Do you think it is possible to call the events in Turkey between 1918 and 1923 a 'revolution'? ■

Discussion The manner in which change came about in Turkey was very different from the 'revolutions' in Russia and Germany in the aftermath of World War I. The major difference was that the ruling dynasty survived military defeat for several years, and the armed conflict within Turkey was less among the Turks themselves but between the Turks and Greek invaders and Armenians. This fighting mobilized the mass of the Turkish people behind the leaders of a new kind of state (it was also extremely savage with massacres on both sides). But even if there was little in the way of armed struggle between the Turks themselves, there was serious confrontation between two conflicting power blocs competing for control of the country: the nationalists of Kemal, and the government of the Sultan. Finally, while the Young Turks had taken tentative steps down the road of secularization and the westernization of the old Empire, it was not until Mustapha Kemal's triumph in the years 1919–23 that there was a major shift in the structure of state and society.

10 SOME BROAD CONCLUSIONS

Now comes the problem of trying to draw some threads together and suggest some conclusions. Ignoring the Balkan countries for the moment, World War I began with four empires in East and Central Europe, and when the fighting finally ended there were more than twice as many republics covering the same territory – Austria, Czechoslovakia, Estonia, Finland, Germany, Hungary, Latvia, Lithuania, Poland, Turkey and the USSR. In addition, a few small republics like Armenia and the Ukraine had come and gone. In the Balkans the tradition of the victors seizing tracts of land from the vanquished was continued. The scale of the changes in Central and Eastern Europe can be grasped if you compare the maps of Europe in 1914 with the Europe that emerged from the war (see Maps 1 and 6 in the *Maps Booklet*). Compare also the map of the nationalities of the Austro-Hungarian Empire in 1910 with the state structure after the war.

At the end of section 9.5, I drew attention to some of the differences between the revolution in Turkey and the revolutions in other states. This was not meant to suggest that the revolutions in the other states were not, in many ways, different from each other. No one doubts that there was a revolution in Russia, though the word is very loosely used, so that we can read of the February Revolution followed by the October Revolution, but also have the two events conflated into *the* Russian Revolution of 1917. Whether the revolution in Germany was the sailors' uprising in Kiel, the abdication of the Kaiser and the declaration of the republic, the Spartacist uprising, or a mixture of all of these events (and more) is not always clear in some history books. As you have seen from section 7 above, some historians deny that the term revolution is applicable to any events in the Austrian part of the Habsburg Empire.

The definition of revolution with which these units began does enable us to use the term to describe similar political processes in all of the states we have examined here. As a result of the war each of the four empires witnessed:

1   A breakdown of government and particularly of the state's monopoly of armed forces, leading to

2   A struggle between different armed power blocs for control of the state.

3   Finally, the new republics emerged when one of these power blocs had emerged as dominant and was able to reconstitute the sovereign power of the state. In Russia, Germany and Hungary the fiercest stage of the conflict came as a power bloc, having achieved dominance at the centre, sought to reconstitute the state at a time when its frontiers were extremely fluid.

History, of course, is not about proving our definitions and assumptions to be right, but if we can agree on this very broad pattern of political process as 'revolution' within the states were are focusing on, then we can move on to the question of the precise role of World War I in bringing about collapse in these states and in creating the committed rank and file for the subsequent 'revolutionary' conflict.

Each of the four empires suffered serious internal problems because of the war; at different times they also faced varying degrees of desertion and mutinous behaviour by their troops at, or more likely just behind, the front. But the Entente powers experienced similar problems at home – there were food shortages and industrial troubles in Britain, France and Italy both during and immediately after the war – and among their troops and seamen. The French army mutinies of 1917 were the most dramatic of the Entente's problems in this respect, but British and Italian troops also, on occasions, proved difficult and mutinous. From 1917 the general staffs and politicians of the Entente powers were expressing the same kinds of fears about Bolshevism in their armies and about anti-militarism, pacifism and socialism at home, as their counterparts in the central powers.

Exercise   Think back very carefully over what you have read in these units and then note down whether you believe that the troops of the central powers were radicalized politically by the war. ■

Specimen answer and discussion   There is little evidence to suggest that many troops became committed to revolutionary or radical party politics as a direct result of experience in the trenches. In both Russia and Austria-Hungary it appears to have been second-line or reserve troops who took a more radical stance than the front-line soldiers. These men had longer periods of idleness and, if billeted in large towns at home, they had a greater awareness of the problems and privations of civilians. The sailors of Kronstadt and Kiel were similar; they spent most of the war cooped up below decks in ports, subject to rigid discipline, without the release of going to sea or the emotional experience of enemy action. Where mutinies, the shooting of officers and desertions occurred, they appear generally to have been the product of low morale, hunger, battle fatigue, and general war-weariness. □

Exercise   The German Revolution saw the creation of *Freikorps* as well as Spartacist revolutionaries. Out of about 8.5 million German soldiers demobilized in 1918–19, about 400,000 were recruited into different *Freikorps*. The following quotation is from a fairly typical historical analysis; do you find it convincing?

> The most disastrous effect of World War I, finally, consisted of the miseducation of a whole generation toward solving its problems in a military, authoritarian manner. The war generation fought in volunteer military units (Freecorps) against Polish irregulars and domestic revolutionaries right after the war. In the 1930s they flocked to the Nazi Party, and other rightwing organisations, bringing along a whole ideology of what it meant to be a front-line soldier fighting in the trenches. (Peter H. Merkl, *The Making of a Stormtrooper*, 1980, p. 15) ■

Discussion   So the war produced a generation which was both Bolshevik and fascist? If one in twenty of the demobilized German troops went into the *Freikorps*, how many of these went into the Nazi Party? And can we really start making simply causal connections between front-line soldiers and political activists? Perhaps some historians (as well as politicians and journalists) have been rather too willing to blame unpleasant post-war political behaviour on the 'war generation'. Thus all kinds of Red Guards, German *Freikorps* and Nazis, and Italian fascist *squadristi* have been labelled as somehow the products of the trenches. If Nazis and fascists made much of the supposed brotherhood of the front-line soldier, this does not mean that such a brotherhood actually forged their parties. Current research into the political attitudes of soldiers during the war, based largely on the reports of the military postal censors, does not suggest that the war politicized, let alone radicalized, front-line combatants. Rather the men who were conscripted or who volunteered to fight for their countries regarded the war as an interruption to their normal lives in which politics was significant for only a few. The French troops who mutinied in 1917 sang the *Internationale* and threatened to march on Paris; French generals and politicians feared for the state, but as one of the mutineers put it: 'If we have refused orders this is not to lead to the revolution which will be inevitable if we should continue, but to bring peace to the attention of the rulers of the state.' The generals feared that the Russians' example would infect their troops, but the French military postal censors found front-line troops writing home and abusing the Russians, since their revolution meant that there would be more German divisions available for the western front.

If problems on the home front and on the battle front were similar for both the Entente powers and the central powers, then the reason for the escalation of these problems into revolution may, perhaps, be found in military defeat. In the introduction to these units I quoted Hannah Arendt's 'noteworthy fact' that we do not expect states or forms of government to survive defeat in modern war. Defeat worsened the problems created by the war: it undermined the authorities' faith in themselves; it undermined the military, the last line of defence of the established order; and significantly it undermined the military in home garrisons first. None of the old regimes were physically overthrown by a massive popular insurrection directed specifically to this end. Rather the old regimes could no longer cope with serious internal emergencies, and it was this which provided the opportunity for groups and individuals, who believed in their own abilities to provide policy and leadership, to struggle for control. Yet here too we must be beware of taking a too mechanistic view of events. In Turkey the military government of Enver Pasha did not survive the war, but the sultanate did and looked like continuing. It was a new war, against the Greeks, which initiated the revolutionary changes in Turkish politics and society – and this was a war in which the Turks were victorious.

Much of the analysis of revolution has concentrated on 'forces' and 'movements' rather than on leading individual actors. Of course, popular aspirations expressed through demonstrations and 'movements' are important, and I am no advocate of a return to the 'great men of history' school, but individuals too can be important in shaping events. Kerensky was unable to establish and maintain control in Russia arguably because of his determination to continue the war in the teeth of popular hostility, and because of his inability to provide land for the peasants and food for the population as a whole. Lenin and the Bolshevik leaders rejected theory and historical inevitability when they set out to capture mass support with the slogan 'Peace, Land, Bread'. Mustafa Kemal was cautious not to alienate supporters of the Sultan until he and the nationalists were secure and victorious; he then acted swiftly and decisively. It is a truism to conclude that it is the leader and the group which is the most determined and totally ruthless, but also politically astute enough to know when to compromise, that shapes the political system emerging from a revolution.

REFERENCES

Arendt, H. (1963) *On Revolution*, Harmondsworth, Penguin.

Arshinov, P. (1974) *History of the Makhnovist Movement (1918–1921)*, Detroit, Black and Red (first pubd 1932 in Berlin by Russian Anarchists).

Bauer, O. (1925) *The Austrian Revolution*, trans. H. J. Stenning, Leonard Parsons (extract reproduced as document II.27 in *Documents 1*).

Borkeneau, F. (1971) *World Communism*, Ann Arbor, University of Michigan Press (first pubd 1939).

Bottomore, T. and Goole, P. (eds) (1978) *Austro-Marxism*, Oxford, Clarendon Press.

Brinton, C. (1965) *The Anatomy of Revolution*, St Paul, Minnesota, Vintage Books (revised and expanded edn).

Carsten, F. L. (1972) *Revolution in Central Europe 1914–18*, London, Temple.

Chamberlain, W. H. (1965) *The Russian Revolution*, 2 vols, New York, Grosset and Dunlop (revised edn).

Deak, I. (1977) 'Shades of 1848: war, revolution and nationality conflict in Austria-Hungary 1914–1920', in C. L. Bertkely (ed.) *Revolutionary Situations in Europe 1917–1922*, Quebec, Interuniversity Centre for European Studies, pp.87–94.

Ellis, J. (1973) *Armies in Revolution*, London, Croom Helm.

Feldman, G. D. (1966) *Army, Industry and Labor in Germany 1914–1918*, Princeton, New Jersey, Princeton University Press.

Ferro, M. (1972) *The Russian Revolution of February 1917*, London, Routledge and Kegan Paul.

Ferro, M. (1980) *October 1917*, London, Routledge and Kegan Paul.

Hardach, G. (1977) *The First World War 1914–1918*, Harmondsworth, Penguin.

Harris G. S. (1967) *The Origins of Communism in Turkey*, Stanford, California, Hoover Institution Press.

Hobsbawm, E. J. (1971) *Primitive Rebels*, Manchester University Press.

Hovanissian, R. G. (ed.) (1986) *The Armenian Genocide in Perspective*, New Brunswick, New Jersey, Transaction Books.

Janos, A. C. (1982) *The Politics of Backwardness in Hungary 1825–1945*, Princeton, New Jersey, Princeton University Press.

Jaszi, O. (1929) *The Dissolution of the Habsburg Monarchy*, Chicago University Press.

Kitchen, M. (1980) *The Coming of Austrian Fascism*, London, Croom Helm.

Koenker, D. (1976) 'Moscow workers in 1917', unpublished PhD thesis, University of Michigan.

Lenin, V. I. (1964) 'Opportunism and the collapse of the Second International', in *Collected Works*, vol. 22, London, Lawrence and Wishart (first pubd 1915).

Macartney, C. A. (1929) *The Social Revolution in Austria*, Cambridge University Press.

Merkl, P. H. (1980) *The Making of a Stormtrooper*, Princeton, New Jersey, Princeton University Press.

Mitrany, D. (1930) *The Land and the Peasant in Romania: The War and Agrarian Reform (1917–1921)*, London, Oxford University Press.

Mitrany, D. (1936) *The Effect of the War in South-Eastern Europe*, London, Oxford University Press.

Moeller, R. G. (1981) 'Dimensions of social conflict in the Great War: the view from the German countryside', *Central European History*, vol. XIV.

Pearson, R. (1983) *National Minorities in Eastern Europe 1848–1945*, London, Macmillan.

Pinson, K. S. (1966) *Modern Germany: Its History and Civilization*, New York, Macmillan (revised edn).

Raskolnikov, F. F. (1982) *Kronstadt and Petrograd in 1917*, London, New Park Publications (first pubd in the USSR in 1925).

Redilich, J. (1932) *Austrian War Government*, New Haven, Conn., Yale University Press.

Roberts, H. L. (1951) *Rumania: Political Problems of an Agrarian State*, New Haven, Conn., Yale University Press.

Shaw, S. J. and Shaw, E. K. (1977) *History of the Ottoman Empire and Modern Turkey*, Cambridge University Press.

Spence, R. B. (1981) 'Yugoslavia, the Austro-Hungarian army and the First World War', unpublished PhD thesis, University of Michigan.

Stone, N. (1975) *The Eastern Front 1914–1917*, London, Hodder and Stoughton.

Taylor, A. J. P. (1948) *The Habsburg Monarchy*, London, Hamish Hamilton.

Tobin, E. H. (1985) 'War and the working class: the case of Düsseldorf 1914–18', *Central European History*, vol. XVIII.

Vernadsky, G. *et al.* (eds) (1972) *A Source Book for Russian History from Early Times to 1917*, New Haven, Conn., Yale University Press.

Wall, R. and Winter, J. M. (eds) (1988) *The Upheaval of War*, Cambridge University Press.

Wegs, J. R. (1970) 'Austrian economic mobilization during World War I, with particular emphasis on heavy industry', unpublished PhD thesis, University of Illinois.

Wegs, J. R. (1976/7) 'The marshalling of copper: an index of Austro-Hungarian economic mobilization during World War I', *Austrian History Yearbook*, vol. XII–XIII.

Zeman, Z. A. B. (1961) *The Break-up of the Habsburg Empire 1914–1918: A Study in National and Social Revolution*, London, Oxford University Press.

INDEX